THE SEVEN
A Family Holocaust Story

THE SEVEN
A Family Holocaust Story

Ellen G. Friedman

WAYNE STATE UNIVERSITY PRESS
DETROIT

© 2017 by Ellen G. Friedman. All rights reserved. No part of this book may be reproduced without formal permission. Manufactured in the United States of America. Published by Wayne State University Press.

ISBN 978-0-8143-4413-2 (paperback); ISBN 978-0-8143-4414-9 (ebook); 978-0-8143-4439-2 (hardcover)

Library of Congress Cataloging Number: 2017953472

Wayne State University Press
Leonard N. Simons Building
4809 Woodward Avenue
Detroit, Michigan 48201-1309

Visit us online at wsupress.wayne.edu

For Sam, Simon, Joseph,
Angela, and Iris

CONTENTS

Preface ix

Map and Time Line xii

1. Who and Where 1

2. Dov 13

3. Josef 55

4. Itzak with Lola Interrupting 101

5. Eva 165

6. Katja 209

7. Legacy 255

Acknowledgments 259

Notes 261

PREFACE

The Seven, A Family Holocaust Story is a different story of the Holocaust, one that is lost to history and needs to be told. Most Polish Jews who survived the war did not go to concentration camps but were sentenced by Stalin to "banishment" in the remote prison settlements and gulags of the Soviet Union. Fewer than 10 percent of Polish Jews survived World War II, and Soviet exile was their main chance for survival.

The title of this book, *The Seven,* is the name other refugees in the prison camps of the USSR gave to the original seven Polish Jews of this story. The Seven were from Warsaw, and I am related to six of them. Beginning in 1984, I interviewed those of the Seven who were still alive, as well as others who had entered their sphere and became part of a more metaphorical, extended Seven. Set side-by-side and in juxtaposition to one another, their voices tell a new Holocaust story—one that resonates with the experiences of today's exiles and refugees.

After Hitler invaded the Soviet Union in June 1941, the Polish government in exile made a deal with Stalin to liberate Polish citizens from the prison settlements in the USSR. Many Polish Jews went south to Soviet Asia, looking for better living conditions than they had in the cold northern territories of their banishment. That's where I was born—in Kyrgyzstan, within sight of the Tian Shan Mountains of China.

I have been asked about my methodology. It is not one I recommend. It was an organic process that began without a plan. In 1978, when the television series *Holocaust* aired, American attention finally turned to the horrors of Nazism. I always knew I was born in a small Kyrgyz hamlet outside of Kant, a village near Frunze (now Bishkek), to Polish-Jewish parents on the run from Hitler. But my family did not describe themselves as Holocaust survivors. American culture, indeed everyone and everything—books, news media, film, and television—defined Holocaust survivors as people who had come out of death and concentration camps, people with numbers tattooed on their arms. Although I was busy raising a family and pursuing my career as a professor of English, occupied with courses and literary scholarship, it was clear to me that the time had come to record the stories of my family.

They allowed me to record them when I told them the audio tapes were for a book I wanted to write about them, a vague notion at first that gained ground and clarity over time, much time. As this material began to take hold of me, I tried to put their experiences into fiction and with my husband to write a novel about them, but good intentions could not glue together our two different imaginations, and the collaboration fizzled out—though the marriage held. With the new millennium and the deaths of some of the Seven, I began this memoir in earnest. I re-interviewed the ones who were still alive and recorded spouses for the first time, as well as some of their children. I hired undergraduate and graduate students to transcribe the dozens of audio tapes that held their stories. After the transcriptions were finished, my plan was to correct them, since the many place names and multiple languages involved were foreign to my students. I also applied for a travel grant to put my feet on the landscapes where the stories had taken place. The Soviets blocked access to some of the places I wished to see, such as Nyuvchim in Komi, to which the Seven were banished in 1940, and Kant in Kyrgyzstan, but I got close enough to these geographies to get a sense of them. In the meantime, I read as much as I could about the history of those years and I pored over maps. In the end, I just began to write because the work of correcting the transcriptions, it seemed, would last beyond my lifespan.

Sometime near the beginning, a voice in my head took over the writing and I finished a draft. Writing a book takes a long time, at least this book did, and as I wrote, memories, news stories, things I read and felt, and my daily life worked their way into the text. Writers have said that at a certain serendipitous moment in a book, the whole world seems to collaborate in its composition. Everything seems relevant and begs to be included. My manicurist, rock and roll, Esperanto, Michel Foucault, whose work I teach, President Obama, Bob Dylan, and Arthur Murray—all of them slipped into my manuscript. That's how this book acquired its unconventional form, a pastiche of past and present, of them and me and a Holocaust history that has finally found the opportunity to make itself known.

This memoir is personal and if intent counts, universal. To preserve anonymity and privacy, I have changed names, some identifying characteristics and details, as well as occupations and places of residence. I have compressed and edited the interviews to fill logical gaps and reflect historical circumstances, and for purposes of the narrative, I have added and emended material. Although

PREFACE

based on interviews, this memoir is my account, my history, my version of their stories. Each of the people described in this book, if they had been so inclined, likely would have portrayed themselves differently than I have portrayed them. I have kept the names of my parents, Itzak and Lola, as a way to memorialize them—although they would not have approved of how I present them, as you will see.

THE SEVEN
A Family Holocaust Story

Pechora

Syktyvkar
Kotlas • • Nyuvchim

•SCOW

RUSSIAN SFSR

Chelyabinsk •

SOVIET SOCIALIST REPUBLICS

Stalingrad

KAZAKH SSR

GEORGIAN SSR

AZERBAIJAN SSR

Caspian Sea

UZBEK SSR

Tashkent •

Frunze • Kant

KIRGHIZ SSR

Aravan
Samarkand • Pachta Abad • Osh

RKEY

ARMENIAN SSR

TURKMEN SSR

TAJIK SSR

Tian Shan Mountains

CHINA

This map reflects the division of land between the end of World War II and the collapse of the Soviet Union.

|—— 200 miles

44	1945	1946	1948	1949	1950	1951	1952	1956	1961
	Brest Stettin (now Szczecin, Poland)	Düppel Center DP Camp, Germany		Berlin, Germany		New Haven, CT USA		1955/56 moves to New York City	Vineland, NJ USA
	Szczecin		Frankfurt-Main, Germany				Vineland, NJ		
	Brest Szczecin	Düppel Center DP Camp			Cincinnati, OH USA	Bronx, NY USA	Vineland, NJ		
Camp, slovakia	Prague, Czechoslovakia Bregenz, Austria Konstanz	Berlin		Berlin airlift	Married Dov, Berlin		New Haven, CT		
	Frankfurt-Oder Potsdam, Germany Magdeburg	Wittenberg, Germany		Berlin		Wittenberg, GDR Berlin, FRG		Paris, France New York City	Vineland, NJ

I

Who and Where

They were seven Polish Jews from Warsaw and it was 1939. I heard their stories when I was already married and a mother. I don't know if they told them before then; I only know that's when I began to pay attention. It must have been around the time of the American awakening to the Holocaust in the late 1970s and 1980s, with TV specials and movies suddenly giving status to their European accents. This attention encouraged my father and his two brothers to talk more about what happened to them, even though theirs wasn't a Holocaust experience of the first order. The stories captivating Americans were about concentration camps and gas chambers and death. My family stories, about how they outwitted their circumstances and survived, were the kind that did not count as about the Holocaust, until now.

This, then, is a Holocaust story plucked from the least known yet most common of the stories of Polish Jews who survived World War II. Most Polish Jews still alive after the Holocaust spent the war in the Soviet Union. So it's a story of exile. And it's also a story of family—my family. Most of the people you will get to know best are survivors who lost almost everything important they had—parents, brothers, sisters, and one would say "homeland," but it seems Jews do not have a homeland, and even Israel, the default homeland, has its problems. Once the Seven escaped the Germans in Warsaw, they did not return, even after the war, but kept going, out of the Soviet Union, out of Poland, out of Europe.

For sure, death was there, too. Of these seven Polish Jews who left Warsaw for exile, six lived out a natural life span. But another sixty, according to the statistics, 90 percent—parents, grandparents, sisters, brothers, aunts, uncles, cousins, nieces, nephews, an entire family network, almost the whole of the *mishpokhe*—did not. Did not go to school, fall in love, and get married to have children and then grandchildren, did not go once a week to the *shvitz*, did not play soccer and ride bicycles, did not go dancing or to the opera or catch the latest film at the cinema, did not do their tailoring or bookbinding or make gefilte fish or light the Friday-night candles for the Sabbath. When I woke up to my connection to this history, I began to record those I could on audio tapes, and as best as was possible, given Soviet restrictions on foreigners' travel, I retraced the steps of their exile.

My first trip to the USSR to find the past was in 1985. Eight hours in flight and two and a half hours in Soviet customs, and I was in Moscow, greeted by Luba, an Intourist guide, a young woman of about twenty-five. Before *Glasnost* tourists were required to have an official guide. I brought books as gifts, one of them Erica Jong's *Fear of Flying*, something I thought Russians couldn't get from the Soviets—very American and sexy, feminist. As I handed her the books, Luba showed alarm and then when I began to talk about them, she shushed me. She quickly covered them with her coat and then slipped them into her satchel. I had not foreseen this response, the fear that forbidden reading excited. So too, when I went to another stop on my trip, Irkutsk, a city in Siberia, and handed my guide a *New York Times* magazine article about his region, I caught him off guard. He lost his tour-guide decorum and barked, "Are you crazy?" He took the paper and made it disappear under a seat pillow in the touring van. I was bringing contraband into the USSR. On that side of the Cold War, small gestures felt really dangerous.

After following the footsteps of my family's Soviet exile during WWII, I returned to Moscow and took the overnight express to Brest-Litovsk. My tiny sleeper compartment had a sink that folded down into a table, complete with a tablecloth. My ticket included linens, so a *babushka*, the train attendant, came and delivered sheets, one towel, one pillowcase, and in the morning, tea.

Right off the train I went to find my great-uncle's house. In 1939 he opened his arms and his house to the Jews his Warsaw brother, my grandfather, sent to him—Jews who were fleeing German-occupied Poland. Among them were four of his brother's children and three others they had invited, making up the Seven whom Stalin then sentenced to banishment along with thousands of others. Once in the remote prison settlement in the forests of frigid Komi to which they were sent, the other exiles began to call them "the Seven" because there were no other groups in the gulags like them, a group so close to one another, who had one another's backs. The group included three brothers—Dov, Josef, and my father, Itzak—their sister Sonia, my father's girlfriend, Lola, who became my mother, as well as Josef's girlfriend, Henya, and his best friend, Chapka. Through the safe harbor my great-uncle provided, all but one of them dodged the German killing machine.

The wooden house where my great-uncle had lived—19 Ulitsa Bialostoskaja—no longer exists. That's the thing about the present. Its debt to the past is often invisible. So many pasts have marched through these streets between then and now. How to excavate mine? All street names were changed by the Soviets to mark the new world they were creating, a world that had no past at all, only a future.

I asked the hotel receptionist how I could find out where the street of my great-uncle's house used to be.

"Perhaps at the museum of local history."

"Where is the Jewish section?" I asked.

"Jewish section? There is a cinema where the synagogue used to be."

Brest is now a town of 250,000, with many Soviet-style modern buildings. As I wandered around, I found an old two-story wooden house with an attic on Ulitsa Sovietskaia, in front of which a bent old woman with a birch broom cleaned the street. I took a photo. From the descriptions I thought my great-uncle's house could have looked like this, although this was the wrong street. Using what little Russian I had, I asked people on the street if they knew Bialostoskaja. No luck.

I had hoped to lay my eyes on this place as it had been then, when the Seven arrived by various routes from Warsaw to elude Nazi anti-Jewish actions. Just as the character Austerlitz, in the W. G. Sebald novel of that name, writes about developing film, I was looking for "the moment when the shadows of reality, so to speak, emerge out of nothing on the exposed paper." But it did not happen.

A bit later I went to the Brest open-air market, where the Seven had so cleverly made a living by selling goods to the Russians. The Russians were starved for the Western goods readily available in prewar Poland. The Soviet collective factories produced shoddy, boring goods, replicated ad nauseam so you would see yourself coming and going, if you were lucky enough to get something at all. The goods the Seven sold were black market, the clothes by real tailors and not made in collectivized factories. The Russians bought everything the Seven had, even lingerie. They bought nightgowns and wore them as evening dresses. Russian officers' wives dressed in nightgowns at official events, to the astonishment of Westerners, has become an iconic image of this sudden encounter between Western and Soviet economies.

On this day, the day of my visit, the market was a sorry place, especially in the rain. It was marked by a wooden banner on two sticks. Through this gate I saw a few scattered people in a large, dirt-floored area. A few boxes of tired wild strawberries, a small heap of anemic cherries, and a few items of clothing were the entire offerings. I decided to come back when it wasn't raining.

At the *kraevedcheskii muzei,* the museum of local history and records, a thin, dark-haired man of about forty-five graciously helped me when I wrote the name of my great-uncle's street, Bialostoskaja, and the date 1939. He consulted an old map and said that Bialostoskaja had changed to Sovestikh Progranchnikov. I spelled out my family name in Russian, *znecep,* said *"semia,"* meaning "family," and drew the Star of David. He and his colleague consulted for a while. I caught *"evreiskii"* or "Jewish" in their back-and-forth conversation.

They sent me to a short, stocky blonde woman in a storefront jewelry repair shop. I upset her with my questions. Was she Jewish? In the end, she pointed to my ear lobes and wrist and said in Russian, very close to my face and very loudly, "We fix earrings and watches," and then turned away from me, disappearing behind the curtain that separated the three-by-seven-foot "shop" from what I assumed was a workroom in the back. This was, after all, the Soviet Union. And I was looking for Jews.

I found the renamed street of my great-uncle and walked to no. 19. The two-story wooden house with an attic had been replaced by a brand-new seven-story apartment building. But I took photos of the wooden houses around it and across the street. Hoping for a miracle, I asked for "Bialostoskaja" from people I saw who seemed old enough to have known wartime Brest, but they just shouted back the new street name. Nevertheless, it is a good-looking, tree-lined street. The trees must have been there when the Seven walked by or took cover from the rain under them. I could imagine Dov, the only one of the three brothers who would rather read than make money, sitting and leaning against one of them, absorbed in a book.

That undeveloped film, though, would not yield its secrets, despite my efforts. I had to settle for other traces, and sometimes, invention.

Like me, the children and grandchildren of survivors have a living connection to the memories that were passed on to them. Survivors' memories become our memories, and to some degree, they hold us captive to the past. We are caught between absence and presence, between our elders' past and the lives we are living. Some have said that absence is our present.

The legacy that binds us to it also requires that we pass these memories on. I can't help thinking, as others have before me, that even though we are the stewards of those memories, we are also charlatans, pretending to own them. Or voyeurs who look through the window at experiences not our own. And then we are the flawed ventriloquists on whom this history depends if it is to last beyond us. Even though we may be the puppets of someone else's history, we become the puppeteers as we push it forward into the future, as we rewrite this history on our own terms.

I walked to the Brest Hero Fortress at twilight. It was made in the oversized Soviet style, with jagged, angry heads of concrete emerging from the base. Orange ribbons commemorate the soldiers at the fortress who held out for almost a month against the Nazi Panzer attack that began June 21, 1941.

I walked through the forest to the river Bug, a central character in the Seven's escape from German-occupied Poland. Each of them had to cross it, under threat of imprisonment or death, to get to my great-uncle's house. It looked to me like a tame, narrow, brown little river, bordered by tall trees that made it seem even more diminutive. The guard stations and searchlights on both sides of the river, which still marks the border, disclosed a contemporary drama of escape and capture that echoes the past.

The market on a sunny day was still a sorry, desolate place. I was about to take a photo, when an officious, thick-bodied, bleached-blonde Russian woman about my age and height stepped directly in front of me and shouted for me to stop, spraying saliva as her words came out. Although I did understand her, I said, "*Ne ponimayu.*" I don't understand. She said, "Français," and then, "Non photo." I asked, "Pourquoi?" She said in Russian, with that overbearing Soviet assurance, "*Tak kak,*" meaning "because." That was it, "*Tak kak.*" Then she followed—well, stalked—me all over the market, making sure I did not open my camera again. Defiantly, although I was terrified, I shot a final photo at the exit of the market as I left.

I had come to Brest feeling entitled by birthright to be there. My grandfather had had a share in my great-uncle's house. Other relatives had owned businesses and their own homes in Brest. But the market woman made it clear that I was an interloper, that I did not belong, that I was suspicious. It struck me that the feeling of being a stranger in the midst of people who are home must be what exile is like, something resembling what the Seven experienced time after time. You could sense the absence in them—especially in my mother and my father's younger brother Dov.

On my father's ninetieth birthday, I invited the family over to celebrate. Everyone—almost—came to his party. Twenty-four people came. We put together the dining-room table, with the extension and a folding table and a card table. All at slightly different levels, covered with a single tablecloth for the unconvincing fiction that it was only one table. We borrowed folding chairs from the neighbors, and in the end, to accommodate twenty-four, we added the piano bench.

My father left his ninetieth birthday party before we brought out the birthday cake and before we took the family picture. He took NJ Transit and then the E train, then the Q55 bus, and then walked uphill for two blocks to get home. He is missing from the family photo commemorating his ninetieth year on Earth. I have noticed that no one has framed that photo. Why did he leave? His wife wasn't there; his two brothers were missing. Despite the twenty-four who came, some from as far away as Texas, there weren't enough people at the table.

My mother emerged from World War II without a single relative. At her funeral, I was surprised at the full chapel. Almost every conversation I had with her when I was an adult included the plea, "I have no one but you. No one." I resisted her hugs; I don't know why. In the funeral parlor reception room, with plush flowered couches and deep armchairs we didn't use, two old women approached me before the funeral began. They were both American, no Eastern-European accents. My daughters and I were lined up against the wall in the somber reception room, elbow-to-elbow, when one brown-haired, popeyed woman in her seventies took hold of my shoulders and said into my face, "She was my best friend." My mother had a best friend? She had a friend? It disturbed me until a second woman, filing past us a few minutes later, also said to me, "She was my best friend." My mother always seemed so alone, so by herself, impenetrable.

One day, years ago, before her heart attacks, we were walking down the street from the parked car to Thomas Sweet ice cream shop in Princeton. I turned around, and she and my father were holding hands. I kept focusing on their hands; the affection it showed—I had not guessed it was there. Usually, they ignored or insulted one another. My father, a short man with a comb-over, now white, would rise up on his toes to the height of my mother, point his finger at her face, and shout—what would he shout? "What's the matter with you? Don't you know better?" Almost Ralph Kramden–style. And she would respond fearlessly, "Chip, chip, chip, chip, chip, chip." They carped relentlessly at one another. He was stingy, so she spent freely—at least until she couldn't work anymore. Then she squirreled away five- and ten-dollar bills out of grocery money. We found bills in almost every pocket of her clothes when she died. I was always on her side because her complaints were about desires and his were about denying them.

The sweet moments of handholding were so much rarer than their airing of grievances. My father especially, but my mother too, I have to confess. The loss at the center of their exile fed the resentments they had in the present. For sure, resentments against history, against Hitler, against the Poles who made them feel despised in the country of their birth, and as I saw so often growing up, against one another and against almost everyone else, including those in the family.

My mother harbored so many resentments. She was always mad at Josef, my father's older brother. She got in the habit early and he gave her no reason to quit. He had a chicken farm and was indifferent to mean to his wife and kids, something I witnessed on the many weekends I spent on his farm while my parents made a living. They sold men's work clothes at the Columbus Farmer's Market in central New Jersey. Those are the durable gray, green, and brown chino pants and shirts laborers used to wear before jeans and T-shirts became the standard. Josef respected my mother—a *baleboste*, a good cook and housekeeper. She may have reminded him of his Polish mother, Brandla.

My mother loved Dov, my father's only surviving younger brother, but when the past came up, the one story she told about him was negative. In the displaced persons camp in Schlachtensee, near Berlin, after the war, Dov was a driver for an American officer and often got chocolates. She resented that he never gave them to me but always to his girlfriend, Eva, who became his first wife. "*A shikse un a daytshe*," a non-Jew and a German, my mother said, her Yiddish lips pursed and tight. He also gave Eva the stockings that my mother would have loved for herself, but she would never say that. Such open self-interest did not fit her image of proper motherhood.

The glue of secret resentments that keeps families together. Don't forgive and don't forget and for sure don't tell anyone. Grudges go as deep as love.

She resented Dov's second wife, Katja, as well, who didn't call enough and was uppity. Who was beautiful and thin and tall and dressed well and spent money on Gap children's clothes for her daughters and on the Ralph Lauren collection at Bloomingdale's for herself. Both my mother and father agreed, "They'll end up in the poor house, *vart*"—Yiddish for you wait and see. They just about did. Dov went bankrupt and when he died, he left no life insurance. Katja then lived hand-to-mouth, making minimum wage as a babysitter to the kids of the Long Island rich.

The resentments went beyond family to friends. My father's best friend, Asher Dorn, for instance. My father would spend a lot of time at Asher Dorn's grand house a few blocks away. My parents lived in a Queens one-bedroom stuffed with furniture and tchotchkes rescued from my father's Berlin business, where he bought antiques for cash from starving postwar Germany. Asher Dorn was also in the antiques business but now with a Fifth Avenue store. They talked about the stock market. My father was a player. But when I said to him, "It's nice that you have such a close friend," he answered mysteriously, "He's no friend. You should see what he did to us."

My mother loved me, her only child, unconditionally. I hold tight the memories she bequeathed to me. I was born in Frunze, now Bishkek, in Kyrgyzstan. It's currently an independent republic, but at the time it was in the USSR. Once my parents got to this Central Asian city of 800,000, they were surprised by the poverty and lack of food. My mother talked about midnight winter raids on surrounding fields to dig up onions to eat from the hard mud. Kyrgyzstan is on the northern fringe of the Tian Shan Mountains and is bordered by China. The people are a mix of ethnic Russians and people of Turkic descent. My mother, Lola, admired the fierce horsemen with their robes flying backward as they galloped through the dirt roads of Frunze, men with funny hats and facial hair. As I sit typing in my New Jersey suburb, I can't imagine it without reference to movies—somewhere between *Dr. Zhivago* and *Braveheart*. My mother playing the long-suffering woman in the wilderness. But I know it wasn't romantic at all; deprivation and poverty and loneliness in an industrial Soviet outpost, with the Chinese mountains as backdrop and alien men on fast horses as bit players.

The only family photograph from that period is a studio sepia print of a woman, a man, and a baby I don't recognize but who are my parents and me. I'm the only one who looks well fed. My mother was grateful to her Muslim neighbors, who would leave food for infant me on our windowsill or outside our door. So I was born there to a starving mother and a father who worked for the Soviet secret police, the NKVD, accompanying train cargo and skimming from it and making some money. That's how he got to see the celebrations in Moscow in 1944, when the Soviet army beat back the Germans, and how he missed my birth, a failure my mother would remind him of from time to time.

My cousin Danny has a blood sister, Idusha, and a stepsister, Brigit, who are the same age, born only a few months apart. Danny's biological mother is

Henya, one of the Seven. Rather than running away from Warsaw and Hitler, Henya was running to her lover Josef, Danny's father, the oldest of the three brothers. She died in an insane asylum in Germany, where Josef left her in 1948. He divorced her in 1950. Brigit's mother, Lina, was the hired help, a German *shikse* farm girl who got pregnant and was abandoned by her Mexican-American soldier lover, and who subsequently married Josef. Her options had diminished by then. Before she arrived, Danny's father put him and his sister in an orphanage. My mother taught me to never forgive him for that.

When Danny was in his fifties and his father was already dead, I told him the story of his rescue. My mother threatened Josef, warning him that she would take his kids out of the orphanage and raise them herself. He was shamed into hiring someone to take care of them. There is also a younger brother called Pavel. He never even knew his mother. He was the product of advice from a doctor who told Josef that if Henya, who was already institutionalized for schizophrenia, had another child, she might be shocked into sanity. So now Josef had three small children and no one to care for them. The German farm girl with the child of the Mexican-American soldier rescued him, just as he rescued her. Where was this? Frankfurt-am-Main, 1949.

Henya, the mystery woman. A fuzzy black-and-white photograph of a tanned young woman in a dark bathing suit sitting astride a motorcycle. She's squinting at the camera, her eyes avoiding the sun. She's gripping the cycle's handles. Henya, the story goes, was made crazy by war. She saw and heard the SS at her door in 1946 when the war was already over. She screamed and cowered and forgot that she had children. "They're coming; I hear their boots; they're coming," she whispered, pleaded, and then screamed until Josef had had it and walked out the door for a while, leaving his babies to endure. The SS came even more often to her after that—in 1947, 1948, 1949. Her gravestone had only her name—Henya G—and a death date. When my husband and I visited it, we had it properly inscribed, as her son Danny had asked us to do. The stone was provided by the postwar Jewish community of Munich, who knew only when she died, not when she was born.

The scraggly cemetery with stones leaning against stones is in the suburb of that city. At least she had a grave one could find. Where were my grandparents buried? In the ovens of Treblinka. Or starved in the streets of the Warsaw Ghetto. They were faces in a family photograph. They were stories my mother or, more often, Dov told. There is something comforting about the real estate of a gravesite.

Dov died a few years ago. I loved Dov. He had all the family charisma. Gentle, romantic, the youngest of the three surviving brothers. During family get-togethers, the three brothers—my father, Itzak, Josef, and Dov—rarely agreed on anything whatsoever. Not even on whether egg yolks are yellow. On those very rare occasions when they did agree, it was usually a received idea they dragged into the present, some rag of past wisdom. My father or Dov or Josef would say: "If the communist revolution had happened in Germany instead of Russia, it would have been good. It would have worked. Just a shame that Germany got Hitler instead." Despite Hitler, the Warsaw Ghetto, and the death camps, and all their suffering and loss, they held on to the idea of good German efficiency.

I gave the eulogy at Dov's funeral. Dov wanted me to write this book while he was still alive. He said maybe a movie could be made out of it. So many World War II movies, why not this? One about him. I asked who should play him, and he laughed and said Pierce Brosnan. Although charismatic, Dov was about five-two, bald, and with the biggest of the family noses, the kind the Germans put on their anti-Semitic propaganda posters. When he walked, it was from side to side—like a duck—so that his back, a disaster, would not be involved. Despite all that, he was charming, and women liked him. In the eulogy I said he should be played by Jude Law because Pierce Brosnan was too old. That got a laugh.

You've now met most of the Seven: the three brothers—Josef the oldest, Dov the youngest, with my father, Itzak, in the middle; Josef's first wife, Henya, who went insane; and my mother, Lola. You haven't met Sonia, my father's sister, or Chapka, Josef's best friend. Dov wanted me to call this book *The Seven* since their unity in exile is what distinguished them from the thousands of other refugees in the gulags of the USSR and what earned them that moniker, the Seven.

The prime number 7 is magical in mythology and legend. There are seven directions: north, south, east, west, up, down, and center. The human body has seven endocrine glands, which I mention because I have had thyroid cancer. There are seven colors of the rainbow. The Hebrew alphabet has seven double letters. Antiquity recognized seven planets; there are seven chakras, seven heavens in the Kabbalah and Islam, a maximum of seven lunar and solar eclipses annually, seven virtues, and seven deadly sins. Seven for the unknown numbers of the missing, also the loved ones who stayed in Warsaw and died—Motel, my father's youngest brother; Rachel, his older sister; my mother's beloved older brother, Natan; and her pesky younger sisters, Felusia and Nata; and my four grandparents, whose names are Sala and Wolfe, Brandla and Chaim. Well, that's more than seven; the dead are always too many.

I was able to interview the people whose names head the sections of this memoir. Three are among the Seven. Well, four if you count my mother, whose voice is in my father's chapter, interrupting and superseding his, and whose presence is everywhere in my life and my book. The other two names represent the two wives of Dov. Only war could have catapulted these women into his arms.

As the seven urbane city-dwellers were shunted here and there in the Soviet Union, they looked on the people in the backwater towns they wound up in as rubes, gullible marks to be used to make a profit so that they could eat. The Brest market was their initiation. They loved bragging about their success, when they had it. It was such a contrast to the indignities of lice, malaria, typhus, starvation, and abuse, which is most of the story.

My father must have told that nightgown story—the one about how the Russians mistook nightgowns for evening gowns—a thousand times. He told it with such pride, the way they traded on Russian naïveté. It was a story I hated to hear. It made me feel uneasy, though I did not tell him. The Soviet Union had saved their lives. Despite the corrupt and bureaucratic Soviet system, individual Russians sometimes gave them breaks when they needed them, to keep from starvation and death. He did not see, could not see, how the story demeaned not them, but him. It was his blind spot, and in those murderous times, it was also his strength.

Not Dov. Of all the stories Dov told, he never repeated that one. He did not have a mean bone in his body. He did not have to. His brothers and the cocoon of the Seven shielded him—at least for a time. Then, as for many Polish Jews who left Poland for refuge in the Soviet Union, his life, the lives of all the Seven, spun outward and collided with other, unrelated lives. The original Seven disintegrated as a unit—lost to death, to madness, to various geographies and encounters. The Seven was an idea, a romantic idea of togetherness and solidarity that they grabbed for. It substituted for their missing family and home for a time. They held on to the poetry of the Seven until they no longer could.

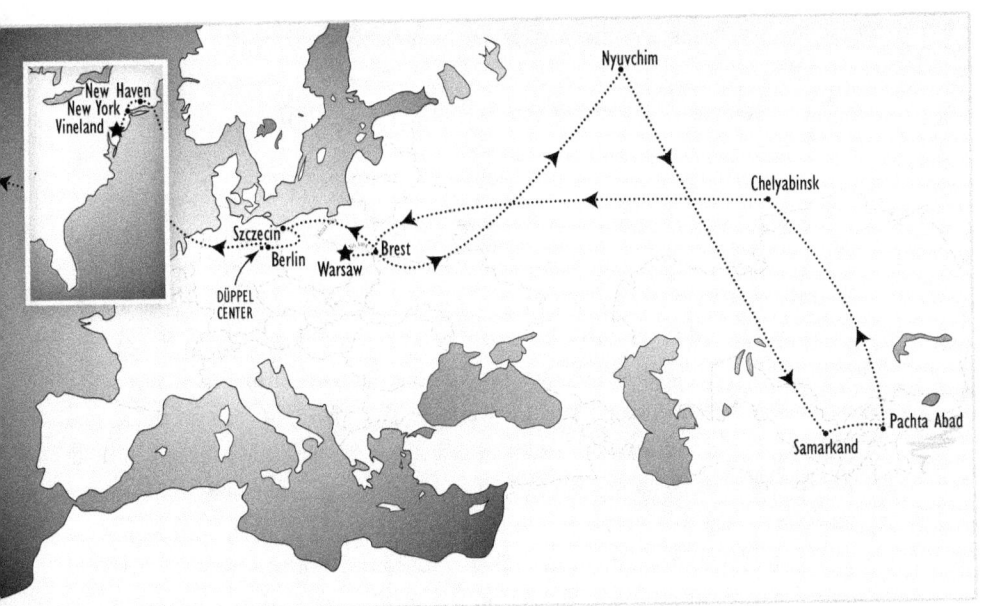

2

Dov

Dov was the first person I interviewed. He was separated from his second wife, Katja, living alone in a one-bedroom condo in Flushing, Queens. It was the usual Queens brick, seven-story building on a block filled with them. Each building had a short skirt of grass, punctuated by a few trees. The shops stood ready a few blocks away at the big intersection. Visitors had to ring the apartment buzzer in the lobby foyer and then be buzzed into the lobby, where the elevator was. Dov opened the door quickly and said, "Come in, come in." He wanted to talk about his separation more than his experiences during the war. The apartment was sparsely furnished and depressingly bare, almost as if no one lived there. No pictures or art on the wall. No personal objects and just a few pieces of old furniture.

"I never would believe that she leaves me. We always had in common our experience during the war.

"We swore to one another that we would never leave, no matter what. I would never believe that she could leave."

The war formed them both. Dreamy-eyed Dov, communist, soccer player, so absorbed in a book that he was unconscious of the fifty pounds of Polish army uniforms he was carrying on his back as he walked through the streets of Warsaw. He didn't take the tram so he could save the money to finance his pleasures. He was torn away from his late adolescence, from his parents and home. When we sat down, his hands were folded in front of him on the square card table he used for dining. He looked directly at me with those heavily lashed, honey-brown eyes, keeping me attentive to his words about being abandoned by his wife for the second time. The first time his previous wife, Eva, took their daughter and left him for a divorced man with four children whom she had met working as a waitress. Eva had been in the girls' version of Hitler Youth. His second wife, Katja, so unlikely to leave Dov, had left him—Katja, whose mother had sent her off with a family friend to save her life. Katja lived out the war in a basement in the German countryside, a child who had not yet learned to read, all alone in the dark, all day long, for years:

Dov: I'm very lonely. *Ach.* Would you believe it, that she could go? She knows how I felt when Eva left. The one thing we always said to each other, the one thing we had in common was the Holocaust. It kept us together. I never could believe she would go.

This was August 18, 1983, a blistering, blindingly bright New York City summer day. Dov was a spiffy dresser in the casual Queens mode—tight, pressed jeans and a light-blue cotton shirt open at the collar, revealing some chest hair, then still jet black. He had a heavy gold chain around his neck from which hung a big gold *chai*, the Hebrew word for "life." He wanted sympathy and I gave it.

"It's terrible that she's gone. It's a complete mystery to me."

Then there was nothing more to say about it, and he was ready to record the story he had been telling for years, in his Eastern European–accented English, to anyone who would listen.

Me: I never got straight why, exactly, you left, Dov, just a few weeks after the Germans invaded Poland? How could you know it would be so bad?

Dov: Let's see, when the Germans marched in, it was September first. It took them a couple of weeks to reach the outskirts of Warsaw. I think they were at the outskirts of Warsaw about September thirteenth or fourteenth. And things got so bad. You know the German high guy, Goering. He ordered one thousand bombers. Of course, Warsaw didn't want to capitulate, so they give ultimatum to surrender. But the mayor, I remember his name, Starzyński, he refused to surrender. Then of course they send across so many bombers. They leveled off all of Warsaw. All Warsaw was leveled except those neighborhoods where Germans would want to live. They knew exactly where to bomb, would you believe it? Today's, what you call 'em, smart bombs, hah! Not to compare.

The blitzkrieg that razed Warsaw began on September 1, 1939. Warsaw capitulated on September 28 and the entire Polish army a few days later. As early as September 21, Reinhard Heydrich gave a secret order to concentrate Jews in conquered Poland into ghettoes. And in Warsaw the *Judenrat*, the Jewish council convened by the Germans that governed the Warsaw Ghetto, was formed by October 4, a scant week after the Germans marched in. German efficiency.

"And of course then Warsaw surrendered. I remember exactly when they gave announcement on the streets and spread, you know, paper flyers."

"And what did the flyers say—in German or in Polish?"

"In Polish, in Polish. That the German army's going to march in tomorrow at exactly—with damn precision—at say, seven o'clock. At those certain points it will be given to people food. Now that the German army has liberated Warsaw from hunger. And what do you think, they used to give out bread from the German army trucks. They just threw it out, you know, from the back of the truck like, like, what do you call it—confetti. But then, and then, ha, ha, what was funny about it was you had German newsreel cameras taking films of what was going on. The Germans throwing bread and the Poles grabbing it. And after they finished with the movie cameras, what do you know, they took the bread away. *Ach*, propaganda.

"And then when they got back home, they showed in Germany how their army had liberated Warsaw, the starving people of Warsaw, gave them food."

"How old were you then?"

"In 1939, about eighteen years old. Yeah, eighteen."

He laughs, "I can't lie to you about my age."

"So you were eighteen years old. You were just a kid! And you were working. You weren't going to school anymore."

"Yeah, you had in the educational system seven grades, seven years. I went to four grades and then no more. And then I went to work."

"And were these schools integrated with the Poles?"

"Yes, Polish Catholic kids. We all wear uniforms. All schools in Poland, you wore a navy-blue jacket with shiny silver buttons on the uniform.

"Even then I was crazy about a little girl, her name was Selena."

Even then he was crazy about a little girl. That's Dov. In telling their stories to me, each of the three brothers created a character for himself. Dov is the romantic one, the dreamer, the poet.

"Selena?"

"I used to carry her books."

"Really?" We both laugh.

"Did you take photographs with you when you left Warsaw?"

"From Warsaw, I have one picture left. I have a picture of myself. See? I always used to walk with a book in my hands as I walked the streets because I love to read."

"What did you read?"

"Many things. Dostoevsky, Tolstoy. Upton Sinclair. Many others. Of course, *Uncle Tom's Cabin*."

"Did you?"

"Oh, yeah! *Chata Woja Toma*, that's the title in Polish. *Chata Woja*—*Woja* means 'uncle.' *Chata* is 'hut.'"

"Anyway, this is the only picture of me in Warsaw."

"That looks like you. Is that a newspaper you are holding?"

"It was a left-wing paper, you know. *Dziennik Ludowy* it was called. I really liked this paper—*The People's Daily*. Yeah. In fact, I was in a group of people, they were very leftist, communist-like, you know. And you know why? Only because maybe I believe in justice, and of course we were all fooled by the idea of communism.

"Even as a kid, my interests were much different than my brothers'. I used to always read and discuss. Ever read *And Quiet Flows the Don* by Sholokhov? How innocent he was. He believed, he believed in a great ideology—communism. But in real life it was different. It's so far from the truth, it's not even funny. In fact, this guy in the book remind me so much of me when I was in my youth. And fighting for a good and for justice."

At first I thought Dov may have belonged to the Bund, a Jewish socialist organization that had a far from unified program and kept morphing. Many of the Bund's tenets had been communist: nationalizing industry, redistribution of wealth, including the land. It was the most popular of the socialist Jewish organizations and the one that had a large youth movement. It was anti-Zionist, anti-religious. Its members saw themselves as Poles and believed in minority rights within Poland. Dov could have signed on for all of that, I think, but by the time it counted for Dov, the Bund had moved right. Perhaps he joined the left wing of Poʻale Tsiyon, a volatile party with a large youth movement, or even the Communist Party—Jewish Warsaw was so alive with politics, particularly the politics of hope.

"In this group, you know, you yell a lot, discuss a lot, you talk a lot at this time. Mainly we talked about the injustices against the Jews and about the system in Poland. I got into what you call a youth socialist group.

"Now, you know, in Warsaw the streetcars, they run on electric wires. They had big overhead wires up in the air, and the car had to get in touch with the wires overhead. Then the train would run. So I learned to cut them—the wires. Also what the communists used to do, just to show that they are fighting for rights, they used to throw over those electrical lines a red piece of cardboard, like a placard, with the words *Vive liberté*. You know, whatever would anger the government. Three guys, they would stake out, to see if no cops are around, and the others would do the job—zoom, and it was done. Now the streetcars couldn't pass anymore. [Laughs.] Right, so the train had to stop—the police had to come with a special truck to fix and to remove whatever we put there. Sometimes it was a communist flag.

"About a dozen of us once a month, in different neighborhoods. From the time I was fifteen until the war broke out. If you got caught, forget about it.

"We used to go to the park, read books, you know, and have discussions. We used to go outside Warsaw and take a boat trip down the Vistula River, talking the whole time. We would sleep in people's barns, on hay, you know. In the morning, we were covered with flies."

"Where did you live, what was your apartment like?"

"Do you know the book *Mila 18*? Well we lived on a street near that square—Muranowska 34. The apartment was no. 85. A three-story brick building. On the street level was a bakery, which I knew very well, believe me, very well. I liked sweets, still do. Also because I used to go for *Shabbos*. Every Friday my mother used to prepare Friday morning early the house for *Shabbos*. She used to cook *cholent*. At four or five, before sundown, I went to the bakery, stuck the *cholent* in the oven, got a ticket, and Saturday around eleven it was finished!"

Cholent is a stew, slow-cooked in the oven on a low temperature: a *Shabbos* dish because you could put it in the oven Friday before sundown and then take it out the next day and feed the family. The bakery was convenient because its oven was always on. One could not work on *Shabbos*, and turning on an oven or even a light switch was forbidden. *Cholent* solves the problem.

It's an ancient Jewish dish with variants all over the world. Some speculate that it was cooked by Jews in ancient Rome. For Ashkenazi or Eastern-European Jews, it's a dish of *schmaltz*, beef, potatoes, beans, vegetables, and grains. Someone asked me to make it once. I remembered the succulent dish my mother used to make, not every *Shabbos* but on special occasions. I'm a pretty good cook and I consider myself my mother's daughter. No need to seek a recipe, just a spiritual mind-meld with Lola. As it turned out, the stew was dried out and tasteless, and no one ate it.

The invention of memory—with its betrayals.

Cholent was one of the dishes my mother was famous for. The other was cheesecake—that is, cheeseless cheesecake. At holiday dinners everyone hoped for *cholent* and the cheesecake that had no cheese in it.

On the map of the Jewish ghetto in Warsaw, Niska Street is just north of Muranowska. That's where my mother, Lola, lived with her family. Niska 39. When they were courting, my mother and father lived a block apart. My mother's street would mark the boundary of the Nazi-defined Jewish ghetto. There were cousins, too, with the last name of Rais. They lived at Franciszkańska 5. My family's lives were spread all over the ghetto. At the end they lived in the northeast. Earlier they lived on Nalewski, near Krasinski Ogród, a park, a bit south of Muranowska. There was the Jewish school that Josef went to. Rachel, my father's affluent married sister, lived in the more posh, more Christian section of Warsaw, on Ulica Pańska. Rachel and her husband had an indoor toilet. Pańska was near Twarda, where Wasserstand, the guy to whom Dov delivered the pants his brothers and father sewed, lived.

"We lived on the top floor. That would be the third floor. There were two apartments on each floor. My neighbors, I remember them well. A big family with five children. The father was Hasidic.

"I liked the daughter, Frania. But I was too shy to talk to her."

"So you had two rooms?"

"Yes, that's all. That's what we had. Two rooms."

Pointing around the room we were sitting in, he said, "I would say about this size."

"A kitchen and then another room. Yeah, a little hallway, there's where I slept—the hallway. There was a big king-sized bed. Of course, my mother and my father and Motel and Sonia, they slept on the big bed. And then we had cots, you know, individual cots, except me and Josef slept on the same cot in the hallway. I remember once he brought a girl into the bed while I was sleeping in it. Would you believe it? Then he went into the army and I had my own bed.

"Josef was in the *Polska Armia*, the Polish army. I even know his regiment. It's the Fifty-ninth Regiment. You know, he had to go to the army. He was drafted. And he came back for vacation. And he walked in with uniform of the Polish army. Oh, I was so impressed. Like they say, they made a man out of him. The army, right? Discipline, you know. And what the army does. The exercises, getting up four o'clock, five o'clock in the morning and running and learning how to shoot. He looked good, you know. Rosy cheeks. His eyes gleaming."

I had always wondered why Dov stuck more closely to Josef through the war than to my father. It had always stung me a little bit since I felt close to Dov, and I took his preference for Josef over my father personally. Josef is colder, more unpredictable than my father, has even less need of others. It was these qualities in a soldier-brother that drew Dov. In a family of sedentary men, Josef is the one with a bit of macho glamour by way of his uniform and aloofness.

We continued to talk about the family apartment.

"A bathroom, too?"

"Nah, a common toilet all the way down. All the way down, forget it. Behind the building. In the courtyard."

"So how did people get out in the morning?"

"What do you mean, how did they get out in the morning?"

"You know, when they had to go to work?"

"It wasn't like here, that you had to go for jobs. Everybody was in his own apartment. Yes. In the apartment, that's where your father used to sit and Josef used to sit, behind my father a little, you know, by a table, sewing.

"They would start, let's say nine in the morning. But when five came—boom, Itzak is out to see Lola, your mother. 'Oh,' my father said, 'Oh! You know, he's going already to see Lola.' Itzak would answer, 'How else am I gonna see her if I don't go now?' My father would answer, 'Tomorrow, you'll see her tomorrow.' But, no, you know how stubborn your father is, goes in one ear and out the other. And Itzak, he just ran out.

"They liked to dance. They used to go to club Rendezvous to dance, somewhere in midtown Warsaw. Oh, boy, did your mother love to dance."

The truth is my mother did love to dance. She was a natural and would come to life when she heard music. One of my childhood memories is of her grabbing me when a tune she liked came on the radio and whirling me around the room. I inherited this passion. As a teenager, I was a rock-and-roll fool. I would go to any dance, any time, with anyone who was willing. I would dance every dance, even if I had to dance by myself—which I usually did not have to do.

In those days, my teenage days, in a small South Jersey town, there was de facto segregation of all groups. Forget about race. That was a clear matter of railroad tracks separating white and black. I'm talking about religious and ethnic segregation. I don't even know where the Latinos were. They were migrant workers on all the big farms for sure. But where they went after work, I don't know. The largest ethnic group in Vineland was Italian. There was even an annual dandelion festival. My mother sliced the population as Christian and Jewish. She was punctilious at demonstrating respect for those others, the Christians. She didn't hang wash out on Sundays because it was *their* day of rest. My sweet mother whom all the non-Jewish neighbors adored.

When invited by a great dancer—yes, he went to Sacred Heart High School, the beautiful gothic-style Catholic school at the other end of town—to go all the way to Philadelphia to dance on the TV show *American Bandstand*, hosted by Dick Clark for so long that his face lifts left him with a permanent smile, I had to say, "No." When I asked her, she gave me that look, "*Mit a goy? Gevald! Vey iz mir. Ikh gey khaleshn bald avek. Gotenyu.*" Yiddish, the language of my ancestors, along with that hurt look she fixed on me, her one and only child, defeated me. "I lost my whole family so you could go with a *shaygets*?"

Hers was a love that strangled as it nurtured. It's still the kind of love I know best. I resented her refusal for a long time, much longer than I should have. Yes, she loved to dance and so do I. I am good at it, just as she was.

"What was the main street in your neighborhood in Poland? Where all the shops were?"

"Yes, that was the Zamenhofa Street. You know Zamenhof?"

"No."

"You're kidding! Zamenhof was Jewish scientist. He was the one that created the language, the universal language, Esperanto. That's how we got the street name. It was Dr. Zamenhof. We used to call it Jica. It was changed to Zamenhofa."

Esperanto? When I was an undergraduate, I did a research paper on Esperanto for a linguistics course. The professor gave me a B for the paper or maybe even lower, which shattered me since I usually got As on papers. His complaint was that I was not critical of the Esperanto movement, that I didn't see how ridiculous the idea of a universal language is. He expected me to have his own grown-up cynicism. As an undergraduate I never would have dreamed that an English professor, with the idealism that implied for me, would be contemptuous of the idea of a universal language, one which, in Zamenhof's scheme, would not supplant the native language but would be a second language used to promote world peace through common understanding. It seems even stranger to me now, as I think about the fact that this happened in the sixties, the moment for idealism in the United States.

L. L. Zamenhof published his book on Esperanto in 1887 under the pseudonym "Doktoro Esperanto," meaning Doctor Hope. Zamenhof was a Polish Jew, and on the grounds that he was a Jew, Esperanto advocates became Nazi targets. Hitler's *Mein Kampf* argues that Esperanto would be used by Jews to advance their international conspiracy to achieve world economic domination. The Germans killed the Zamenhof family and hunted down Esperanto-speakers for imprisonment or murder. Stalin was also against it. The Esperanto movement, though, lives on internationally and has an affiliation with the United Nations and UNESCO, as well as MENSA. It is even one of Google's translation languages. Dov was drawn to the etymology of the street name Zamenhofa, to its association with the desire for a better world.

"You know, come to think, there was a house of prostitution in our building in the basement. We saw men always go in and out. You see, we live very close to a certain area, Krochmalna. Was considered like the East Village. Of course there was no drugs then. But lots of crime, and if you stole something, you went to this place. There these people would buy it from you, all the hot stuff. And no. 7 was a famous building. That's a famous place for all the criminals, where the Jewish criminals used to live. Purse-snatchers and pickpockets, you know, the criminal element."

When I looked up Krochmalna Street, I was led to Isaac Bashevis Singer, the Noble Prize–winning Yiddish writer. In 1908 his family moved to Krochmalna, where he set many of his stories. He talked about it as "the center of the universe." His autobiographical book, *In My Father's Court*, describes growing up on this street and about the rabbinical court his father sat on called *Beth Din*. Singer brought home to me the poverty and Jewishness of the neighborhood. Crowded cobblestone streets holding up tenement buildings and small shops, a confusion of the sacred and the profane—the rabbis and kosher kitchens, like that of my grandmother, and the thieves, prostitutes, and drunks, like my grandfather who, full of beer or vodka, would bribe his children with chocolates when he came home late from the bars. There were children everywhere, of course, like the baby of the family, Motel, who ran through the courtyards and streets with the other kids. And troublemakers like Dov and his buddies. Not all of their activities came from an idealistic impulse. They would bore holes into the stinking wooden edifice that held the garbage of his building. Why? To see what was there and to be chased away, doing it for the thrill of being bad.

The neighborhood helps to explain why Dov got left behind a grade in school. He went to school for five years, but finished only four grades.

"I was left back one year in the same class because I didn't pass for some reason. My mind was always on something else, maybe I think about playing football, you know, soccer, dreaming. I forgot the name of the teacher. I can see her before me. Always with a ruler in her hand and hitting you over the hands. Or pulling your ears. Oh, yes."

This compulsive reader drifted off into his own world at school. The schoolroom for him was not a passport to possibility. Beyond elementary school, you had to pay. His was a family that could barely make the rent, even with all the kids working. The only way out, the hope that boys like him held on to, was a new and different future world through politics, through revolution. He got his wish but not in the way it was promised.

"Dov, you did tailoring too?"

"No. My mother and father tried very hard to make a tailor out of me. So I sat down, I tried—I used to sit down without a thimble, you know.

"'Come, I'll show you how to sew,' my mother always said. But I never like a thimble; it bothered me. It fell off. I stuck myself always anyway. So I took it off. My father—'He cannot work without a thimble! He cannot be a tailor without a thimble. He has to have a thimble.' And I say I can work without a thimble. 'No! Just forget about it. You'll never make a tailor. Get out of here!'"

In the 1930s home-workers, consisting of 25 percent of the Jewish labor force, were common. And 85 percent of that group were tailors or shoemakers. Most worked by contract, as did my grandfather. Common also was child labor. Dov's two older brothers, Josef and Itzak, my father, worked in their father's trade as young teenagers. Tailoring sustained both of them for much of their lives. Dov, however, gleefully told me:

"And I never did become a tailor.

"Well, I didn't miss nothing. I was more into mechanics. I was fascinated with cars. And with planes. I told everyone I wanted to be a pilot."

Like Bigger Thomas in Richard Wright's *Native Son*. Bigger, an innocent, poor, black boy with dreams of flying who got mixed up with a rich white family, to his destruction. That's what I thought of. Neither one had a ghost of a chance.

Dov had no talent for tailoring. He had a talent for reading, for languages, for soccer, for romance, and for dreaming.

When it was clear that Dov would not follow his brothers into tailoring, he tried various apprenticeships to learn a trade, ones he could get for free. He tried to become a toolmaker.

For Dov, the romantic, most adventures involved a girl. He was no Don Juan, no seducer. Girls chose him. And he was not afraid to give his heart away—although he was picky.

"So that was the trade I was going to learn, toolmaker. And if I would have learned this trade, I could earn like four *złotys* an hour, which was a lot of money. A lot of money. That was the going rate for men who had this trade. And once you knew this, you could shape different types of things.

"This man, his name was Greenberg. I remember that name. He had four daughters. One daughter—they all liked me—but one, let's say, was crazy about me. I didn't like her. And he used to threaten me, 'If you don't go out with my daughter, I won't teach you this trade.'

"So that was the end of that."

As he drifted in and out of apprenticeships, he worked for his father delivering pants.

"So when we finished a batch of pants for this contractor, Wasserstand, right? My father gave me fifty pair of pants to deliver, and he give me like twenty cents, *groshn*, for the tram, but I walked. I saved the twenty cents and bought chocolate! I was a terrible *nasher*—you know what *nasher* is? I couldn't live without chocolate. This was one of my passions, chocolate.

"Yeah, also I joined what you call a sports group, like a club, a soccer club. It was called Maccabi. You know, like Maccabi in Chanukah and the revolt of the Maccabees?"

The club Dov is speaking of sponsored a Jewish form of the Olympics, which inspired its formation. The first games were held in 1932 because it marked the eighteen-hundred-year anniversary of a famous revolt against the Roman Empire called the Bar Kochba revolt. You can still find these youth sport clubs attached to Jewish centers around the world.

"My brother Josef belonged to a club, too. He was bicycling. So was your father. But I was soccer player. In fact, when I came to the US, I played for Yale University in New Haven. Would you believe it? Somehow they heard I had played in Europe, and they signed me up. Paid me fifty dollars for ninety minutes every Sunday, more than I made in forty hours of work at Winchester Arms."

"Was it possible to make friends with Polish kids?"

"No. Never, never. All I thought was why? Nothing else. Why? I don't do nothing wrong. I understood it was against everybody, all Jews. This I understood. Not just me.

"We used to go Saturdays—we used to go to a swimming pool, the only public swimming pool in Warsaw at this time, which was in some kind of a school. I went with my group, my social group, who I used to hang out with. There were Christian boys. They used to try to chase us out."

"How did they know you were Jewish?"

"See, that's a good point. Now, the popular idea of a Jew at that time, which most Jews was not really living, they are the ones with the big black caftans, with the big fur hats, with the *peyos* and the *tsitsit* sticking out. This how the Jews was depicted, right?

"Now we were dressed European—like the gentiles. But how did a Pole know that you were not? Of course, me, they could spot me a mile away that I am Jewish because of my nose, right, because my physical looks. I look like, they say, typical Jewish.

"Now, if they were in doubt that you are not a Jew, then they would take off your pants, see if you are circumcised. This is what happened in Warsaw, mainly when the Germans came. The Polish gentiles, the young kids and the older ones, they used to be with the Germans, and they used to point out Jews. If they were in doubt about somebody, they told him take off his pants, see if he's circumcised, *umgeshnitn*.

"The Germans used to go through the streets, grab people, take them to work. They took me to the river to clean their trucks. They took once my sister Sonia, grabbed her, and they made her clean their quarters with her underwear.

"They just go into the streets—you know, you were afraid to say no. 'You there. Come, *Jude, komm*! Come with us.' You wouldn't say no. You were afraid."

"Did you know any adult Poles?"

"The only adult Christians I came across were all nice. My father's customers, you know. My father was a specialist in dressing the Polish officers in pants. They had to be very tight below the knee. The Polish officers were mainly from the—what they called the Polish good blood—aristocracy. You couldn't be just an officer because you were a good soldier. They were big playboys, they were gamblers, they liked to fool around with women, and my father always helped them with money, go to the racetrack and so on and so forth. This is why they liked him. They used to come to my father to lend them money, and they'd write checks, and my father used to give them cash.

"He'd give the shirt off his back. And I am like him 100 percent.

"My sister Sonia could have dated those guys—they wanted to date her—those Polish officers. But no, no, no—*a goy*!

"And in fact, those same officers, when the war broke out, they told him, 'Chaim, move out of here, things are no good, move out, move out.' They warned, 'Get out of here. We'll help you if you need. They told him to go east, to his brother in Brest-Litovsk.

"But my father said, 'I don't believe.' He should have believed, but he didn't believe it. My father in the beginning said he remembers the Germans from World War I. 'They also talked many things then, but it wasn't bad at all. You don't listen to rumors. It couldn't be what people say.'

"You know, there was chaos. Warsaw was chaos; people were running from one place to another. Like my mother, she was worried about my older sister Rachel and her two kids, a boy and a girl, so she used to walk from where we lived to where she used to live, which was a long walk—over rubbles, over bombed buildings, over ruins."

"No telephones?"

"No, no. We never had a telephone. Rachel, my sister, had a telephone. She had a toilet; what a luxury! In fact, when I worked for this guy Wasserstand, you know, when I was delivering pants there, I used to go up for lunch to Rachel's, yeah? And this was an experience I'll never forget. I loved the toilet. I could sit there for hours if she let me. It was such a luxury. I cannot describe to you that feeling of having your own toilet.

"First of all, there was a fight to get food. Food. So let's say after about September 7, 8, 9, 10, 11, 12—they were bombing every day. Dead horses—people used to cut meat out of the horses, which was something new, you know, it was something new. You were just a little in disgust how people could do it.

"*Ach*, look how we used to live! If they hit with the bomb a warehouse, we used to run, everybody straight to the warehouse, and we used to take anything we could lay our hands on, right? I believe Josef took a motorcycle. A motorcycle! Right? I took a bag of food, which was salty, it was so salty! We soaked it in water for hours, for days, and it was still salty. I don't know what it was, but it was so much salt. I said what the hell is it—it looked like meat, but it was so salty! Forget about it. So I took something unusable."

Dov's impracticality was legend. He could romance a stone, but when it came to survival, all he did was blunder and laugh about it. He proves the truism that poets have to be kept or they are in danger of starving. He struggled for money his whole life.

He cared the most that I would write this book, that his stories would not be lost. His worry that he would be forgotten reminds me of the words the poet John Keats had put on his gravestone, "Here lies one whose name was writ in water."

Sixteen days after Germany invaded Poland, beginning World War II, the Soviet Union invaded from the east, following an agreement with Germany. After it surrendered, Poland was partitioned. Germany occupied Poland's western half, and the Soviet Union the eastern half.

"The Germans got tougher every day, the new orders given out, the Jews shouldn't do this, shouldn't do that. Let's say, the Jews must surrender all the radios.

"We had a Philips radio; you know the brand? It had a magnetic eye, was some radio. You know it's like you buy a new, very high-tech television, but the difference was even greater than here because in Poland it was a luxury to have a radio. And to surrender it, we hated to do it, but if you didn't, you heard you would be shot. Everything then is death.

"Yeah, you know, I didn't know what classical music is. There was no access like here. We had a few stations only. And the first time we bought a radio, and I came across Beethoven's Fifth Symphony. This struck me so much, like you give somebody a punch, you know. And then I got interested in classical music."

"Whose idea was it to leave Warsaw?"

"Oh, yeah. Rumors say the Germans killed last night fifteen people. Rumors, rumors are flying, every minute a different rumor, right? But of course, the people didn't make them up. They were more true than they made them up. So we heard shots, you know, at night. Everybody's heart was pounding; you had no peace."

"What finally made you leave?

"What made me leave? All right. Rumors were flying. Germans are gonna do this, they're gonna to do that. In fact, I was once caught in what they called a roundup in the neighborhood, you know. They roped off three or four blocks. Everybody on the trucks to work on digging, remove rubble, dig. Which we did. And then, on the way back, some people say, 'What happened to the other people?'

"And so they used to whisper—they got shot. Must have been *geshosn*.

" *'Ikh gleyb es nisht.'* I don't believe it.

" *'Ikh hob gehert shisn.'* I heard shots. You know, the people's rumors!

" *'Vu iz Yoysef oder Menakhem?'* Where is Josef or Menachim?

" *'Ikh ze zey nisht.'* I don't see them.

" *'Iz geshosn gevorn.'* Was shot.

" *'Vu zenen zey?'* Where are they?

"The Germans were there just a few days, and when they take the Jews out on the trucks to work, some Jews didn't come back. So, of course, the Jews didn't want to go there anymore, voluntary, to work. Not knowing what's gonna happen. Some people were taken away, you never saw them again. Who knew who was where? You were just looking out for yourself.

"So my father had family in Brest-Litovsk. Well, it was now in Russia. You know, Poland was partitioned again in World War II. The river Bug was the border with the Russians. East of the Bug was Russia, west of the Bug, the Germans. Brest-Litovsk happened to be east of the Bug and became Russia. So my family in Brest-Litovsk became part of Russia. They didn't like it! But they said, better with the *Russen* than the Germans. Which was true. The *Russen* didn't kill you. At least they didn't kill you. They let you live."

Dov was wrong about that. Stalin's policies were murderous. Read Timothy Snyder's book *Bloodlands*. None of the Seven, though, died at the hands of the Soviets. The Soviet Union saved their lives and so gave me my life.

Dov gets us some beer. We are where? In Queens, but he has moved back with Katja, and they are in their lovely, lovingly decorated one-bedroom apartment. Their daughters are grown and out of the house. This would be their final home. The beer reminds him of when he worked for Wasserstand in his married sister's neighborhood, and she made him lunch. He remembers being reprimanded for his eating habits by his brother-in-law, Simon Drexler. He put a stop to Dov's slurping.

"And when you cut, you know, take fork and knife to cut your food, you put the knife away and you take the fork, pick it up, and you eat. So the days when I used to go to Rachel's, I did all those prescribed etiquette of eating. I was so uptight; the whole time I was hoping I'm not doing nothing wrong. Then I said I'm not going to come. 'No,' my sister said, 'you must come. I demand that you come.' Because my mother used to say, 'Please take care of my Dovela.'

"My sister's husband, Drexler, was tall. He must have been five-nine. To me it's tall. Me only being five-three or five-four, it's tall. The biggest joke about my family is that I'm the tallest in my family. To me, he was tall. Skinny and tall. He was also kind of an artist. His job was to decorate the windows, you know, showcases, outside windows for big stores in Warsaw. He made lots of money. He was very talented. Very talented. He used to sing and perform. I heard many times his imitations of Al Jolson. *Mammy, Mammy, How I love ya, my dear ol' mammy.* In fact, my sister was also an actress. She was performing on the stage. We went a few times to see her perform on stage. This I remember."

"Why didn't Rachel and Drexler go with you to Brest-Litovsk?"

"You know why? All right. Let's put it this way. He talked very fluent German. Also, my sister spoke German because of knowing him. So he thought he was gonna get away. In fact, he did some business with the Germans. Nobody wanted to believe what they gonna do.

"And of course, Chamberlain came in and talked about this white piece of paper to bring eternal peace, remember? When Chamberlain went to Munich to make peace. And all those stories, everybody believed. Maybe it'll be avoided—the war, right?"

Dov is talking about the Munich Agreement, signed by Hitler and Neville Chamberlain, prime minister of Britain, on September 29, 1938, ceding the Sudetenland part of Czechoslovakia to Germany in return for Hitler's agreement not to invade the rest of Czechoslovakia. Although Chamberlain returned from his meeting with Hitler thinking he had accomplished something, Hitler invaded anyway. Chamberlain's policies have gone down in history as deluded, and Chamberlain himself as a Hitler appeaser. Dov remembers the hopeful atmosphere in his home and in Poland, after the calming statement Chamberlain made as he returned to London with the agreement, delaying an Allied response:

> My good friends, . . . there has come back from Germany to Downing Street peace with honour. I believe it is peace for our time. We thank you from the bottom of our hearts. Now I recommend you go home, and sleep quietly in your beds.

"But all of a sudden we were all afraid that something was going to happen to us. So my parents said, 'Ah—you better go to my brother in Brest.' And 'Maybe we'll come too. Maybe.' You couldn't go altogether, too many people, and they were afraid to leave their furniture—their brand-new mahogany furniture. Can you believe it?

"Everything came all of a sudden. Everybody felt the atmosphere of the war. Mobilizations and Polish radio blast the march music, getting the people prepared for war."

Dov and the rest of the Seven left German-occupied Warsaw in 1939, shortly after the Germans occupied Poland. In the year after they left, here's what they missed:

The destruction of the synagogues.

Strict curfews for Jews.

Requirement for Jews to wear a star on their clothing.

The freezing of Jewish bank deposits.

Travel restrictions for Jews.

Registration of all property held by Jews—including furniture (mahogany or otherwise), jewelry, and even clothing.

The building of the Warsaw Ghetto wall.

Despite the many deaths from typhus and starvation, the population rose after the Warsaw Ghetto was sealed because the Germans were liquidating the ghettoes in surrounding towns and transporting Jews to the Warsaw Ghetto. By the summer of 1941, the Warsaw Ghetto had about 450,000 Jews, but by autumn that number had been reduced to 415,000. In 1940 about 9,000 Jews died in the ghetto, but in 1941 more than 43,000 died, many in a typhoid epidemic. The Germans kept squeezing the boundaries of the sealed ghetto, snatching the better streets and buildings in exchange for fewer and poorer ones. At one point in 1941, houses on the even-numbered side of Krochmalna were to be emptied. In the same year, Jews were forbidden to accompany their dead to the cemetery because it was outside the revised border of the ghetto.

The Seven left Warsaw separately or in pairs. So from Warsaw to Brest, they hoofed it or biked it or paid for rides when they could get them, and they each, in their own way, made it across the Bug River to the Soviets.

From Brest to Kotlas with stops in Minsk, Moscow, and Yaroslavl, they went mainly by train—lice-infested cattle cars really—then by steamship to Syktyvkar, where they were put on a truck and driven to the small taiga town of Nyuvchim, the location of their prison settlement.

Each brother remembers the journey vividly and also differently from the others. I believe them all.

Of all the people they left behind, Dov regrets most leaving their youngest brother, Motel, with whom their mother refused to part; she wanted to keep at least one of her babies.

In his final illness, Dov dreamt about Motel:

"I dream a lot about my youngest brother, who was about seven years old when we left. He was born in 1932, I believe. I used to take him to school. He was so afraid. And I told him, 'Don't worry. I was the same way as you.' And he was very nice little guy. Very friendly. And I pick him up from school. And today, very often, in my dreams I see him.

"How would he look when he would be my age? What would he do? What kind profession he would have. Even today, when I look at his picture, right away I start thinking about him. Was a very good-looking, handsome guy like my father. Like me. [Laughs.]"

The Seven had to sneak across the border, which was closing tighter and tighter each day. The three brothers left German-occupied Poland by different routes. Josef was first. He crossed the Bug River, which marked the border, into the USSR with his army uniform on and shrapnel in his knee. Then he went back to Warsaw to retrieve the others and returned to Brest with Sonia. My father left on bicycle and got stuck in the river's muddy bottom. The others were more game than Dov for the deceptions involved in illegally crossing the border. Dov traveled with Henya, then Josef's girlfriend. They walked, they paid for wagon rides, and when they negotiated to cross the Bug River to get to the Soviets, they were duped. Dov gave most of their money to a Pole for a midnight boat across the river. The Pole told them to meet him in a certain spot that was safe because he had bribed the guards. He took their full fare and never showed up, while Dov and Henya were grilled by the guards who were supposed to have been bribed. A guard took pity on them, and for the few *złotys* they had left, took them to a rowboat and told Dov where to cross the Bug. The boat leaked, and they abandoned their watery vessel three-quarters of the way across. They slogged through chin-high water with their few possessions balanced on their heads, held steady with one arm, before they found better purchase and waded to reach the other side. Dov and Henya were the fifth and sixth of the Seven to arrive at his uncle's already-crowded house. The last was my mother, who was held at the border with her brother for weeks. When Polish border police asked them where they wanted to go, they knew to say Poland. They were tutored to say the opposite of their true intention: The police sent you where you did not want to go. And so they were eventually sent into Soviet-occupied territory. My mother's life was saved and thus mine became possible. Her brother is another story.

"After I crossed the border with Henya—Itzak was already there, Josef was there, and Sonia was there—all of a sudden I decided to pack my things, the first day I was there. I was very eager to go to the Russians because of communism there. I believed in this. I believe in the real communism, the way maybe it's spelled in simple terms. Everybody is equal. Nobody has more than you. This concept was for me. In fact my clothes were not even dry. I grabbed my stuff off the clothesline and with some buddies took the train for Kiev.

"In that time you just got on a train without paying any money. Then you tell them you are a refugee, *bezhenets*. That was the word for refugee. When you came into like the grand central station in Kiev, there were signs '*Bezhentsy* register here,' right? So I registered. My name, you know. Where I was born. What kind of work I can do. I say I have no trade, nothing. So they put me in a big factory, on an assembly line. I lived inside the factory. They had quarters for us. It was a big room with beds, you know. Like in the army. I must have stayed a few weeks there.

"Of course my days off I went sightseeing with the tram or walking. Was very interesting city. I remember having big discussions. I didn't know nothing then that I have to fear about the way I talk. But the Jews, the Russian Jews say to me, 'Don't talk Yiddish.' They say, 'You cannot talk the way you talk.'

"I asked questions, lots of questions about how communism works there. How come this? How come that? Right? And the answer was 'Oh, it's too soon.' The answer was, 'It's only a little more than twenty years after the revolution.' 'Give us time,' right? But forget about it, you know. These people, Jews, dedicated to communism!

"The guy who talked to us was called political commissar. Every factory has political commissar, you know. It's part of propaganda, part of teaching. They teach you good things. If you ask them the question, 'Why the money is worthless? Why they live fifty people in the same room, why can't everyone have an apartment?' He will give you the answers about productivity and the future, right? 'Why do you have to do it this way.' Didn't make me feel better. But I got the answers to my questions.

"You were disappointed with communism."

"Right, was disappointed. The work was very hard. So I was among thousands of young guys who went there voluntarily, and then decided they gonna go back. They wouldn't let us. Then some of the guys, they lay down across railroad tracks, you know, for protest."

The romance of ideas and the mendacity of reality.

"And then they just shipped us back. So I came back to Brest-Litovsk. Oh, they said, '*Er iz aher tzurik,*' he came back. And that was still in 1939. I remember when I got to my uncle's house—in December. It was bitter cold. We wanted to stay inside, but the uncle chased us out to work in the market, to make some money. My father's family lived in Brest-Litovsk for many, many years. They were bookbinders. They had their own house, a cow, and so forth. So we lived there very peaceful, everything was fine. We used to trade, sell clothes, watches, lots of different stuff at the bazaar. And the Russians used to buy the watches, six watches on one hand. Two on the feet! Suits, they didn't even put it on. 'Give us. Give us.' They didn't care. Shoes. 'Give us.' If it fits or not, just 'give us.' And watches, watches, watches, and more watches. We did make a very good living while we were in the Russian part of Poland, in Brest-Litovsk.

"My uncle was a cripple, He was an invalid from first world war. I mean part of his leg was chopped off. He had a wooden leg. Is a story with his wooden leg, too."

The story Dov tells about his uncle's leg is the beginning of the story of the Seven's exile to the Soviet prison settlement in Nyuvchim.

"So the Russians wanted the Polish refugees to choose. They say to us either you become a Soviet citizen and stay here, or we must ship you out of here. We don't want any undesirable characters living in the border. But you must register. So we register, but we never agree to become a Soviet citizen, right? I figured things are going to change. Eventually I was going back to Poland, right? That's what we always thought about. We didn't know what's going to happen—never thought of the slaughter of all those Jews.

"But we didn't want to become Soviet citizen. So after we registered, we didn't know what would happen. Soon after, we hear that the Russians are rounding up every single Polish Jew—those who had just registered but did not become citizens—and they're gonna ship them out. So we all went into hiding, right? The next night—always at night, never the daytime, at night, right—we hear a big knock on the door. We could hear trucks coming up to the house. And we were in the attic already. Up in the attic. The Russians, two Russians come in, one in uniform, one civilian. And they go to the uncle, 'What's your name?' He says his name. And he says, 'Where is?' and say these names: Josef G., Henya G., Itzak G., Lola G., Sonia G., Dov G., Natan F.—where are they? And we were of course in the attic, and we heard every word."

"Lola G.? So my parents were married by then. Otherwise they would have asked for Lola F., no?"

"No, they were not married."

"Do you know if they ever had a wedding?"

"I was never invited to one. I let slip out something once, and you were there, and Josef gave me a look. And later we laughed about it. Lola was always pressing Itzak, 'We need to get married.' Anyway, it's unimportant. You know, if a Jewish boy and girl, if they left together from Warsaw, it was like a marriage, except that the rabbi didn't perform the ceremony, or put a ring on her finger; it's like being married."

Yes, it is *like* being married. But it is *not* marriage itself, not to her. No ring, no rabbi, no wedding, and therefore no marriage.

Jewish law views marriage as a contract between two people. A rabbi is not technically required, but my mother could care less about "law." She was all about following proper custom. As it looked to others, so it looked to her.

"Don't tell your mother; she would crucify me! But I know they were not married in Berlin, they were not married in Russia—if they were, I would have known about it. I never paid attention because to me, they were married."

I was stunned. Stunned. And then immensely delighted to have something on them. Well, not them, but her. Who was so puritanical; her, with that dreaded look she gave me to communicate her disapproval. Mouth held tight, she sideways-glowered at me and shook her head in profound disappointment.

I could not let this new, spectacular information go unused. So once on a Sunday visit, when my parents were both in the room at the same time and I could study both their faces, I asked my mother if she still had her marriage certificate. They exchanged looks, and I knew Dov was right. By the time I interviewed my father, they had agreed on the story they would tell me about their marriage, including a date. Improvisation and chutzpah were survival arts my mother perfected while on the run from the Germans. I was a piker in comparison.

The whole family came to the fiftieth anniversary party I then had to throw for my parents based on the invented date of their marriage. Catered dinner, cake, candles, presents, and in the aftermath, the complaints: Katja's new jewelry from Dov and the way they waste money—*a shande*; the *shaygetses* both their daughters married—*a shande*; Josef's youngest son, Pavel, and his recent divorce from his only Jewish wife—*a shande*. But the true legacy of that party for me is the falseness, the lie it put between my mother and me. It lay there every time

I saw her or thought of her—though it has lost weight since then. Her lectures about "boys" and their evil intent, her rigid moral judgments about others—regarding not only sex but also all the rules about being proper—seemed, well, hypocritical. She practiced a double standard.

Writing her story, I understand that her attitudes were shaped by having to hold on to something as history dislocated her, hurled her free of all that had connected her to this earth and made up her identity. The persona of correctness she created for herself linked her to the prewar stability of her religious, bourgeois, shopkeeper family and formed a shield of sorts, a steady way to be in a world in which she was repeatedly dislodged, and a means to navigate the disparate cultures and the confused succession of languages through which she moved or more accurately, was shoved. It provided respectability despite unspeakable loss, a difficult husband, many miscarriages, factory piecework, strokes, and then finally the heart attacks. Through all that she held on to her dignified female role of moral rectitude.

"So to the question the police asked of where are they, my uncle says, 'It was three days ago they went out to the country. They're not back.' And the Russians again say, '*ty lgat*,' you lie. 'You, old man, you lie.'

"'I know they are somewhere hiding here; you are not telling the truth. You better tell the truth because if it's not true, you know what's going to happen to you.'

"So he said, 'I swear by my health and by Russia that it's true. Look at me,' he said. 'I lost a leg. I was in the Russian Army'—you know, to get their sympathy. That he fought for their land and sacrificed.

"'All right,' '*ya polagayu tebe*,' I believe you. And they walked out.

"They rounded up every Jew they could in Brest-Litovsk. I don't say we were the only ones that were, you know, hiding. They never get 100 percent.

"So then one day passes by. We're afraid to go out. The second day passes by; we were discussing what to do. What are we going to do if the Russians see that we have no Soviet passports and are not citizens? What will we do if they find us? If we tell them we just came back from the country, will they believe us? So we all decided to save my uncle trouble—to just volunteer.

"Right. So we went to volunteer. So we went to them and volunteered.

"They asked, 'Who are you?'

"So we told them. 'We are the G.s. We came late. We want to volunteer to take us out.'

"They tell us, 'We don't want you. If we want you, we know where to look for you.' They were too proud, the NKVD, to admit that the Russians ever fail. If we want you, we'll find you. So we couldn't go. And then we bribed our way onto the trucks, loaded them with all our garbage, our stuff, you know. So we just bribed the guard, and we went to the train with the trucks—off we went."

"Did your parents know that you were leaving Brest-Litovsk?"

"They didn't know at all. There was no correspondence. It was all chaos.

"At this point, some people who were in Brest-Litovsk decided to go back home, to German-occupied Poland."

"Lola's brother Natan went back, I think?"

"Yes. He went back because of Josef; Josef chased him out. In fact, Lola blamed Josef that he is dead. This I remember. I always used to hear them fight.

"She used to say, '*Du bist shuldik, az er iz nisht do. Du bist shuldik.*' It's your fault that he is not here. You are guilty."

Most of the way to Nyuvchim, in Komi SSR, they traveled by train. Dov describes the trains as cattle cars, with thirty to forty people to a car, but they had sleeping berths. He makes the point that they always got the coveted lower berths because of my pushy mother. Just like in Brest, where she sold more than anyone else.

According to Dov, who rarely left the book he was reading to go to the market, Lola sold the most.

"*Pani* Lola, we used to call her. *Pani*, Madame Lola."

"Why *pani*?"

"It's something better. It's something higher. It's not common. Because she always walked very brisk. Very sure of herself. Very nicely dressed, very clean. And that's the way she is today."

Dov gives these compliments, but there's something sardonic about his tone. Then comes what he really wants to say:

"She has big elbows. Your mother knows how to push. I've seen her in action. [Laughs.] She wouldn't give a damn. What she used to do, I couldn't do. You know, very pushy. If there was a line, she would elbow her way in, not in the back, but up front. Yeah. She had the guts. She'd just go right to the front. When we used to go in Brest for something in a line. '*Bist meshuge,*' she would say. 'Are you crazy staying in line?' Boom! 'Come with me.' Up front we go. That was Lola."

Dov's harping on my mother's pushiness begins to annoy me. For one thing, she *was* pushy, and for another thing, I have been accused of that once or twice.

I have become reconciled to my own pushiness. Look, I took over my small college's women's studies program when it was little more than a line in the academic bulletin, and grew it to be one of the largest in the country. It's the old saw: What's described as assertive for a man is described as pushy for a woman.

And don't argue with me.

"I once missed the train. *Echelon* was what was called the whole trainload of cattle cars. While I was standing in the line to get the food, the train took off. Nobody came up and told we're going to leave in a moment or two. So I missed it. And I was upset because I didn't know how the hell I gonna catch up to them. But I knew the direction they were going, so I thought I gonna catch it up at the next town. So I smuggled into the next train. But it took a long time, days, maybe longer before I met up with them. And while waiting for a train to come, I was hungry. So I go inside Russian restaurant—which was, you know, for the Russian military. I used to go bare feet. I left the shoes probably somewhere, and I was dirty—you know—not shaved with a torn shirt, a dirty shirt. I used to go to the tables, to eat from the tables what the Russians left. They used to look at me like a wild animal. I can still see them looking at me, and of course you know what they say. The one who is fed doesn't believe that you can be hungry. So they looked at me as if I were an animal. Let's say that if you eat at a very fancy restaurant, and all of a sudden a bum walks in and grabs food from the tables. That's what I used to do. But they didn't do nothing—they just look. 'Oh, they said *'besprizorniki,'*" which Dov translated as "refugee," but it means homeless or street kids.

"I did that until I caught up with my brothers with the train. When I did, they thought I took off for another adventure like when I went to Kiev. They didn't believe I missed the train.

"On the train we had nothing to do but crack lice and talk. We were blacked out of any kind of news. The only news we had was rumors. This guy heard this; this guy heard that, this guy this, and the other guy that, right? Nothing else. Poland will never be back the same. Forget about Poland. We'll never go home. Nothing is going to be like it was. Some used to say, 'Oh, you're crazy; war's going to be over in a few months. We're all gonna go back. It's going to be back the same.' And we said, 'How the hell can it be the same? No one even knows where our homes are. They are all bombed out.'

"Even the place where we lived was bombed, but not bad. They used to bomb systematical, house-by-house. You could tell what would be next. Here goes the house no. 44. Here goes no. 46. We knew exactly when it's going to hit. I was going with my father to the apartment, and we heard a shooting sound. Then BOOM! After a minute, another BOOM! So we just took cover in a corner, right? And of course a shell exploded about two hundred feet from us. But we were not hurt. Our apartment house also still kept standing.

"Right, so we're on the way to Nyuvchim. The trip took us some weeks, I'd say. The seven of us were together, except when I missed the train. That's what people called us—the Seven.

"So when we got to Syktyvkar, the trucks came. We went in them to this Nyuvchim. Other people were taken to the next little town, right? We were lucky, I must say, because some people had told us that they went very far east, where there were swamps and the people got eaten alive by mosquitoes. People who went to Pechora used to say '*Du host mazl; bist nisht in Pechora.*' 'You are lucky. You are not in Pechora.' Many people died. They died like flies in Pechora. If you look at the map, you can see how far east they went, how we were lucky. In fact, the refugees there always comment on our luck—the luck of the Seven. Our place, Nyuvchim, was not so bad.

"We got to Nyuvchim, maybe it was June in 1940. They led us to the barracks. And then ask us of course to register. 'What kind of training do you have? What do you do?' And of course the political commissars. They used to come tell us, 'Don't worry. If you work, it will be good here. The better you work, the better you gonna have it.' And of course they were very hungry for our trades that we brought with us. In fact, when we were liberated, they begged us to stay there. They cried so we should stay because we brought a lot of knowledge to them. We enriched them. In our group were carpenters, tailors, shoemakers, bakers. There's a shortage of everything there, right? We even had a barber, which they never saw in their lives.

"In fact, in this place was a big, big factory. They made wheels, you know, for wooden carriages. That's where I used to work, making wheels. I worked with a smith, you know, to put the iron around the wooden wheels and the spokes. But the quality—very, very poor. After few days they used to fall out. All the spokes used to fall out. When it was assembled, you used to drive, and, BOOM! Off went this—off went that.

"But since we came, and we had so many trades, we used to put out a good quality of a wheel.

"Of course, your father had it fantastic."

"Why?"

"As a tailor? Are you kidding? Itzak had a goldmine there. They had no tailors there. This is why he had it easy. Before I went to the wheel factory, I always chopped wood, up to my nose in snow. Worked eight hours cutting woods. Not with a chainsaw, with an ax. Later I worked as a land surveyor. I worked my way up! We did topographical expeditions. You know, they find so many riches there—copper, uranium, zinc, you name it. They had so much wealth, but don't know how to take it out."

The prison settlement in Nyuvchim was one camp in a system of labor camps in the wilds of Russia. They dated from imperial times, and were called *katorga*. Nyuvchim was in northeastern Russia, seated in the taiga, the area deeply planted with birches and pines, firs and evergreens, and mottled with lakes and threads of rivers and streams filled with fish. They stayed there until the Germans violated the Hitler-Stalin pact by invading the Soviet Union in June 1941. The Polish government in exile, formed after the German invasion of Poland and headquartered in London, then made a deal with Stalin for the release of Polish nationals in the USSR who could form military units against Hitler. That's when the Seven left Nyuvchim, after about a year or so, depending on who's talking—only by then they were six. They did not join the Polish army in the USSR.

As Dov related the adventures of the Seven in Nyuvchim, he was ebullient, like a former high-school football star recalling his days of glory. Nyuvchim sounded like summer camp, summer camp in a Soviet gulag during the Holocaust.

"The food was also something. We used to go in the woods. Oh, mushrooms plenty. Plenty. And blackberries. Oh, delicious. Not like here. When you ate one, your mouth got black. And your fingers got stained black. This is the real ones. And so many fish. *Ach*, they made a fish stew, *ucha*, like—what do they call this in French—bouillabaisse? They chopped up the fish into a big pot."

Looking up at me a bit shyly, he added, "That's where all the funny things happened."

The Seven in Nyuvchim were among two hundred "undesirable aliens" who lived in one-room barracks, each housing about eighteen to twenty-five people, mainly in their early twenties. Dov remembers the carryings-on among the couples at night and the bed-hopping of those not already paired off. In one common room, discretion was impossible.

Dov depicts the Varsovians as sophisticated city folk bringing culture to the backwater. But in Nyuvchim it wasn't a case of targeting their marks for profit as in Brest-Litovsk. There was real affection for the Russians in Nyuvchim.

"We introduced to them European dances. They used to be crazy about them. Oh, they drove us nuts. Dancing, dancing. That's when my sister Sonia used to sing. She had a beautiful voice, Sonia. You know there is musical talent in our family. I sang also. I used to belong to a group, singing and dancing, and at night, the brilliant moon over us—cold, but we all enjoyed it, holding all hands and singing.

"They had a special place. They call it *Palats Kul'tury*, palace of culture. On weekends everybody came dressed up. They played balalaika and harmonica. And that's how we used to dance and sing. There was a guy in our place in Nyuvchim. He was a Tatar. He was in love with my sister, with Sonia. Yeah, he was big leader in this little town—political leader, political instructor. Very handsome, black eyes. He was a frequent visitor to our barracks!"

Not only Sonia's Tatar but also other Russians were tempted by the young Jewish refugees. The oldest brother, Josef, visited the Russian woman doctor almost daily and came back to the barracks with documents excusing him from work the next day.

And Dov of course had a romance:

"Yeah. There was a girl. Her father was a fireman. Her name was Maya. That was her name. She was Russian. But she was a head taller than I am. Black eyes, black hair. And of course I was in love with her. But I was very shy to tell her, I guess. I used to dance with her a lot. I know I was crazy about her. That's for sure. I know she could feel my excitement when we danced, but she never slapped me. I hated to leave her."

Dov looks at me, and I can see he is gauging whether he should say what's on his mind—not my pushy mother again!

"When we came home from our eight-hour shift, we wanted to eat. And the women all wanted to feed their families. The stove, you know, there was only one. It had only four places for pots. It was a wood stove, and the burner was a hole that you put a pot on. So there is always a struggle about who gets to cook first. Already at noon, they were all walking along the stove; everyone trying to be first. They spoke Yiddish, right? This is '*mayn lokh*'; this is '*mayn lokh*'—my hole. Lola was the first—this is '*mayn lokh*!' And it was so funny. 'You can't have this. I have seven people waiting.' There must have been almost twenty people who stay in this one room, but Lola was always the first to cook. Always first in line."

All right already, Dov.

Then Sonia left the Seven.

"We were always determined to stay together. No matter what, we were the Seven. We felt good about it, and the other refugees knew us by that. In the meantime Sonia had been writing to her boyfriend whose father made suits for the NKVD. We had all sold the father's suits while we were in Brest. The boyfriend convinced her to come back to Brest, and with the NKVD connection, he could make it happen."

The Seven decided it was a good idea to send Sonia back to Brest because maybe she could help their parents and also could help the rest of them get back to Warsaw after the war. The news took flight so quickly that all the Polish Jews in Nyuvchim and the surrounding prison settlements knew Sonia had gotten a pass to go back to civilization, to Brest. Everyone knew and they were jealous, Dov said.

The luck of the Seven was the talk of the exiled Jews in the entire region:

"Oh, are you the relatives of Sonia G., who went back to Brest-Litovsk?"

Luck can be either good or bad.

The *Einsatzgruppen*, a murdering force drawn from the SS, followed the German army across the border and liquidated Jewish ghettoes.

"We didn't know what the Germans did. All we knew was that they marched into Russia in June 1941. We heard the speeches from Stalin on the loudspeakers in the camp. All we knew was that Germany attacked Russia."

That was the end of the Hitler-Stalin pact.

Sonia's letters ceased.

Given their liberty in the deal the exiled Polish government struck with Stalin, the Nyuvchim Jews longed for a warm climate and fruit that was not berries. The idea of moving to Asia—with its promise of better weather and more food—spread like wildfire. General Władysław Anders's army, consisting of Poles liberated in the USSR, was forming in Asia, which somehow provided another motivation for them, even though they did not intend to join. They had free passage to wherever they wanted to go, and Dov wanted to go to Uzbekistan:

"Because I once read a book about Tashkent, 'the City of Bread.' Yeah, in Poland, I used to read this book *Taszkient miasto chleba*. So I thought, 'Okay, let's go to Tashkent.' It is in Uzbekistan."

Aleksander Wat, a Polish Jewish intellectual, talks about the book in his classic memoir, *My Century*. He writes how the book's idyllic description of Tashkent spread like a virus among the gulag Jews, causing them to race there, only to be greeted not by bread but by typhus and malaria.

Just as each of them talked about how they were known as the Seven, how they got across the Bug River to their uncle, how they made friends with the Russians in Nyuvchim, and how, tragically, Sonia went back, they each told the story of how they got separated. As family lore has grown around this event, it has become known as "the Separation."

For Dov, the Separation happened when the train stopped in Tashkent.

"There was no room in the car for all of us. Josef wanted me to go with him. He was with Henya and Chapka, and your father wanted that I should find with him and Lola a car to stay in. They argued over it. I went with Josef. It didn't make difference, I thought, because we all wind up in same place anyway.

"But in Samarkand, what is in Uzbekistan, the train was stopped. In middle of the night, train started again. It woke me up. In the morning I stepped off the car, it was in Osh in Kyrgyzstan, and half the train was missing. I realized Itzak and Lola were gone. They were with the other half of the train."

The Seven, now six, had counted on staying together, on keeping a protective watch on one another, but this plan broke apart with the train's capricious separation. No more Seven, no more six. They were atomized and more vulnerable. Once separated, the brothers did not do as well at first as they had done together. Everyone starved—literally—for a while.

Dov, Henya, Josef, and Chapka went by oxcart to a place called Pachta Abad, near Aravan, where they lived on a collective farm in clay huts. It's unclear whether Chapka had met his wife-to-be yet, but he was assigned to a different hut. Dov, Henya, and Josef lived in a single big room covered with carpets, with a stove in the middle by which they slept in the winter.

It was in Pachta Abad that Dov picked cotton.

"I used to wake very early in the morning. The big-shot Russian CEO on a horse used to wake everybody: 'Up! Up! Go collect cotton. Collect cotton in the fields.' So we went, but we just were only sitting and talking. We didn't collect much cotton. When we saw him coming, we started collecting again. So time passed by, days and weeks. And then we got a little advantage; they gave a better place to put in the cotton, big cloth bags. Just like you stomp grapes with the feet, so we used to stomp the cotton down in big, nice beautiful bags. Used to do it like you were dancing in it, to pack in as much cotton as you can in one sack."

Left outside, the bags became wet in the rain, and the cotton rotted.

"Then they gave us some tools. They had humongous loads of cotton outside, big bales, two-stories-high bales. Two stories high. And we used to pluck out the rotten cotton. Why was the cotton rotten? Because they didn't have anything to cover it up from the rain. Millions of dollars' worth of cotton, and we had to go like rats digging holes, like a tunnel, to find the rotten cotton. So once we got out the rotten cotton, we all took a nap. And very often, we used to take those bags where we used to stomp the cotton, wrap around our bodies and take them out; we used to sell them. That's how things went." In telling this story, Dov wants to illustrate the Soviet system's failures. Not only its inefficiency and wastefulness, but also its inability to attract buy-in from the workers. Nobody cared. Since the system did not take care of them, they took take care of themselves as best they could.

Rather than seeking out adventures, easygoing Dov usually waited for them to find him, but in Pachta Abad he acted to right a wrong.

"Josef was always floating around somewhere with a knapsack on his back. With good foods to trade, to make business. Sometimes he didn't come back for a few days.

"I really don't want to talk about this.

"And he had a big valise with food. Locked. Only he had the key. Mostly filled with grain. So he used to give us like seven spoons for me and Henya to use to trade for food. Which was like, I will say *gornisht*, nothing. Which wasn't enough. Once I took the nerve when he was away; I opened up his valise and took out the grain. From this, we used to trade it for big meals. Because I used to work for it, too! I wanted my share. So finally our bellies were full, me and Henya, and at this time, Henya was pregnant with their son Danny, right?"

Grain was the currency there, and they were supposed to trade it for food to sustain themselves. When Dov finally broke open the valise for more grain to trade, he felt defiant and angry, but also criminal, despite having justice on his side.

I can make sense of his timidity only by thinking about what the philosopher Michel Foucault wrote about the panopticon. Picture it as a prison in which there is a central guard tower surrounded by the prison itself. The tower has a 360-degree view of the imprisoned. Although the prisoners cannot actually see the tower guards, they assume they are being watched all the time and therefore regulate their own behavior accordingly. For Foucault the panopticon serves as a metaphor for all the mechanisms that lead to self-policing in contemporary society. What was the mechanism for Henya and Dov? Josef had kept them in line, but how? Why didn't they challenge Josef and open the suitcase as soon as they had the need? Fear, for sure. Would he abandon them in this alien land? I confess that if I were Henya, I would not want to depend solely on Dov, whose worth was more immaterial than material. She was pregnant and probably already mentally fragile. How could his sweetness and stories help her? I would never marry a poet, though I might love him.

But the Jewish refugees and Kyrgyz natives were eager to adopt this charming boy.

"You know, Tevye and Heniek, a couple of shoemakers, wanted me to marry their sister Zoshia. They would have accepted me into their business with open arms. They always left me alone with her, but I never liked to kiss her. Boy, did she get mad. She called me worthless and threw me out of the house.

"I was crazy for a Kyrgyz girl. She was very young, no more than fifteen or sixteen. Her family liked me and invited me to the circumcision of her brother, aged thirteen. What a festival!

"I made friends with the natives, the Kyrgyzians, not the Russians. They were Mongol-looking, with slanty eyes. You should have seen their clothes. The men wore red and black caftans, with gorgeous hand embroidery. And such tall boots. Their hats were what you call pillbox."

He remembers them thundering down the roads on horses. The women wore loose white pants and blouses, over which they put embroidered vests. Although Dov made an inroad, Polish Jews generally were avoided by the Kyrgyz people, who associated them with the Russians. "Russians, no good," they said in their language. The men would cut off fingers or toes to avoid being drafted into the Russian military, but they liked Dov.

His connection to the Muslim girl was severed when the Soviets drafted Dov for the labor front in 1943. He was sent to Argostroy to build a dam to provide power to Chelyabinsk, a project of which he was proud. Before shipping him out, the Soviets did not reveal to him where he was going, so he left without Josef or Henya knowing his destination. Each brother was now in the dark about where the other two were. From the enveloping cocoon of the Seven, Dov was now alone.

He did all right.

Dov landed in a barracks with about twenty other single young men who all lived on rations, and he launched his career as a driver—fate's poetic justice for his brother Josef withholding his bicycle from Dov. His first vehicle far surpassed it. He began as the motorman on a small train with about eight cars, which he would drive up a hill so that excavated stones could be dumped into them. Then he drove the train down the hill and piled up the stones to create a dam. Another job he had was driving a cement truck. From then on, Dov spent his exile behind the wheel. First a train, followed by trucks, jeeps, and finally his own taxicab in New York City.

He came to Chelyabinsk alone, but he was not alone for long.

"You know, the first night I came there, I went to their social hall, their *Palats Kul'tury*, to meet people. Wouldn't you know it, as soon as I walked in, Emma Ivanovna, she took me and did not let go."

Not for two years, when he wrenched himself away.

The European Jews again brought their dances, for which the locals gave up their indigenous circle dances. The Jewish Poles taught the natives the pleasures of the polka, tango, foxtrot, waltz, and a British dance that was hot in Warsaw before the war, the "Lambeth Walk."

Here's how you do it, according to Arthur Murray's instructions of 1938:

Forward 8 steps, link arms with your partner, and circle right 4 steps, and circle left 4 steps

Back 8 steps and circle out 4 steps

Slap your thighs for 4 counts and yell "Oi!"

Where did that Yiddish "*Oi!*" come from?

"Lambeth Walk" refers to a street in a London working-class neighborhood that gave its name to a song-and-dance number in the 1937 musical *Me and My Girl*. The plot turns on a Cockney boy who inherits an earldom and as a result nearly loses his working-class girl. But it all works out in the end as class warfare is trumped by love. This fantasy plot provided comfort in a world that was shredding apart. The dance helped deny the coming disaster. The *New York Times* captures the mood with its October 1938 headline, "While dictators rage and statesmen talk, all Europe dances—to The Lambeth Walk." The British Ministry of Information used the dance to lampoon the Nazis in a 1941 propaganda film. The film manipulated footage from Leni Riefenstahl's notorious *Triumph of the Will* so that the goose-stepping German army was doing the Lambeth Walk.

The men of the region were all off fighting the war, so these young guys, like Dov, were very desirable. Emma Ivanovna was about forty, and Dov was twenty-one. "She was a sex maniac," he said. Her husband, a Soviet general, had been away for two years.

"The people in the town looked at me like I was a criminal. Her husband was very sincere and well liked. I can picture her now like it was yesterday. She was a blonde and well built, with some meat on her. She was famous in this place, locally, you know. She performed in Chekhov on the stage in this *Palats Kul'tury*."

The first thing Dov remembers about his life with her, after the sex, is the food. She had a cow and chickens—lots of food.

"Many guys who lived there, they envied me that I had such a good life. So I used to tell them, 'What do you worry about? You are benefitting too from it.' 'Yes, yes, Dov. Good boy, good boy.'"

"Like your father, you shared with your friends."

"What a great house she had. It was all on a single level and made of wood. It was painted white with three bedrooms and a basement. They had there also another building, a shed to keep the cow and the chickens.

"She had two sons. One was very handsome. He was in the army. The other son was eight-year old boy. I liked him very much. He remind me of my little brother that was left in Warsaw. He did not want to let go of me."

"You were happy there."

"Yes, I was. I was building a dam and I liked it. I had a truck for myself. You know, I got Chelyabinsk driver's license, which I had it until 1973. First I must have a learner's permit, before real license. With this permit, I was learning car mechanics, not only how to drive, like here with permit.

"I always carry wood with me for the roads. They were so muddy. If you didn't have wood to put under the wheel, forget about it! You wouldn't be able to move out of the mud."

He lived day-to-day and did not think much about his brothers or his family in Warsaw. His time was organized by a whistle marking the beginning and end of work. He came home to Emma and her younger son, who loved Dov.

"You know her little boy cried when I left. Of course when her older son came home on furlough, I stayed away. I didn't want any trouble."

The labor front disbanded at the end of the war in 1945. The men had to wait for permission from the Communist Party to go back to Poland. The Soviet government put pressure on them to stay, to build another dam somewhere in Central Asia. Some of the men married Russian girls, like Dov's friend Avram Petrol. Emma wanted Dov to stay, and when he refused, she wanted to go with him, but he said he didn't want the responsibility. Dov was twenty-three, and Emma was approaching her mid-forties.

Some months before the end of the war, Dov and Itzak found one another. Dov told me that Itzak began to stop by from time to time as an NKVD train courier when he passed through Chelyabinsk. He ran into him one day, he thinks, though he could not remember the details of this reunion.

The next thing Dov remembers is being on a train with Itzak, Lola, and me—a passenger train to Warsaw. Josef was not with them yet. They stopped in Brest-Litovsk to find Sonia and their uncle before going to Warsaw.

"So all of a sudden we stopped on our way back to Poland. We stopped off in Brest-Litovsk. This I remember explicit. Where we used to live with our uncle, right? Before they shipped us out to Russia. Now it was all fenced in. A six-foot wooden fence. There was a guy there, he came out. He was a gentile guy. I guess he lived there, and we asked him if he remembers my uncle. His answer was, 'I don't remember.' All he told me was that after the Germans crossed over the river Bug, they rounded up all the Jews and killed them all off—all of them in one day. And among them of course was my sister Sonia. That was the first shock—by the way we found out. In Russia we didn't know nothing about any atrocities. We didn't know about concentration camps or gassing. We didn't know about such things. So this was the first shock, when this guy told us that the German army came in and rounded up all the Jews. And he mentioned somewhere—a little place where they took them out for executions. I guess outside of town. They never did a slaughter inside a town. Always out of town.

"Then we got back into the train to go to Poland. Your father had a fur coat that he wanted to sell in Warsaw to get some money. We paid for the fare to go to Warsaw. So we went to the compartment and there were lots of gentiles. And they looked us over. '*Oh, Zydy,*' Jews. And they walked out of the compartment, not wanting to sit with us together, right? We felt very depressed, of course.

"Now as soon as we crossed the border—across the Bug River into Poland, there were kids and grownups throwing stones, greeting us with stones. Now mostly on the train was Jews who are coming back from Russia into Poland. It was the greetings. '*Zydy do Palestyny,*' Jews to Palestine. Also '*My was nie chcemy,*' We don't want you.' We said to each other, 'You see this? After all this, what they did to the Jews, and now the coming back to Poland—this is how they welcome us.' So after this we felt even more depressed, so instead of making a longer trip—we shortened the trip. Instead of going to Warsaw, we went to Lodz. He sold the coat."

The Seven, now six, began to regroup in Poland, in a town called Stettin, close to the German border. After some months they used the coat money to buy illegal passage across the border into Germany. I was with them.

"We went in a military truck. There were some guys, the Jews were always like a network. Mouth to mouth. *'Vilst geyn tsu Daytshland? Ikh bin der makher.'* 'You want to go to Germany? I am the guy who arrange whole thing.'

"They told us when it gets dark, come to this certain place. And of course you had to pay them in advance, with monies per head. Truck was packed. And of course everyone had some bundles and wooden suitcases. And so we were stopped at the border, of course. My sister-in-law Lola had a little baby called Ellen, about a year old. So we came to the border, and my little Ellen started to cry. 'Shh, shh, quiet, quiet,' but didn't help, and Lola stuffed her mouth with a cookie not to cry.

"There was an exchange of words. We could hear them talk Russian. Over the border was Russian-occupied Eastern Germany. I guess they bribed them. And this is how we got across, must have been three in the morning.

"And then they dropped us off in an empty field off the highway, and we all got off, and—yeah, there was one guy who was supposed to lead us to the railroad station, which was part of the Berlin network of commuter trains, right? The first train left at 5:30 in the morning, right? So we all followed him, right? Forty people following this guy like geese to the train station. And then this guy was walking faster because he was afraid to be caught for smuggling us across. So he ran away from us. We couldn't follow him. We all had things to carry. And I carried the most always. I was bundled up with four suitcases. And Lola was carrying her pots, what she cherished, and you on her arm. Oh, it was a nice bundle to carry.

"People with their bundles couldn't keep up. All of a sudden, there was no one to follow, and we couldn't find our way. Then we're in a town, and there was an elderly lady. And none of us could speak German except me. I knew a few words. I asked her, *'Vu iz di stantsye? Vu iz di stantsye?'* You know, I just translated literally. I tried from Polish to Yiddish, making it sound German. But *stantsye* in German means nothing. I had to say *Bahnhof*. I didn't know the word *Bahnhof*. So she looked at us, like we were dumb you know. [Laughs.] '*Stantsye, stantsye? Was, was, was?*' What kind of people are you? So I said, 'Nach Berlin, nach Berlin,' toward Berlin.

"'Oh, *der Bahnhof.*'

"Then it dawned on her we wanted the train station. And she told us.

"So we were at the station, right? And it was loaded with a lot of other people already. There were Germans waiting for the trains. We had more than an hour to kill. All of a sudden, the police walked in with their flashlights—it was still dark, there was no light. And they looked in everyone's face. There was big movement at this time. People are going and coming; they were going to or coming from, right? So they asked us, 'What are you doing here? Where are you going?' So Itzak told them we are going back to Poland. This is what you learn—never say that you want to stay where you are. You always say you are going to go back to where you don't want to be. 'Nein, nein. Sie können nicht zurück gehen.' You can't go back. Do you have papers to go back? So we said no, and they left us. Then the train came within a few minutes. We bought, of course, tickets, which were very cheap. And within another twenty minutes, we were in the French sector of Berlin, Gesundbrunnen.

"That was the first stop. They told us when you take the train, get off at Gesundbrunnen because over there, people from the refugee camp were waiting for us already as we got off. And they took us down with military trucks from the UNRRA, United Nations Relief and Rehabilitation Administration—you know, for us refugees.

"They took us to the DP camp in Berlin—Schlachtensee."

The Schlachtensee displaced persons (DP) camp, one in an international network of DP camps, was run by the Americans. In 2008 a group of scholars at a Humboldt University (Berlin) seminar put together a website to help memorialize this DP camp. Whether they had been repulsed by postwar Polish anti-Semitism, like my family, or wished to escape the cemetery that Poland had become, or hoped to enter the waiting room for emigration, especially to Palestine, Jewish refugees flowed into the camp. The camp, my camp, was officially called Düppel Center, and it was a marvel of the indomitable cultural force of its population. Within a year it had a Yiddish newspaper, *Undser Lebn* (Our Life), a school with teachers from the refugee population, theater, music, a cinema, a library, its own tribunal, and a synagogue with three rabbis. I'm thinking of the marriage opportunity my parents did not take.

Dov belonged to the camp sports club, Herzilay.

"And you know, I joined a club right away, playing soccer in the camp."

"Here you had another language to learn. You didn't speak German."

"No but I caught on very fast. The first thing I did was buy newspapers. I always walked with papers and books. Always a book under my arm.

"I also got friendly with an RAA officer. The guy who was in charge for supplying food for the camp, right? I was his driver. I had a jeep to my position. I used to drive him all around to wherever he had to go: to get food for 3,500 people in the camp, all right? And then he would go to army headquarters, and the food went on trucks. We would go ahead of the convoy and move it to the camp. That's how I always got lots of food. His name was Murphy, an American officer in the army.

"I met Eva through him. He had a girlfriend. Her name was Ursula. After work I used to drive him to the girlfriend. And she lived in a villa in Wannsee. Was a very, very rich suburb of Berlin. Like Great Neck or Port Washington or Scarsdale. In Wannsee there is also a little lake. There was a song about Wannsee. 'Wannsee, Wannswe, wir geyen baden im Wannsee.' In fact, the German plan of total liquidation of the Jews was made in Wannsee, somewhere in one of those villas."

Dov is referring to the gathering of the Nazi hierarchy on January 20, 1942, in a beautiful villa by the lake, and the crafting of the "Final Solution of the Jewish Question," which solidified plans for the mass extermination of the Jews. By that time one million Jews were already dead.

"And that's how I met Eva. She and Murphy's girlfriend were going together to a language school to learn English and shorthand. Eva was there in Wannsee, in the villa where Murphy had his girlfriend. She was stretched out in her white bikini on the edge of the veranda. You know, the sundeck. And it was love at first sight. [Laughs.]

"And of course, Lola, your mother, she said: '*Shemst du gornisht mit a daytshe tsu geyn?*' 'Don't you shame yourself for going with a German?'

"Yeah, well, then I was in a cloud. You know, everything was not clear, what you heard. You didn't know what to believe, right? She was just a girl is what I'm trying to say. She was born in 1929 right? She was ten years old when the war broke out, seventeen years old when I met her. And I was twenty-seven. I was ten years older, yeah. I think it's a nice difference.

"Don't forget, the German girls, they were sick of the typical German type, Nordic type. Blue eyes, blond. That's all you see there. So when they saw somebody a little dark with curly hair, like me, they went bananas. The German girls were going bananas about *die haar*, hair, *lockigem haar*, means curly hair. They were going bananas.

"She was stretched out, taking a sunbath, in a white bikini, and that did it."

When Schlachtensee disbanded in 1948 because of the Berlin blockade, Dov gave up his dream of going to Israel so that he could marry the *shikse* but not before an adventure in smuggling and jail time as an American spy.

"Before the camp Schlachtensee was dissolved, they transported all the things from the camp into West Germany, right? I was part of the convoy. Was about fifteen trucks. And they told me to take some sewing machines on the way back. Take sewing machines from West Berlin through the Russian sector into West Germany."

"Who told you?"

"Smugglers. Which I did. Guys knowing that I'm going in a big IRO, International Refugee Organization, convoy to West Germany. They said, 'Dov, I'm going to give you some sewing machines. And for every sewing machine you sell, we'll give you a certain amount of money.' I was supposed to go only one way. One way, not coming back. In other words, we took the truck which belonged to the IRO and just drive to this displaced persons camp in West Germany and surrender the trucks over there. At the same time, they give me sewing machines to sell in West Germany. They gave me a contact there.

"And how do I come back? They say if you want to come back, you're on your own because we had dissolved the camp. So you do whatever you want to do. You want to go back, you go back on your own into Berlin. That's what it was. All right, so I did. We did sell the machines. So I had money. Now I had to go back to Berlin, right, back to Eva.

"Because of her I didn't go to Israel. How can I take a girl with me to a country that has a war going on? How could I take a gentile girl to a war, which is not her war? Not only this, how can I take a girl with me to Israel, and I'm probably getting shipped out to a war? Not knowing if I'm going to live or die. Did this make sense? Right?

"All right, so of course there were again connections—people who knew how to get back and smuggle across into Berlin, right? Of course, for money. There were two guys being smuggled, me and this other guy. Now, first, before we met the German contact to get us on the railroad, we had another guy who smuggled us across the border by foot, right? Through a mountain pass. We paid the guy money. Yeah, a thousand marks, I guess. Now, he got us across, and he told us, 'Don't go into any restaurants. Don't knock on doors. People look for refugees. Stay hidden.' We could see the railroad tracks, right, and the station, of course. 'Just go and buy tickets to Berlin, that's all.' Just keep it simple.

"Now, this guy with me, I didn't know him, but I got to know when we crossed the border, he saw a small restaurant. A bar, right—*eine Kneipe*, a kind of bar. And he was very thirsty. And I told him, 'Let's not go inside, let's do what the guy told us.' 'Ah, it's two in the morning. Who's going to be there?' I said, 'It's a border. Let's not do it.' Anyway, he talked me into it, right? But me, he shoved in first through the door. And like a damn fool, I open up the door. And there are the Russians sitting at the bar facing the bartender, with their backs turned toward the door. But when they heard the door open up, what did they do? They turn to look, to take a look at who's coming in. And they were all Russian soldiers. They turn around, they take a look at me. The minute the soldiers saw us, the other guy ran. He ran away. And I couldn't run anymore. And what was the Russians' reaction? 'You dogs, you. We don't have to guard the border, you come to us.' That was what they said to me. [Laughs.] 'You *sobaki*, you dogs, you. You make it very easy for us; you come to us.' And they caught me. The other guy ran away. Supposedly, he stayed two nights up a tree. A tree, and he escaped. They didn't catch him, but me they caught.

"And they held me in their barracks, interrogating me. Supposedly, I was an American spy. Ask me questions, how many tanks in West Berlin? How many trucks? They held me in the barracks, in the cell, with rats."

He could not have picked a worse moment to be caught behind the Iron Curtain. He was imprisoned by the Soviets during the Berlin blockade, and thus became tangled in the faceoff between the postwar superpowers, each of them raging with paranoia and global one-upmanship.

"This is what I don't understand, about how could they ever think a spy would walk into a bar. Didn't make sense, right? A spy wouldn't do this. They kept me for two days there. And then they shipped me over to Eisenach, a town in East Germany's Black Forest, into a prison, and they kept me there for five days. Of course interrogating with same questions: Who sent me here? What mission do I have? One guy and an interpreter.

"I talked in Polish and a little Russian. So he asked me, 'How come you know a little bit of Russian?' So I was afraid to tell him I was in Russia. This made me complicated. So I said, 'I learned it after the war, when the Russians liberated Warsaw.' So I talked to them mostly Polish, and also German with the interpreter. How many tanks? Who's paying for my work, and how many planes, how many troops? They were interested in American troops only.

"And I told the truth. I was going to West Berlin. 'Why?' 'I'm going to get married,' I told them. 'How did you get here?' I told them, 'I couldn't go across, so I smuggled across the border.' Then they transferred me from Eisenach to East Berlin. But once I was in East Berlin, I called up your father. I was entitled to a phone call. And he had the antiques store on Alexanderplatz, close to where I was. And somehow, with money, he got me out."

Itzak, my father, was making up for a future betrayal. Dov is reluctant to tell me about it.

"I don't want to tell the truth."

"No, it's okay. Tell the truth."

Dov was trying to buy his own medallion, a license to operate a taxicab, in New York City, which at the time cost $17,500, including the car. This was much later, about 1957.

"I asked my brother Itzak to lend some money, which he did. He gave me $2,000. But then the check bounced. He stopped the check without telling me."

I'm glad my father rescued him, pulled him to safety when it really counted, because otherwise I don't think I could bear it. He also bought Dov his gravesite when Dov couldn't afford his own. That's a kind of rescue, too. It gave Dov peace of mind.

Another time my father helped him was when Dov went bankrupt on his chicken farm, after Eva had left him and he was remarried. He was trying to scratch out what he could from the farm before the bank foreclosed on it.

"I used to lose on every dozen of eggs, I use to lose five cents. I did anything to stay alive there. I even bought an egg route. Deliver eggs to New York City every day to certain stores to break even, which I couldn't. I owe the supplier of the chicken feed, I owe them like $18,000 for it. So I decided to smuggle my chickens out at night, that they wouldn't take them. I wanted to smuggle them out and say goodbye to the farm.

"And I made a deal with a guy in the business, a Jewish guy my brother Itzak knew. Okay, we decided this certain night to go, load the chickens, bring the trucks, and load up maybe six thousand chickens, all the good layers, at $3.50 a head. We loading up all night. When the daylight broke, all of a sudden this guy wanted to shake me down. He said, it was at night and he couldn't see so good. But now the chickens, they look so pale at daytime. I said, 'You know what, you're right. Let me ask my wife.' I didn't need to talk with my wife. I made my own decision already. I went back. I called my brother Itzak. I took out my two dogs and put my rifle in the car. When my brother came, we faced the guy. Itzak told the man, 'What are you doing to my brother? How dare you tell him such stupid stories, they look pale?' The man was embarrassed that he did it and said, 'Dov, they look better now.' And he paid me the money."

Although Dov rarely complained about him, my father complained about Dov relentlessly. He discounted the poet in Dov, saw only the holes in his pockets through which money disappeared.

I could see his point sometimes. Despite his mechanic's training, Dov bought a car from Jimmy, who was popularly known as "Jimmy the Gyp," a "beautiful-looking" 1937 Studebaker. It was at least 1953.

"But when I got into the car, and put my foot on the floor, I fell right through. Was only cardboard."

Dov saw the poem, the beauty, but not the material car itself.

When he first came to the United States, he went to an armed forces recruiting office in Battery Park, New York City. He had given up Israel, the land of milk and honey, for the USA, the land of opportunity; maybe he could still be a pilot. They asked him if he had a high school diploma. So instead the CIA—it didn't care about the diploma—tried to recruit him because he spoke so many languages, but he couldn't see doing it after being a communist. He may not have learned to fly a plane or be a spy, but he did take a job as a shill at the Sahara Hotel Casino in Las Vegas while he was waiting out the time to get his quickie divorce from Eva.

He spent most of his working life in New York City, driving a taxicab. Some of his best stories came out of it. For instance, would you have guessed that Jackie Kennedy was a bad tipper? My favorite story, though, is about when President Harry Truman got into his cab. Dov was driving north along Madison Avenue, when the doorman at 35 East 76th Street came out and hailed him. It was the Carlyle Hotel. The doorman who hailed him said, "I have a passenger for you that you wouldn't believe, but I'm not going to tell you who." Then Dov says to me, "Who walks into my cab? President Truman. My favorite president." Dov said to him, "Mr. President, Mr. Truman, how come you are riding with me? Don't you have bodyguards?" Truman answered him, "Never mind the bodyguards. And don't call me president, call me Harry." Dov then said, "Mr. Truman." Truman interrupted, "Don't call me Truman; call me Harry." Dov continues, "Okay, Mr. Harry. Thanks to you I came to this country." "How come?" asked Truman.

"In 1949 the Congress said no more refugees. That's it. But the Democrats, you asked for special permission for another 150,000 people to come to this country. The Polish quota was eight thousand a year and I am Polish. In order for me to make the Polish quota, I would have had to wait a thousand years. So thanks to you, because you vetoed the congressional bill, I am here. I want to thank you for vetoing the bill so I could come here."

Truman quipped, "Dov, if I had known I was letting you in, I would never have given my veto."

That's Dov, full of the poetry of the past. Someone who lived not in the moment or for the future but in the past. When he came to my class on the Holocaust, he told the students he would never forget. He did not say whether he would forgive. But I think he would because that time, while he was running from Hitler, was the time of his youth. He built a dam in Chelyabinsk, he had an affair with a Russian general's wife, he drove an American army jeep in Berlin, he was jailed as an American spy, and he married the blonde *shikse* in the white bikini. Like the rest of the family, he had resentments, but unlike them, they were not formed during the war. It was the present he resented, the present that did not have an adequate story, the present that did not live up to his idea of himself. That's when his exile truly began.

If you are ever at Ellis Island, look for us on the Wall of Honor. It was Dov who put us there, who paid for it, who cared that our names and that history were written in stone.

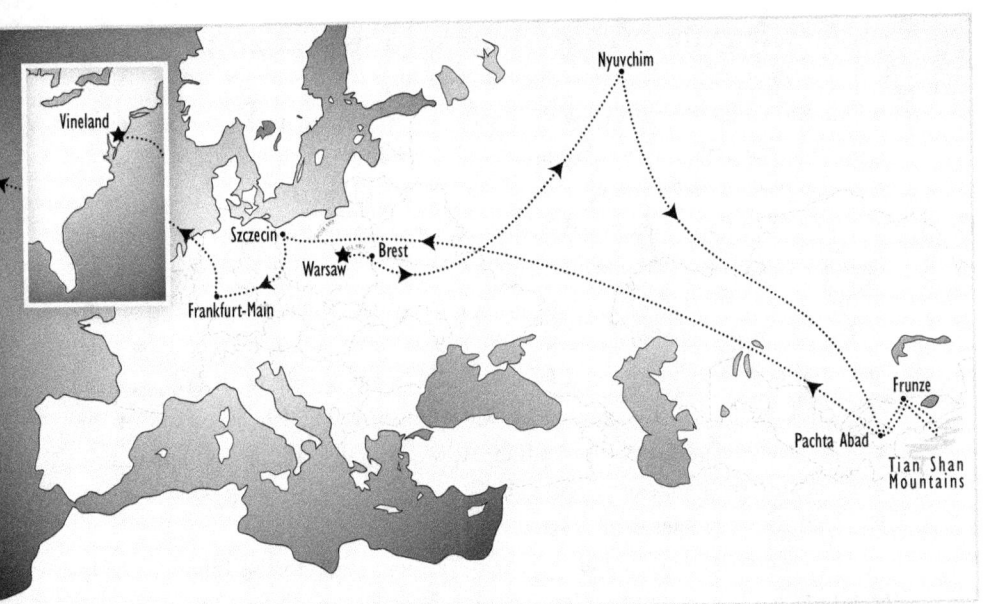

3

Josef

Josef, the eldest of the three brothers in this story, is apple-cheeked and just as short as the other two brothers, standing about five-two. He is slim, and when I was a teenager, the top of his head was already bald. His smile does not register enjoyment but something negative. The first thing that comes to my mind is lasciviousness. When I was twelve, he grabbed my ass. I told my parents and they talked to him and he denied having meant anything. After that he stayed away from me, didn't talk to me directly until I interviewed him for this book.

I was stuck on his chicken farm for many weekends as a kid because my parents' living was selling work clothes at a farmers' market and that happened on weekends. Well, it started Thursday afternoon and ended on Sunday. Sometimes I went with them, but it was boring. I would sit on that grabbable ass and read. But they stayed there from 10 AM to 10 PM, and twelve hours at a stretch is a lot of hours to spend reading, even for me. I could walk around the market, but the goods and ambience fell below my idea of myself. Sometimes I tried to sell the clothes in our stall, but how would you like to be served by a mouthy twelve- or thirteen-year-old who thought she was too good for you?

Josef's smile was executed with his cheeks rather than his eyes or mouth. Besides lechery, the other quality it communicated was condescension. In answer to my interview questions, he replied with a tone of studied patience. His implication was, "I don't believe you don't know this" or variations thereof. Dov called him "the professor," meaning a know-it-all. He did not show affection. Period. Not publicly. Not to his wife or his kids. Never. His kids were afraid of him because when he paid attention to them, it was negative attention—demands for work, insults, or threats of the belt.

Can he really have been all that bad?

His English was German-accented, no doubt due to the influence of his second wife, Lina, who was German, and that was their shared language—not counting English, which never fit that comfortably. Unlike him, she was very appealing, always good to me. She taught me to drive, and she made my Halloween costumes—from scratch. My favorite was a hula dancer. She thought it up all by herself, sewed it on her Singer, and gave it to me without my asking. She knew that at thirteen I wanted to be sexy above all.

When I asked Josef a question, he often interpreted it as a question of general fact rather than a question about his personal experience. That gave him license to doubt my intelligence and knowledge—the answer was something I should know but did not.

Josef was honest about a lot, but not everything. He wanted to control the narrative. He portrayed himself as the wise rescuer, the one who saved his brothers from the Germans and then the Russians. Despite his slight size, he was a tough. He owned guns and knives. There was a sense of icy self-sufficiency about him.

Who would play him if he were cast according to his idea of himself? Someone with grit, a fighter, a man of few words, emotionally cool. Daniel Craig, perhaps? The most raw and least suave of the 007 James Bond movie leads. Although it is filled with improbabilities and danger in an international setting, Josef's story has no glamour. Survival seems to be the goal driving his life from the beginning of the war to his death. Ironically, of the Seven I was able to talk to, he seemed the least enamored of life. He told his younger son, Pavel, that at seventy he was ready to die; each additional year was gravy.

I knew that Josef did not give his kids a Jewish education, which made me curious about his, so I asked him, "Were you bar mitzvahed?"

"Yah."

"What did that mean?"

"What did it mean? It's a Jewish ritual where boys, when you reach thirteen, you take total responsibility of a man by himself."

Did Josef really think I did not know that?

"Were you the only one who had a bar mitzvah?"

"Who said that? I don't know what your father told you."

"Dov said he didn't have one."

"He made bar mitzvah. All of us had bar mitzvah. I was the only one who went to a Jewish school. Itzak and Dov, I believe they had a private tutor."

The Jewish education, whatever there was of it, must have been driven by my grandmother Brandla. In stark contrast to his Hasidic next-door neighbors, my grandfather Chaim did the minimum to observe the proprieties.

"My father, in fact, in this whole apartment building, in the whole thing, he didn't care about the *shul*. Only the most important holidays like Rosh Hashanah and Yom Kippur. This he couldn't ignore, so we didn't work, and we went to cemetery where they had a big chapel there. And it was so common to go there; we all, the prostitutes too, everybody was there. Everybody. It was the biggest Jewish cemetery in Poland."

When I visited Warsaw, I saw the cemetery on Okopowa Street that Josef talked about. The jumble of weeds, trees, and tilting, unruly old gravestones reminds visitors of the despised status of Jews in Poland. Newer, brighter monuments—put up by American Jews to recognize their Nazi-murdered relatives—point an accusing finger by their contrast.

About 260,000 bodies are buried here in single graves, and about 80,000 are buried in mass graves. As the conditions deteriorated in the Warsaw Ghetto, Jews died in such numbers that they no longer could be individually buried. In the mass graves, women are separated from men and Orthodox Jews from the others. A low wall near the entrance is constructed of pieces of broken gravestones. It records the anti-Semitic vandalism and destruction to this cemetery committed both during and after the war.

I met the cemetery caretaker, Boleslaw Szenicer. He told me that he inherited the job from his father. He said that he wanted to leave Poland to go to Israel to find a wife since there are so few Jews left in Poland, but he was afraid to leave the country because he might be prevented by the Polish government from ever coming back. What would happen to the cemetery then?

Josef does not judge his father for his drinking, but he is less forgiving of his father's demands on his kids, as well as his generosity to his friends, which deprived his own family.

"According to his theory in those days, everybody has to work. Everybody, regardless of age, as long as you can do something, you have to help. And if other kids had more freedom, we couldn't have it. All the time he fought with us. Let's say, when my father was here across the room with his iron and pressing and things like this, and I would say something to him, and he wouldn't like it. He could take a big piece of wood—what they are putting down on pants to flatten them. That's it—right in my head!

"Oh, we had a lot of battles, always. Because I didn't like the things what he was doing. He had friends, and he gave them money for which we had to work very hard, and I was the oldest and I understand the whole thing. The others were all younger; they didn't understand, and my mother even agreed with me, but she couldn't say nothing. The arguments was about money, what he borrowed away to the people. And always about the hours what we had to work."

Josef had more awareness of real material conditions than Dov, whose head was in the clouds. Dov did not calculate the consequences of his father's generosity for his own family.

"You see, one more thing is here to realize. The conditions of living, they were so frustrating in comparison, if you compared it today. For instance, we worked seven days a week. And not only eight hours a day, but sometimes fifteen, sixteen hours a day. And when it came to collect the money, the debtors couldn't pay us the money. So everything, everything what we made went on the book. Then we went into the grocery store and we bought on the book. Whatever you did need, you have on credit. You know, every week you pay so much and so much. You couldn't have the opportunity, the chances to save up and pay for it in one time. And the debt on the book came higher and higher and higher. It never came down. Always more and more and more on the book. Because the Jewish trade was in a ghetto. You living in a ghetto and you have to deal between yourselves, and nothing outside comes into the ghetto. Nothing comes so that you can make a better living.

"We lived in a time where the persecution of Jews was very bad in Poland. When you came into the Polish sector, you were a Jew; you were no good: 'Go, go to Israel.' They didn't say then Israel. They said Palestine. 'Go to Palestine, you don't belong here.' And the pogroms. I remember pogroms in other cities where they killed Jews on the street. They killed women, they killed babies. For no reason at all, they just killed them. And the Polish government, they do the same thing. If you went to complain, they put you in jail."

His wife, Lina, interrupts us. She wants to make lunch. I say to her, "I hope you didn't go to any trouble."

Josef responds, "No, what trouble? What trouble? All right, Ellen, for a person like you, with your intelligence, we should be able to cook."

He calls me intelligent while he is implying I am stupid. Josef has a hard time being gracious, though I understand he is trying. Okay, Professor Josef, let's have lunch.

After lunch, I ask Josef when he started riding a bicycle.

"I started bike riding when I was fifteen."

"How did you get your bicycle?"

"My parents bought that bike."

"Did they buy the bicycle? Dov complains bitterly to this day that he never got a bicycle."

"[Laughing.] Well, I know why. Because my father was upset with me with this bicycle because I didn't want to work. I always want to go away with my bicycle. When I want to go, I lower the bicycle out the window so he wouldn't know.

"We belonged to clubs, and we went on all kinds of excursions. One club was Zionist because it was for the future of the country in Israel. And then it was a group *Hapoel*, it was a Jewish soccer team. But they had other games like bicycle riding."

I looked up *Hapoel*. Even now it is associated with a Tel Aviv soccer team, and historically it is connected to the *Histadrut* trade union movement, which had strong communist sympathies. At matches its fans often wave banners that have the face of Che Guevara on them. The youth movement associated with this name was known as *Hapoel Hatzair* or "young worker." It was Zionist, socialist, and advocated Yiddish because that was the language of the Jewish proletariat. It had a volatile history, merging with similar Polish groups.

"When did you first hear about Hitler?"

"I heard about Hitler the first time in 1933. Well, in the first place it was coming already Jews from Germany into Poland and telling us about the changes what they made. Things like that. And actually there's a book *Mein Kampf*. I was reading the book, *Mein Kampf*. This was 1933 and I was twenty-one years old, and I was involved in a lot of political activities. Well, you know, it was there a communistic party. Well, I wasn't a member. Let's say I was a sympathizer and doing all kind of things, all kind of crazy things. Like going out in the street and throwing flags where the electric lines for the trolleys are. Up high. Like a red flag. Like from the Soviet Union, you know? For this they put you in jail, and they never let you out. Also, we went out in the street and writing on the walls with all kind of slogans."

So much for Dov thinking that he was unique in his family for his political activism. In urban areas such as Warsaw, the *Komunistyczna Partia Polski* (KPP), or Communist Party of prewar Poland, did have a large Jewish membership. More than half its leadership was Jewish. Part of the attraction for Jews was the stand against anti-Semitism taken by the KPP. The authorities, however, used the association between communism and Jews for the stereotype of the Commie Jew, *Żydokomuna*. This connection was reflected in who got thrown in jail in cases involving communism. More than 90 percent of the accused in such cases were Jewish, a much larger percentage than were in the KPP.

"And sometimes without any warning, it came the police. With their billy clubs and canines, they came and took us to jail for a day or two, and then they released us. You see, they didn't have any hard proof that we did something wrong."

He told me that his best friend, Chapka, whose life he saved by folding him into the Seven, was in the same club.

The pull of the Communist Party for young, poor Jews must have been strong—so strong that Dov left his family in Brest for a Soviet communal factory in Kiev. None of the three brothers remained socialist-leaning. Dov's socialist ideology did not hold against the realities of a communal factory. He voted for Bush, the younger, when he was an old man, and my father voted Republican much of the time. My father identified with the forces of the stock market. I doubt that Josef voted much.

Chapka, though, was an exception. Unlike my family, Chapka stayed in Poland and even rose in the communist government hierarchy. In about 1968 he moved to Paris because Poland had become uninhabitable for Jews. "Move or die," he said. But he was still a believer. I told Josef, "He calls his son a capitalist."

"Chapka calls his son a capitalist? [Laughs.]"

Chapka, Josef's best friend, one of the Seven. I tracked him down in Paris in the late eighties. He made me dinner and introduced me to his grown children. His son married a Moroccan Jew. When the couple left, Chapka asked me whether in the United States people also feel prejudice against dark-skinned Jews. I felt he asked the question out of genuine curiosity, to see whether this phenomenon was French or more general, a question that I think came out of socialist idealism rather than bigotry.

JOSEF

Josef talked freely about his sex life in Warsaw, which did not surprise me. Even at his funeral, his sons talked about his "side" relationships, something they knew about, and his touting the strong inherited sexual drive of the family men. Nine years older than Dov and brazen, Josef either thought Dov would not know what was going on when he brought a girl into their bed or he did not care.

"In those days you have to be more careful. If you got involved with a girl, you have to be very careful not to get her in trouble because you know if you get her in trouble, you have to marry her.

"Oh, yes. I had a lot of girlfriends, not only one. Well, I had girlfriends what I talked every day to them. With no strings attached or something like this. No responsibility. And I have a girl that I was very close to her. In the same place where we lived, I had a girl. Her name was Estusha. I was then maybe sixteen. She lived on the same block. And sometimes I went into her place. She made manicure. She came with bunch of boys and when she saw me, she left the boys and she came with me. And you know the usual thing. You could go up three or four stories in a building, and there was a place to go in there. You stay there and you fooled around, that's all.

"Now, after her came a girl, her name was Natcha. I was about nineteen and she was maybe seventeen. She lived on the Sventoyerska. She worked for her aunt, and sold things like to write in school, books and pencils and all kind of things. I met her through the club. She came there with a couple girls and we met together. I was planning to marry her. Yah, I was planning to marry her, and she would get herself a place on her own where they sell all kind of things, books and pencils and thread and all kind of things. I had in mind, too, that it's a possibility that I would open myself a small store specializing in men's pants—all kind of pants, breeches, and then for military also.

"Well, it didn't work out with her. When I was in the army, I start getting letters from my friends that she's going out with other guys, and things like this. Which I didn't like it. And no matter how much you loved a girl, you had your own pride not to give in. You didn't want your girl to have anything to do with someone else. And those rumors kept going around. I stopped seeing her and she start seeing another guy, and she got married to him. Well, she took a long time to try to persuade me not to do it. That she's innocent and she didn't do any wrongdoing. But she didn't persuade me."

"Were you disappointed?"

"Oh, yes. Very disappointed. You know, it was a love affair when you are young. And you like somebody, love somebody. All of a sudden, out came the letter from your friends, and they telling you she did this, she did that. And I did regret it later."

"That you left her?"

"Yah. But it was too late."

I go to a nail salon every couple of weeks. Usually the manicurists do not talk beyond a cursory "How are you?" but this Korean woman asked a lot more questions. She wanted to know what I did for a living—all about me. So I also asked her about herself. She told me that she had married young in Korea and had a baby boy. Her husband came to the United States and worked in a nail shop owned by his brother-in-law. Then abruptly she asked, "Where does all the love go? Where does it go? Where is all the love?" The question flummoxed me. She talked about love as if it were material. It's there, and then it's not. Where did it go? Her husband fell in love with a white manicurist in his brother-in-law's shop. He no longer loved the mother of his son, and she hated him for that betrayal. Once she came to the United States, she had no option but to live in his house and work in the same shop he did, but where was the love now?

Where did the love go?

I asked Josef if he remembers any of the films he saw before the war, and he remembered the 1936 black-and-white film *Rose Marie*, which he described as "a beautiful movie about the Canadian Mounted Police"—with Jeanette MacDonald and Nelson Eddy, who sing the haunting duet "Indian Love Call":

Oo-oo-oo-oo, oo-oo-oo-oo
When I'm calling you
Oo-oo-oo-oo, oo-oo-oo-oo
Will you answer too?
Oo-oo-oo-oo, oo-oo-oo-oo

That means I offer my love to you to be your own
If you refuse me I will be blue, waiting all alone

But if when you hear my love call ringing clear
Oo-oo-oo-oo, oo-oo-oo-oo
And I hear your answering echo so dear
Oo-oo-oo-oo, oo-oo-oo-oo

Then I will know our love will come true
You'll belong to me, I'll belong to you

Then I will know our love will come true
You'll belong to me, I'll belong to you

Josef carried Natcha's photo with him through enemy fire, the frozen tundra of his Soviet exile, starvation in Central Asia, near-death in the Tian Shan mountains, the lice-infested cattle cars that brought him from place to place, the black markets of Eastern and Western Europe, and all the way to a chicken farm in South Jersey. He gave her up in a common way—to keep his pride. He gave up love when he felt it most, when he had plans for the future, when he had hope and some optimism despite poverty and anti-Semitism and the coming war.

His favorite movie describes a utopia.

"In those days I also saw the *Lost Horizon* movie. It's a movie about the mountains in the Himalayas where some scientists got lost. They hiked there, and they found a paradise. Everybody who lives there, lives a life forever and never gets old. And the moment they stepped down from there, they got old, they died."

Josef talked a long time about *Lost Horizon*. This 1937 sci-fi adventure-fantasy film by Frank Capra, starring Ronald Colman and Jane Wyatt, concerns a group of airline passengers stranded in the Himalayas in a utopia called Shangri-La, an Eden without death or deprivation. Although all but one of the passengers who leave it die one way or another, one of them, the film's hero, played by Colman, returns to it in the end. From one perspective, it was an escapist vision for the times. It was a terrible moment: post–World War I, the Depression, the Spanish Civil War in progress and European fascism on the rise, and the looming war against Hitler. In these circumstances who wouldn't want to contemplate Shangri-La rather than the world as it was? But utopias such as Shangri-La are also last resting places. As a space for eternal life, Shangri-La can be construed as a kind of death, for everlasting life is also death. Heaven is a nation of the dead. The film received seven Academy Award nominations and won two.

For Josef, unlike the Colman character, there was no going back. The process that eroded his love of life, that slowly soured him, had begun.

"Do you remember being drafted?"

"Well, when I was age twenty, I had to register, and they went through all the inspections. And there was a lottery, and a card came and told me I was taken. It was a big surprise for me. Oh, boy. My, my, my, my. I was the only one from my friends taken. The army sent you a free ticket. I had to report. It was about two hundred miles from Warsaw. Was an army base in Inowrocław. This is not far away from the coast of the Baltic, you know? It was in summertime."

I looked up this unpronounceable city. Wikipedia mentioned Inowrocław Synagogue, so I clicked on it. The entire synagogue was built with the money of a Dr. Leopold Levy. The Germans tried to turn it into a swimming pool, but when that failed, they destroyed it. The site of the synagogue is now called John Paul II Square, its Jewish origins kept alive only virtually by Wikipedia.

About 100,000 Jewish soldiers and officers fought the Germans in the seventeen days before Poland capitulated. This figure represents 10 percent of the Polish armed forces. And about 50,000 Jews died in Polish uniforms.

"I was friendly with everybody, but the upbringing from Poles against Jews was always discriminating. When the basic training was over, I was assigned to be a leader of several platoons, which we did ride on bicycles. I went with them for exercises, you know. We went let's say, twenty-five to thirty miles. We had the machine guns and a backpack with maybe sixty or seventy pounds on you. And I kept training them, and I was successful with it."

Bicycles. Never in my fifty years of movie-going had I seen a war movie that depicted a bicycle platoon. Imagine Patton with a bicycle platoon. *Saving Private Ryan*? No bicycle squadrons. In war movies, soldiers flew planes, sailed on ships, rode horses, sat in trucks, tanks, cars, and on motorcycles, and marched. A bicycle platoon seemed to me a Polish joke, an ethnic joke.

I asked Josef why they would have a bicycle platoon.

"Oh, they did have it in the army bicycle platoon."

"What could you do on a bicycle?"

"Well, first of all, you could come to the point a lot faster than marching. I took my bike from home when I was on furlough."

Indeed, many sources confirm that a 1939 Polish cavalry brigade and regiment of six thousand men could well have had a bicycle platoon consisting of maybe forty bicycles.

"You came out of the army in 1936. How did you think of your future?"

"You didn't expect too much from the future, and you didn't expect too much from the present. It was every day with no difference. You knew that you going to get up the next morning, you going to do the same things a week later, a year later. And you didn't see any special perspective in your life, which you could distinguish that something is going to happen."

Where did the love go?

"Oh, you felt that you living in a society that nothing, nothing moves. You have to live this way. Nothing is going to happen because the anti-Semitism was very great."

"Dov remembers you in your army uniform. He was a boy when his big brother came home in uniform, and he was very impressed with the uniform."

"Well, in the first place, I made my own uniform. The uniform what they gave me, I took it and modeled it to my shape, and that's why it looked impressive—because the others they didn't have something like this. I still have the pictures with me in the uniform.

"I was in the army from 1933 until 1939. I was in and out. I spent three years and then every summer for six weeks. Let's say every year, I went to army for maneuvers. I was trained machine gunner."

"When did you meet Henya?"

Josef met Henya, one of the Seven and his first wife, though they never officially married, through his best friend, Chapka.

"I met her I believe in 1937, one year after I came out from the army. She was Chapka's cousin's husband's sister. I wasn't in love with her then. No, she was just a girl. I had already girls before that I was in love with them. And I didn't have for her the same feeling what I had for Natcha."

"Did you ever fall in love with her?"

"Well, you know what they say about your first love. First real love. When you meet a second person, it's not the same thing what it was the first time. We cannot take away from anybody, man or woman, their first love. This is something very special."

But where does the love go?

"What happened is that time went by and by, until it came to this fatal date of 1939. Just two months before the Germans invaded, I went back into the army. They proclaim a general mobilization in July, and all the guys on reserve went to barracks outside of Warsaw. We stayed there, and then we heard that the Germans already are crossed over the borders, and there were fights between the Polish army and the Germans. And then the Germans start coming closer and closer. And then we started defending our position. Was not far away from Warsaw.

"Germans came in and they start taking over the country so fast, that you just kept running away, farther and farther and farther from the Germans to the east of Poland. They came from all directions. The Polish army didn't have any defense.

"I was when they bombed Warsaw. I was when they bombed our units in the fields. And then there was so much chaos with our soldiers. They were so confused that they were shooting at each other from every direction and a lot of things. Before mine eyes, I didn't even know what happened. A lot of soldiers were killed right when running in the ditches. The shooting came from both sides, so a lot of us got killed. And meanwhile we were going always more to the east.

"I was waiting with three platoons of mine command with machine guns, and we guarded a bridge. And the Germans came on motorcycles with machine guns attached to them. And we start opening up on them, and they were flying in the water because we opened at them from all directions. And we had about three or four times like this. And quite a few Polish soldiers were killed. And a lot of Germans, they were killed. But this didn't hold them back. They send in more and more, and then they start coming with the planes. And when they start coming with planes, we didn't have *any* rescue for it. Machine guns, no machine guns, we couldn't hold them.

"They start gaining on us, and we ran into the countryside into—what do you call it—with the hay and the stock inside? We ran in there, a barn. In one case, they dropped a bomb on one side. And they killed all the Poles who were on that side. And I was on the other side. And I got a little wounded in my knee from shrapnel.

"And I managed to get some horses and a wagon, some military horses, and after going a mile or two, I found a hospital. There was so many wounded that mine things didn't even count for a lot. I had to fix with it myself, to take care of it. And this was in a little town near the border from Russia. Now, when I walked out from this hospital, I didn't have nothing to eat. I had no place to sleep. It was Rosh Hashanah, so the Jewish people went there in the synagogue. And I was standing before the synagogue in mine uniform and some people came out, and they looked at me and some, some came closer. They asked me few questions, and I said I go into the *shul* because I was wounded—I talked Jewish. Oh boy, as soon as I start talking in Jewish, the people took me into their homes, and they gave me something to eat and took care there, some bandages and everything.

"And I wasn't too much far away there to Brest, sixty or seventy kilometers from there. So I start walking toward Brest. While I was walking, I met those Polish officers what they didn't want to give up the war."

Josef was referring to his encounter with the *Narodowa Organizacja Wojskowa*. They were an insurgent Polish nationalist group of soldiers, officers, who were against both the Germans and the Russians and who attacked other Polish soldiers. It was an anti-Soviet and anti-German Polish resistance paramilitary group. Competing reports of its activities associate it with both the killing and rescue of Jews. In my Uncle Josef's encounter with the Narodwe, as he called them, it was a near-death experience, one of several in the short time before the Polish army was decimated.

The encounter took place in the chaos while he was on the run from the Germans.

"The Narodwe accuse some in the Polish army; they said that they sympathized with the Russians. There were a lot of cases where they killed them in front of mine eyes. I was with maybe forty or fifty guys, and the Narodwe came out from the woods, with machine guns and said, 'Stay right there. Now, who of you soldiers live in the territory in Poland but near at the border?' Because we were close to the border, they thought that we are sympathizers with the Russians. They took us out from the group. Then they asked me, 'What are you?' I said, 'I'm Jewish.' So they let me go. And they took who they thought was Russian sympathizers out in the woods, and they kill them. They were Polish soldiers in Polish uniforms—all of them.

"Okay, now while I'm going farther and farther away to the east, all of a sudden the Russians are coming out from the woods on the highway. Now they start asking us questions. Naturally, I couldn't talk much Russian.

"But the Polish and Russian had a lot of words that was similar. And one guy, a Jewish guy, was an officer; he start asking me questions. 'Tell me where did you saw those Polish officers?' He knew about the Narodwe and what they did. So I told him the story, what happened. He said, 'If you know about it in so much detail (I showed him on a map where it happened), you must be a Narodwe officer too.' I said, 'Look, I'm not a Narodwe officer.' I was only a sergeant. He didn't believe it, so he said to me, 'Who can vouch for you, that you're telling the truth? That you are what you say you are?'

"So I had from my mother's side her relative living about three miles away from this spot. So he send me over with a few Russians to my relation, and he vouched for me that I was what I am. And then they let me go. And this is how I walked into Brest. And when I walked into Brest, the whole Russian army was already there sitting on their tanks. Yah, sitting on the tanks and throwing down to the people confetti. That's what they did. Well, they tried to get the people on their side, you know.

"That's how I came to Brest. I had there all my father's relatives. And a few kilometers away, about forty kilometers, I had my mother's relatives—all on the east side of the Bug. And the Germans were on the west side, and they went up to the river Bug, and they stayed there. And the Russians went from the east side up to the river Bug, and they stayed there. Yah, this is the way they divided Poland."

"What comes next is mine effort to go back to Warsaw to get my family and to take off my parents from Warsaw and bring them to Brest.

"I went to Warsaw, I would say, in the month of November. And then already everything was very strict, tight. The borders, they were patrolled and I was holded on the border. I told them all kind of stories—that I'm from over there and I want to go there. I told them always the opposite stories. And it worked. Anyway, I went to Warsaw, and it was nightmare because the cattle train had a lot of Poles what they didn't like the Russians, and they escaped to the Germans. And they were talking on the Jews, all kind of things. That the Russians are sparing the Jews. The Jews can get away what they want. And if they would find out that I am a Jew... I was in a Polish uniform, anyway, so they couldn't recognize me, and I was with two other guys.

"And on every station the SS came up looking in your face. They shout *Juden raus*, Jews out. This was the first time that I felt very offended. And I felt persecuted. It was very frightening. Anyway, I went to Warsaw. I bought a cheap ticket, and I went with the cattle car, and it let me off ten miles from Warsaw, on other side of river Vistula. While I was walking, I saw on the street the German patrols walk around, looking to catch people and taking them away. Everything was suspicious with them—going around and searching with a machine gun.

"So I went to mine house. The moment I came in, you cannot imagine the joy from my mother and father. I had a sister there, Sonia, and I had a little a brother, Motel, there still.

"Okay. Now, I don't remember the date, when it was, when exactly the date, but I remember I said to my father. That was the words what I said to him, I said: 'Look, you are not going to believe me, but take my word for it, this what's going to happen.' I said, 'Up till now, me and a lot of young people, we didn't believe that this is going to happen. We did believe that France and the English and the other nations are going to sit down, and they going to give Hitler a few things to shut his mouth, and everything will be all right. But this is not the way it goes.'

"So I told him, 'I read *Mein Kampf*.' And I told him what I read in *Mein Kampf*. What Hitler support, what he wants to do with the world. He wants to make a pure Aryan race. And they going to be built of blond and young people. I said, 'They don't want people like you.'

"So my father told me, 'I'm older than you. I went through the first war. I worked for the Germans, and they were very good to me. I sewed for them. They gave me food; they gave me money. They were excellent.' So I told him, 'This is not the same Germany! They are not the same! Why do you want to stick here?' So he said to me, 'No.' He doesn't believe it."

"How about your mother?"

"Well, my mother she would agree. But my father wouldn't agree. He build up here his business, he had machines, he has new mahogany furniture. You know, like the old people, they sitting on their five cents and they wouldn't move on them.

"Then I had a sister, Rachel. She was married and she had two children. And I told her about it. And I told my brother-in-law about it. I talked to him, and he was a very intelligent man. I would say at this time he was on top, with the education and his moneymaking. He was a man who decorated windows, the most expensive windows in Warsaw. And he had some money and an apartment, and I told him. And he said I'm right. And he start preparing already before even I talked to him. He took all his money, and he exchanged it all for gold and silver. And he made himself a stick. And he put it all in a stick to take it out from the country. They were ready to go with me.

"And then I asked my parents if they will leave me my little brother. He was about seven years old. His name Motel. So they said, 'Everybody's gone.' They said, 'You're going back. Itzak is already gone. Dov is going. Sonia, you are going to take now from home.' And the other sister—Rachel with her husband. All of them. My mother said, 'What are you going to leave for me?' So I said, 'You can have Motel any time; give him to me. If you don't want to go, give him to me. He's young.' They didn't agree."

"So I was in Warsaw three nights. I slept there in our house. In those three nights, I went through scares all the time. We lived in a big complex where you have to come to the big door and push the buttons to let you in. And every night, two or three times a night, came in the German SS, and they look around to take out people. And this got me on my nerves. Son of a gun, I got through the war and everything, and I made it this far. I am not going with them now.

"Anyway, on the third day, when I was ready to go back, we packed a few things, and me and Sonia, we hire a guy with a *doroszka*, a carriage, because the trains didn't go and everything was *kaput*. We were ready to go back to Praga, to the cattle cars. And my sister Rachel told me that they decided that they're not going. Drexler said to me, 'I'm speaking so good German, and I believe that I'm going to do with them business.' He didn't believe in the stories what Hitler is going to do. He didn't believe that Hitler is going to seek out all the generations of Jews and put them in concentration camps and kill them.

"Anyway, so they didn't want to leave, so I grabbed Sonia, and soon we came to this point near the river, the Vistula. Germans came out and said to her '*Fraulein, wohin gehen Sie? Komm mit uns.*' And they took her away to go and clean their offices. I was standing like on hot coals. I mean I didn't know what to do, but I told her, 'I'm going to wait for you at the station there.' They told her to clean with her underpants their offices. With her underpants! Then they give her food and even a few German marks. And they let her go. And she came there and we went in those cattle wagons. And we start going back. On the way back was exactly the same story. I was in the uniform. I was sitting with Sonia and pretending that she is a girlfriend of mine.

"So, anyway, we went to this place when it was nighttime, and we went to a guy there who lived near the river Bug. And we had to pay him for taking us over the river to the other side. And meanwhile, this guy, what he did, he sent somebody to the Germans, and while we were sitting there all bunched into the boat, my sister and some other guys there, maybe some other nine or ten people, they came. They were not the SS, but they were, what do you call them? *Polizei*, police, something like this. And one of them said, 'What are you doing here?' So I told him, 'We are from Brest.' So, surprisingly enough, he said—you know, I used this trick before, too—he said to me, 'No, if you coming from Brest, you go back to Brest. And don't even try to get in the train.' And he told the guy to take us back on the other side, and he told him, 'You have to treat them like people. Give them some food and let them sleep all the night. In the morning take them back over. And if I hear one complaint that you did something wrong to them, I'll come.' Was a nice guy.

"So we went away from this place, and we went to another place by the Bug River, and we hired another guy. We did not trust first guy. And we paid this different guy again, and he took us all to the other side. And the moment we came over to the other side, the Russian patrol came over. And they took us all in, and they put us in a jail there. And they hold us all night, and they ask us the same questions. 'What are you doing here on the border? What do you want to do on the border?' So we told them that we want to go to Poland, to Warsaw. He said, 'You coming from Brest, and you want to go to the Germans? Oh, no, you're not going to go to the Germans; you're going back to Brest.' You understand the trick? They didn't like nobody to escape from them, and they didn't like nobody to leave from there. The next day we were out, and I joined with mine family in Brest."

"Did you take your uniform off then?"

"No, no I still didn't take the uniform off. It took me quite some time until I decided that I don't have to be afraid anymore of the Germans, that they're not going to come in.

"I saw the Russians. What a force; what a might! Oh, boy, they came in on those tanks. They had so many of them; it's unbelievable. I thought they took them from the whole world. And they were going around singing their nice national songs. And they were busying up the bazaar, the market, buying all kind of stuff and things like this."

"So in a period of a few months, between September and December, you fought a war, you went to Brest, they bombed you, you were wounded, you crossed the Vistula River, you crossed the Bug, you crossed back into Warsaw, and you were in jail."

"I went through like a Vietnam."

Vietnam? I thought about why Josef grabbed at Vietnam since he had been through his own war—a world war in which he, as a Jew, was a specific target. Was it the unprecedented graphic television images of the horrors of Vietnam that came to represent all wars to him?

The prewar Jewish population of Brest was 21,518 or 41.3 percent of the total. Jews were so integrated into the town that, although the mayor was always Christian, the vice-mayor was always Jewish. Menachim Begin and his wife lived in Brest, as did his parents. Although the parents stayed in Brest, Begin and his wife, like the Seven, were transported to a prison camp, in his case one of those infamous gulags in Pechora that Dov talked about. Begin, who would later become prime minister of Israel, wrote a book about his gulag imprisonment called *White Nights*.

"As a matter of fact, from all the Jews what came to Brest from Warsaw or from other parts of German-controlled Poland, a lot went back in a special registration. At that time, if you want to go back to Warsaw, you have to go in and register with the NKVD. So they stood there all night long in line. It was so many people want to get a pass to go back, your mother and father, too. After they did this, I had a talk with them, and I also had a talk with my friends what they also register. My personal friends. And I had a talk with them, and I pleaded to them, 'Don't go back, stay here. You have it good here. You have a place here to sleep, you have food to eat, you make a few dollars on the side selling to the Russians.'"

"Lola's brother went back though, right?"

"Yah, he went back, yes. At this time, he went back. But somehow I manage to talk your parents out of it. But I had a couple of friends, my very good friends, they went back. Chapka stayed though."

"What did you do all day in Brest?"

"Well, most of the day we went out on—they call it a bazaar. We always sold some clothes to the Russians. Make good money. We had a friend, he had a store. And since the Russians came, everybody close the stores, so we start taking out goods from the side so the Russians they didn't know."

"Why did they close their stores?"

"Yes, because they were afraid that the Russians would come in, and they would confiscate. This was November, December."

"What did you think about the future?"

"I think only one thought, one thing—going back to Warsaw when the war is over. I thought it is better with the Russians at this time because you were free. You could do whatever you want there. They didn't have any business with private people.

"I didn't thought that the NKVD going to come one day and move us deep in Soviet Russia. I thought the things that were going on up till now, they're still going to go on. But nobody could make any predictions. It came a time that they claim they didn't want to have any undesirable element there.

"The people who lived in Brest, they were citizen, the Russians left them alone. But the people what they came over from Warsaw and from the other places, the Russians all of a sudden came out with a statement that they are an undesirable element to live on the border. And we were the undesirable element. They didn't want it on the border. This happen in June 1940."

"But you didn't think that this was an anti-Semitic action?"

"No, I didn't think of any anti-Semitic action. What I thought then is just plain: that they don't want this element to be there because it was on the border. They don't want them telling things to the Germans."

It did not make sense to me that the Soviets were afraid of Jews collaborating with the Germans, their allies by way of the Hitler-Stalin pact. I checked and Josef's interpretation is largely correct. Although with historical hindsight it seems obvious that Polish Jews fleeing the Germans would likely be the most dedicated supporters of the Soviet state because they knew what was happening to Jews on the other side of the border. But for Stalin, in this case at least, Poles were Poles. His goal was to seal off the USSR with no movement of information either in or out, since information from outside the country could not be controlled by party authorities. Soviets also couldn't be bothered to deal with the housing, employment, and food needs this concentration of Polish-Jewish refugees created, so they dispersed them to remote regions.

I asked Josef whether it was his idea to allow the NKVD to move them away from Brest. "Were you acting like a father to the group?"

"I felt because I'm the oldest. So I told them only one thing. 'Let us go all together where they are going to bring us. Let us be all together.' Not even one of the family what we had there in Brest, uncles and aunts and cousins and things—everybody said against it. Better stay here. And I said, 'No! I'm not going to stay here with you.' I said, 'The Russians, maybe they will let us go this time, but they can come in another time and put you in big danger for hiding us out.' I said, 'You did enough. And I believe where all the refugees are going, we should go with them. And we're not going to the Germans; we're going deep into Russia.' I didn't know how deep we going to go, but I know we going away farther from the Germans. That's all what it counts.

"And besides, we were very young. We had a lot of guts. And we weren't afraid of anything. Now I would think twice."

I wondered if they had gotten tired of Brest, a small town in comparison to Warsaw.

"No, no, no. We didn't get tired. Oh, the time went there, very beautiful. I have uncles there what they were in business. One had a butcher store, and he rented boats on the river there where he lived. And so, we had a good time there. Always going around and having a lot of food and things. And everybody was so nice. And everybody wants to hold me and for me to stay with them and things like this. Like family. It was different, was not family like today. Was *family*."

"When you took the train away from the Polish border, were you still wearing your uniform?"

"Two, three weeks later, when I came back from Poland, I saw I was safe from the Germans. And that's all; I took it off."

Josef added details about the journey to Nyuvchim.

"On the cattle car trains to Kotlas, they had inside an oven. And sometimes they supplied some wood to keep you warm because even in summer months the nights got cold. What they did, the Russian authorities, they called ahead three or four stations to prepare for us some soup and bread when we got there. So we came to a station, we went down with big dishes to take the soup and things. And everyone was on the line. And they divide the food, and we eat it.

"On the train, you could open a little the door and look out and see where you're going, what you passing. We didn't know where we going. We knew that we going north through a lot of little towns. After some time you came into this big station where the trip for the train ended. This was Kotlas. It was more than a thousand miles from Brest. Then in Kotlas, we came out and we were waiting there for ships. The train didn't go anymore, any farther than this. Over there for first time we experienced those—what do you call it? The white nights? Yah, the sun doesn't go down too much, and then comes up again. We were outside. We kept a fire for keeping away the mosquitoes. They would bite us to death, such big ones. I never seen something like this.

"It was like a no man's land. You know? Like it didn't belong to nobody. Nobody almost lived there. Very, very primitive. All the Russian buildings were wood because over there is a lot of wood. You have thousands and thousands of square miles of forest."

"How long did you stay in Kotlas?"

"It was a couple of days, maybe less than a week. Thousands and thousands of people waiting. Not only our train came. It came ten or twenty. Came a lot of other trains."

"The seven of you stayed together. Is that right?"

"We always kept together. We determined to stay together. And then naturally the ships came. And we were going into the ships. We were going in the ships, and we were going on the water. And over there we had a lot of fun with the water. I remember Dov was an excellent swimmer. He and Sonia, both of them, they jumped from the top of the ship into the water, and under the ship. Under the ship! And came out on the other side. Yah, we all jumped into the river. We had a lot of fun there. We were all young people."

"So you all felt you were on an adventure. Did you feel frightened at all?"

"No, no, we didn't have any reason to be afraid of the Russians because we saw the way they treated us. And the Russian people treated us nice. We didn't have any, any trouble with them. So the ship brought us to Syktyvkar.

"We already in Syktyvkar, right? It was June 1940. And in Syktyvkar we stayed there a couple of days or something like this, and then came the trucks, the military vans, and they took us from Syktyvkar to Nyuvchim. Everybody who went to Kotlas went from Kotlas to Syktyvkar. Everybody. And from there on, they start dispersing them all around to all different locations and regions. Us they bring to Nyuvchim."

"How did you get to be called the Seven?"

"Because we were Seven. Me, Henya, Itzak, and Lola is four, Dov is five, Sonia is six, and Chapka is seven. We were altogether seven, never separate, so they call it the Seven."

"Were other people also traveling in groups?"

"No. Nobody except us in this little village has this closeness together like we had."

"So in this little village you came to be known as the Seven. Did it feel like a prison camp?"

"No. It was a little village for natives there; they didn't know about the Russian system at all. They just adhere to it, and they went about their own business. They were people, mostly nature people. They went fishing. They build houses. Not with all those tools what we have today. The only thing what they had was, what do you call it—an axe? There was forest to cover the whole world there. You see white bears. You see wolves. This was all over there."

"Weren't you afraid? I mean, you came from a big city."

"Well, you know, we got used to it. Bears, they don't like people. They don't eat people. They like mainly berries, mushrooms, all those things. We only were very careful when they have their litters. Then you have to make a big circle around them, that's all."

"You lived in a common room there?"

"For us they had a wooden house with one big room. And it was a stove with about three or four places."

"Everybody remembers the stove."

"Everybody remembers the stove. And they were fighting about the stove who wants to go first and cook."

"Tell me about the stove."

"There's nothing to it. You put in wood and make fire."

I need to ask my questions differently if I don't want this kind of "Professor Josef" answer!

"The fire was going almost all day long. Always some woman was there cooking for the next meal, the next meal, the next meal. The natives they always caught fish, and they did sell it to us, very cheap. From time to time it came in sweets from another state in Russia; so much sweets. Like with confectionery sugar and all those things. They gave you ration cards. And when it came in, you get maybe four or five kilos for a person. We didn't know what to do with it, so we made packages and we send it home to Warsaw. And they received on several occasions."

"How do you know?"

"Because we had a letter back. They were short there of sugar and sweets and all kind of things. So we made packages, and we sent it away."

"What did they write in their letters?"

"Oh, they did write that they okay. They still okay; they need only some things, this and that. I don't remember exactly. They couldn't write too much because it was, let's say, censored a lot. But the packages still went through. This didn't last long. We send them maybe two or three times packages. And then, everything stopped. We send them and didn't receive any letter from them at all."

"When was this?"

"In the same year. In 1940. Yah. And the work what we did there is I went working in the woods, cutting down trees. It was cold there, but we had special clothes. The clothes what we wear, they call it *kufiki*. This is a piece of cloth, it was stitched with cotton inside."

"It was quilted?"

"Was quilted, yes. It was a jacket and pants. But on the head we had a special thing, very warm, what they wear in Russia. You can let down the flaps over the ears. And for footwear, we had boots made out of sheepskin—*voulanka*. And this was so warm, you could wear it fifty degrees below zero, and you didn't feel nothing.

"Oh, it was a very exciting and very nice life there. We were all young. We didn't have a worry in the world. We had what to eat, we had to drink."

"Was it a hard life?"

"No, I wouldn't say it was a difficult life. I had the hardest job, and I wouldn't complain. I went in the woods cutting down trees. And this was a terrible job. Then I had to go in the river up to my chest and put together the logs, tie them together and then let them go. I came always home wet. And the others had heaters where they worked. Itzak had a job in the *artel* where they made clothes, and he didn't even have to lift a finger. It wasn't even cold for him. And Dov the same thing, and Chapka the same thing. I had the worst job."

"You never went out of the village?"

"Well, yah. We went to a neighboring village where the farmers hired us. They had their own gardens, right? So they need help. And we were young, young people. So they hired the women, and they hired some men to do for them the work. And they paid them with the crop—potatoes, cabbages, and all kind of things."

"What were the villagers like?"

"Yah. They were just plain peasants. They were not affiliated with politics. They lived there, that's all. I didn't see any churches there. Well, it was Russia; it was eliminated. So they were just plain primitive people, what they lived in this climate. And to them it didn't make a big difference whether it's a Soviet Russia or not. They went about their own work. They did their things; they had their little gardens and lived. They probably lived a lot better than the people in the cities."

The agrarian romance of happy, rural, small lives. As soon as they could, they ran from it as fast and as far away as they were able to go.

"But we missed here a part. You know what we missed here?"

"What?"

"We missed, yah, the time when Sonia goes back to Brest.

"We all thought they had the better deal in Brest. But it turned out that we got the better deal because then they were all killed. She went back, I would say, at least two months before the Germans attack the Russians. Two months before—April 1941. And at this time everybody was jealous. Everybody—because to get out from a wilderness like this, so remote area, she was very lucky. They considered it very lucky. They call it 'luck of the Seven.'

"But I still tried to hold her back. I said, 'Don't go; stay with us. Whatever happens, stay with us.' She said, 'No. I have a chance. I'll go. I want to see him.' Her boyfriend. So finally came the day we took her back. We took her back to Syktyvkar, and from Syktyvkar she had to take again a boat to Kotlas. And from there she had to take the train."

"Did you get a letter from her?"

"Yah, we got still I believe one letter and that's it. That's it. She didn't believe that she's going to go back. But when she received the permission to go back, nothing could hold her. Maybe she wasn't even two months with him together. That's all.

"And meanwhile we lived there in Nyuvchim, we knew a war is going on, we didn't know the outcome until the announcement came that they attack Russia. When the Germans attacked, the Russians ran so fast, they couldn't hold their pants up."

Josef just can't let go of those ideas of German efficiency, even though Germany murdered his life and lost the war, due in large part to Russia.

"What we spend there was from June 1940 until the Germans attacked the Russians. Yah. And then they came with the loudspeakers, and they said, 'You Polish citizens, you are free now to go in Russia any place you want to.'"

After Sonia returned to Brest and Hitler broke his pact with Stalin by crossing the Bug River, Menachim Begin's parents, Zeev and Hassia, my Aunt Sonia and her husband, whose last name was Finkielsztejn, and the uncle, Yosel, and his wife, Rivka, with whom Josef and the Seven had stayed, witnessed some or all of the following events, depending on how long they lasted:

> The city of Brest fell on the first day of the Nazi invasion despite some brave Soviet soldiers' holding out at the Brest Fortress for almost a month.
>
> The German *Einsatzgruppen A*, one of the infamous mobile killing squads targeting Jews, followed the army into Brest—with the special unit *Sonderkommando* 7b doing the killing, helped by *Einsatzkommandos* 7, 8, and 9, Police Battalion 307, and local volunteers.
>
> When the Germans entered Brest in June 1941, they shot at Jews randomly.
>
> About July 5 two hundred Jewish men were imprisoned and eventually killed.
>
> On July 10 the most prominent Jewish families were trucked to a suburb of Brest, where twelve large pits, guarded by the SS and SD, were waiting. They were shot in groups of fifty.
>
> On August 7 all Jewish men had to register with the Germans and pay a tax. In the same month, new rules forbade gentiles from buying from, selling goods to, and trading with Jews.
>
> On September 17 the Brest mayor decreed that Jews would be docked one day's pay per week.
>
> On November 10 all Jews over the age of fourteen were ordered to apply for identity papers with their photographs on them.

I have a microfilm copy of Sonia's passport application with her photograph. She did marry her lover and recorded her last name as Finkielsztejn. A historian at the US Holocaust Memorial Museum found her for me in the Brest Ghetto Passport Archive.

Since Sonia is the only one of the Seven who did not survive the war, I include her ghetto passport with her photo here to offer her the little that is still possible—a symbolic presence in the world beyond the war. She filled out the application on either November 18 or 20—the document has both dates—about

a week and a half after the Polish clerks began the processing of such documents for 12,465 Jews. She had to surrender her passport, thus giving up her citizenship for a stateless identity—that of a Jew. Being Jewish meant being without a country and the protection of its laws. She gave the clerk two copies of her photograph and was fingerprinted. The document also says she submitted her marriage certificate, the only one in my family who had a marriage of record.

The address she gave, Bialostochia 21, Apartment 2, is so close to Bialostoskaja 19—the spelling my father gave me for my great-uncle's address—that I think she lived next door with her husband when she came back to Brest. It's how she met him before the Seven left for Komi. He lived next door.

In December all Jews were forced into a ghetto. They were ordered to replace their yellow Stars of David with two yellow circles, one on the chest and one on the back—over the left shoulder. This requirement was modeled on a practice in medieval France.

If they lasted until July or October of 1942, they were transported 117 kilometers to Bronnaya Gora. Seven trains with about two hundred people per car brought Jews there. From Brest there were two trains in July and one in October. A short distance away large pits were waiting to receive their bodies as they were shot. In March 1944 the Germans tried to hide their crimes by having locals dig up the bodies and burn them.

Where did the love go?

"We didn't go home and start packing right away. We were sitting down and talking about it. And talking about it. So we know that the Germans attack the Russians, that they come so fast after them that Nyuvchim is not even going to be a place where we can hide.

"The enthusiasm from all the refugees there was so strong about leaving that no one, not even one, stayed there. It was a panic. I would call it a panic, yes. We stayed there more than a year in a wilderness like this, and we said we have to go someplace else. We were talking that this is the farthest place from here—to go to Asia border where there is food and other things still plentiful. And life is a lot easier. But when we came there, we met some other problems."

"Do you know how you got to central Asia?"

"To tell you destination to destination, no, I wouldn't remember because there was so much going in circles. Sometimes we came into the same place twice. It's because we had to sometimes move away, go on the sideline for the military transport for troops. And we had to make sometimes big, big circles in order to come to the destination. We went through a lot, a lot, a lot of places. We went out of the way sometimes, I would say, five hundred or a thousand miles. And then came back to the same place in order to proceed. All by train.

"We went through Chelyabinsk. We circled back because they don't always have trains. Oh, yah, we got close to Stalingrad, close to the battle zone. And then all the way down to Tashkent and Alma Ata. Also the highest mountains in the world, the Himalayas. It's the same chain of mountain that goes into India. What goes into Mt. Everest in Nepal. It took at least three months.

"It wasn't given food regularly. You were on the train, and one station called the other station, let's say five hundred to six hundred miles away, to prepare for us soup, and you came to this station but everything was screwed up, and you didn't get the soup sometimes.

"And when the train stopped, and it was a big station and you know that you going to be there staying three, four, five hours, so you went right away on the bazaar. You came out to this marketplace, and over there the people were waiting. They knew we were coming. So they brought out their things—let's say they killed a swine, right? So there were pieces of meat, and you start trading with them. Salt, you gave them salt, you gave them other things, what you had from other places. I remember we went on the way to Asia through the Caspian Sea. And there was salt waiting just to grab it. And we put it in bags, and we loaded up bags and bags of salt, and then we went again five hundred miles away from there, and we exchange it for food and soap and for all kinds of things.

"And this is the way we kept going all the time, all the way to Asia. You didn't have to be the best. Everybody who had something, they went trading; we got always home with something. It was enough for everybody. We always cook for seven."

"After Nyuvchim, it was six."

"Oh, yah, Sonia wasn't there anymore, right."

Whether she was physically with him or somewhere else, whether alive or a ghost—she was always in the count. Chapka, too, even after the war, when he went his own way.

"When we came to Samarkand, it was a dividing point. From here, they could transport you every place to the south. In every direction. And the NKVD took over there, and they did divide us in all kind of places. They put some people to a bigger city like Osh. Us they took to the outskirts, where they had the big collective farms."

"I guess life in the cattle cars was not easy."

"Oh, it was always things wrong with it. All kind of things. When you travel so many people together, it's too close to avoid everything. I remember people dying. They died, first of all, it was a very big epidemic in all kind of diseases. I believe some maybe got cholera. Some had typhus. And then the biggest plague was lice.

"What we did was when we stop at a big place, and we stood there let's say a day or something like this, everybody was running to the public baths. You took all your clothes, and they put in an oven to disinfect, right? You put in your clothes, and then you went back to the same cattle wagon. And an hour later you were all filled with lice again. You couldn't get rid of them. And because of this and other things, people were dying. So what we did, we took those people who had died, and we put them out on the platform. Every train had a platform, in front, you know? We put them out there and the next morning we went out, it was no sign of them. They disappeared. A lot of people died.

"And matter of fact, sometimes, we went through some thousands of miles, and it was very cold, and we didn't have nothing to heat the stove with. So the people went down. We didn't have any tools with us. So they went down and with their bare hands, with their bare hands, we lifted up the railroad crosses, you know what I mean. The railroad crosses. We lifted them up, we pulled them out from the tracks. And we put this wood into the stove to keep us warm. On many occasions. And this was very forbidden. If they catch us, they will send us to Siberia.

"First of all, people died of malnutrition. Sometimes we traveled for days and days and we didn't get a portion of soup because we came to the station where it was ordered, and they didn't have nothing for you, and you had to survive, let's say, days and days without food. But fortunate enough we, our group of seven—no, no, six—always manage to have something. A matter of fact, when we left Nyuvchim, we baked ourselves whole bags with dry bread. You know, you bake it on the oven, and you make it very hard, and this can stay for years. So you always had bags of food like this. I remember we had about fifteen bags of dried foods like this. To be safe."

Josef always remembered more about the food than the other two brothers. Survival was his main goal. It was an aspect of how he presented himself, in his role of older brother, caretaker of the Seven or the six now. His brothers, though, did not always see him as acting in their common best interests.

"And did you stay together? I mean, did you fight among the six?"

"Who is going to fight with whom? Three brothers—two of them grown-up men. And Chapka, that's all."

"Tell me about the big Separation. Are we up to that yet? How did you get separated?"

"I don't even know what that was all about. I don't even remember. I cannot recall the incident why we were separated. I can't recall. I don't remember this incident. I don't remember what it was all about it."

"I don't know." "I can't recall." "I don't remember." Josef, we've seen the movie. Such is the answer of a guilty man—not consistent with the protective big brother of his self-portrait.

"When we came to Asia, we felt safe there. But the thing is in Asia itself, the Asian people, like the Kyrgyz and the Uzbeks, the other peoples what they lived there, they themselves were asking for the Germans, when are they coming? They did want to get rid of the Soviet regime because they had a lot of land and other things before. And everything was taken away from them by the Soviets. So they didn't want the Soviet regime; they want the Germans to come in there.

"When we got to Pachta Abad, Chapka and I, we worked, let's say, making little canals. Which those canals the water would come down from the mountain. Those canals was needed in order to water all the fields. You see, they don't have rain there at all in summer. The water they using is only what comes down from the big mountain. The climate is a dry climate. The temperature goes up to 120 to 125 Fahrenheit. In the winter, they have like monsoon season. You know? About two months in the year it rains. Sometimes you walk so deep in mud there from all of the rain was coming down. Up to my ankles in mud—more. We lived on this collective farm in a little-bitty house what is made out from the things from the cows."

"Cow dung?"

"Cow things. Put together with lot of straw. They make little blocks of it, right? Those little blocks, they put one on top on the other, and this calls a house. In rainy season, in monsoon season, the roof fell down on your head. When came monsoon season, you had all the holes and all kind of trouble to fix it up."

"How did you get this job on the collective farm? I thought you were free to go anywhere."

"Anywhere in Russia. But we had to work. Without work, no food. Like the Russians always said, *"Kto ne rabotaet, tot ne est."* That means, 'This one who doesn't work, doesn't eat.' So let's say, they paid you by measuring meters. How many meters you made in the canal. According to this, you got bread, and you got from the farm extra—let's say, wheat, corn. They pay in grains. And a little bit of money. Little bit.

"Well, in the beginning was very hard. The work was very hard because we getting blisters. And the rations for the work wasn't too good. They gave you only a couple of hundred grams of wheat or corn, or something like this. You took all these things, you went home and you cooked some soup with this. And the rest we have to steal from the farmers there what they grow in the summertime. They had all kind of vegetables, all kind of things to steal.

"Then after this, I worked in a cotton factory. Oh, the beginning was very hard. You had to talk with sign language. They don't understand Russian."

"How long did the hard time last?"

"Well, I would say at least those hard time, it lasted for a year. So for me anyway. I don't know about your father. And, yah, after a year, I learned the language. Speaking and writing.

"So now start communicating with them.

"Then I went to work in an *artel*, in a place where they make clothes and shoes and things like this. And over there I got contact with the leaders from the NKVD, so I had some favors from them. All kind of favors."

"Like what?"

"Well, you make something for them, and they will give, let's say, they had some other sources. They got a lot of vodka and other things, so they keep giving you for your work. Money wasn't object. With money you couldn't do much. But with things like this, like vodka, you could do a lot. And sometimes they got, let's say, a quarter from a cow, or something like this. So they had a little over, so they give you this. So you always exchange, you always get something out of it. As soon we got to know the NKVD and start communicating with them and exchanging and do all those things, we had everything what we want. We ate meat every day.

"The *artel*, what was tailoring and shoemakers, they call it for the people, but the people they don't get nothing of it. Only the big shots they come in and get all kind of things. And while we are doing it for them, you had some favors from it too because they had easy access to food and all kind of things. The only thing was here, food, food, food. No money, just food."

"At this time were you still feeling that you were on a big adventure, like in Nyuvchim?"

"What could you feel good, you were taken away from home. You came to a strange country. And then you came to a very primitive place. Like this, where the culture is a different kind. The nature is different. And you didn't see the end of it! And the whole picture was like, you couldn't believe that you are there. Also some strange things the Uzbeks and the Tatars had. Donkeys. The donkeys were so big; they were seven hundred to eight hundred pounds. And they go behind them with a little stick (swish, swish), and they go for miles and miles and miles and miles. When you come from a city like Warsaw and then you're seeing things like this.

"So all right. We suppose to get passport without a country. And they kept those passports in the police station; the passports were ready for us, and they didn't give it to us because the commissar or how you call him couldn't get over the fact that the Uzbeks and the Kyrgyz and Tatars were all going to the front. And we sort of sitting there, and we working for living. They want to take us and draft us to the army. If it's not to the army, they want to draft us, they call it the front where you working in war, besides the army. They call it the *Arbet* front. You're working on the projects for the government but they also high risky. Not with shooting, but with other things, which I will came to it. And they start chasing after us, so I escape from one farm to a neighboring farm, let's say it was about twenty to twenty-five miles away. So I work in another farm in order for them not to find me, and I came home every week, and I had all kind of bags with wheat and rice and all kind of food. And I left it at home with Henya because she had the little baby, Danny. And this thing was going for a long time."

Josef is talking about the consequences of the Soviets' breaking off diplomatic relations with the Polish government in exile in 1943. Those Polish males who resisted the second offer for Soviet citizenship—the first was in 1940—were drafted for hard labor to help in the war effort.

"Where was Dov?"

"Dov at this time wasn't anymore with us. He went to Chelyabinsk. In Ural Mountains. He was in *Arbet*—labor—front to build dam. But at the time we did not know where he was."

Whenever Dov talked about the dam he worked on, it was as if he had built it himself—he was so proud of it. I tried to find it on various maps and websites and learned that Chelyabinsk is considered by some to be the most polluted city on earth. Beginning in 1948, several nuclear plants were located in the area, and through the years, nuclear accidents and the dumping of nuclear waste into the Techa River—which is likely the river with the dam Dov worked on—have earned the area this distinction.

It was also the site of massive industrialization both before the war and during it, when Stalin wanted to move factories, particularly those involved in weapons and other production for the war, out of the way of the advancing Germans. For a while Chelyabinsk was known as Tankograd due to all the tank-producing factories there.

Dov found all the energy poured into the development of Chelyabinsk exhilarating. Because he was in love with Emma and finally eating well, he could allow his idealism to surface, to undertake philosophical contemplation, to think about the power of man, who could tame a river, and of his participation in that power.

"Yeah, he was drafted to the work front. So now they went after me, and I was hiding until they did caught up with me, and I had a Jewish big shot that I knew. He told me, 'Don't quarrel with them this time. Go where they send you. The war isn't going to keep so long. It's better to go.' Anyway, so they sent me.

"So I had to go. I was to go in Kyrgyzia, past Frunze, to the Chinese-Soviet border. Over there, they spoke about building a railroad to China. This was high in those mountains."

"Okay, now I'm coming to it. Now listen to this. But this you have to listen careful. I'm coming to Frunze. I'm coming to the town of Frunze, and over there I wasn't guarded, just on my own will I have to go there where they want me to go. I came to the town of Frunze. I was hungry. I was dirty. And I had malaria with me, which I had my malaria all the time as long I was in Asia. I came over there and I had on my feet, I didn't have any shoes good. So my feet were wrapped up with all kind of things. And this was monsoon season. It was coming toward winter, you know? And I was walking, and I walked on this bazaar in Frunze. You know what a bazaar is? I was walking in this marketplace in Frunze. I had something with me. I took from my place this dry, sunbaked fruit. They call it *baruc*—little sweet things, which I was going to trade there for something else. They, over there in Frunze, didn't have it. This is the story in all of Russia. There is plenty of one thing in a place, and the other places nothing. So I was carrying this to sell.

"Well, I'm walking in Frunze on this bazaar, and I don't even look up. I'm looking down, not to step in too deep mud. And I'm looking and looking and looking. And there, before me, about ten to fifteen feet before me, I saw other people walking. And then all of a sudden, I saw a woman—with a fur coat. And 'This coat,' I thought, 'Where did I see this coat?' my goodness. And then it came to me. I thought, 'This is Lola's coat.' Lola had a coat like this. But I didn't know it was her in the coat. Maybe some other people had a coat like this. How is possible I'm going to meet her here after so many years, and it's so far away?"

It was almost three years since the brothers had seen one another.

"And I start walking faster, and I'm making a search around to see the front of her. And she looks at me, and she had bought some *kielbasa* and some bread. The first thing what she did, she put in all the *kielbasa* in my mouth. Not a word. And the bread."

"And then we start talking and boy, oh, boy. I said, 'I recognized the coat,' and I told her the whole story. And we went from there with a little train to the place where they were living. And they were living in Kant. Didn't I tell you before, Kant? This little place, Kant. And she comes home, and I believe Itzak was still at work. He work also in an *artel*. Yah. And he came in and said, 'I don't believe it. I don't believe my eyes.' And then we told him the whole story. And I took off all my clothes and we burn it. It was with lice and dirty and everything. And I got some new clothes, and I stayed there with them a day or two.

"And then I said I have to go to the place where they will send me. They will go after Henya, and they will bring *tsores*, trouble, you know? So I stayed with Itzak and Lola, and I gave them the address where we live. Now they know where we are. And I said, 'Believe me. In a week or so, I'll be back here.' That's what I told them. 'How you going to do that? You going to escape there? It's like a prison,' your father said to me.

"I came to the place; it was a very high mountain. And you went in. And it *was* like in a prison. With barbed-wire fence and things like this. Everything guarded. I came in, I register. They took my name. And they showed me where to go. And over there we lived. In the mountain.

"And over there I met a few friends of mine from the same village. And they told me, 'You're here too?' I said, 'I'm here too. But I am not going to be here too long. Let's see how the things are, how it looks here.' Well, the lice was there—the moment you went on your back to sleep. They crawl over you; they ate you alive. You can't get rid.

"They made soup. And five in the morning, you have to walk maybe a quarter of a mile for the soup, and it was so slippery. So bad, so cold, so slippery that on the way back, it spilled out. We didn't have much to eat unless you took it there and you gulp it down. And then they gave you some bread and things. It's not really a prison; they didn't punish you there. They didn't have more to give. That's all.

"And what was the work? Then we went with one what is in charge, and we start going up the mountainside. We went up the mountainside, and on first day, right away before my eyes, it came a sudden wind, and it was ropes there. All the time, ropes to hold you on. Because the wind and the ice and the things was so bad that the slightest slip and you going down, down forever.

"And in front of mine eyes, it came a wind, and three people, like you see in a movie were picked off by it—like in a hurricane. Worse than a hurricane, a tornado taking off everything, so it took off the three people and they disappeared. This was the first day. On the second day, I went there and I saw the same story. People, they were doing nothing, we just staying around there. We couldn't move. It was too dangerous. On the third day, I went again and was the same story. And then when you came home, at least, you wanted to sleep, but you can't sleep. The lice eat you alive."

Josef's service for the Soviet labor front was in the Tian Shan Mountains of Central Asia, a chain that straddles Kyrgyzstan, Kazakhstan, and northwest China. Its tallest peak is almost twenty-five thousand feet high. Nothing he knew could compare to it. He was a working-class city boy who had sat on his ass sewing pants in the bosom of his family except for lovely, rebellious bicycle excursions with his buddies. No reference point existed for him in this malevolent, exotic world.

In the book *Into Thin Air*, Jon Krakauer, describing the 1996 climb to Mt. Everest that killed six people, expressed the feeling of finally standing on the summit of the mountain he had just ascended: "I just couldn't summon the energy to care." Krakauer was a journalist, and he had chosen this assignment. Thrill-seekers, the other men who made the climb, had paid $65,000 each for the expedition, just to die or be too depleted to give a damn.

Josef did not begin with a sense of adventure. He was fighting for his life. Unlike Dov, Josef did not romanticize his experience. Terror was at its heart, and it drove his plan to escape.

"On that third day, I got two friends. And we decided that we going to escape from there. We had with us the tools, what we work there with them, so we took the pliers and we cut through the wires. Make big holes. And we escaped forty kilometers by foot, crawling on the highway. Over there the highway, they had deep ditches on the side, like for the water to drain. We crawled there in the ditches on all fours so that the police or anybody who goes there was not to see us. And this way, we went forty kilometers to the station. To the first railroad station.

"We came into the station. We waited for the train to come. I went in the car where the toilet was and was hiding there until the train start going. And then when the train start going, I came out, and the Russians themselves, the conductors, they had long coats. They had a bench to sit down. I was lying under them and when the *nachal'niki* or NKVD came by, they didn't see me. Why did the conductors let me do it? Because they know a lot of people got killed there. They were good people. They didn't agree that people should risk themselves in the mountains.

"They didn't agree with the things what NKVD did.

"So this way, I escape back to this little town Kant. I stayed with your parents a whole month, and during this month, Itzak tried to get me in a paper, a transit paper, that I can go on the train back to Osh. It was false but with a piece of paper, you could make a stamp to make official-looking. And this is the way I went back to the town where I came from. And when I came back, the authorities knew that I came back. But they close their eyes because I said to them, 'I went there in the mountains. I went there. This is impossible. This is worse than to go to the war.' Anyway, I convince them. And they said, 'Don't let us see you here around. Keep hiding until the campaign from taking the people is over.'

"So this was the way it goes there. They make a campaign. They take us and they send us to work front, and after the campaign is over, it's over. Even if they see you, they don't care anymore, yah.

"This was 1944, and the war ended in 1945, and I was working still in this place as a tailor. And this was going on until maybe winter or spring 1946. And then they start coming rumors that they going to free us. Go home to Poland, back. And this was so unbelievable, like somebody would tell me, 'You going to live two hundred years.'"

"Did you stop in Warsaw?"

"Our train didn't come close to Warsaw."

"My father had a choice. He could have gone to Warsaw."

"Well, I could go to Warsaw, too, after Stettin. The train was for us refugees. And this train went to Stettin."

In Polish it is spelled *Szczecin* and pronounced something like "shtechin." Located in the northwest of Poland, it is about 120 kilometers from Berlin. In 1944 Stettin was hit by a barrage of Allied air raids, destroying most of the city, which had more than one hundred slave labor camps filled mainly with non-Jewish Poles. When the Red Army captured it in 1945, it also had the largest German population of any city outside of Berlin. After the war was over, the Soviets gave it to Poland to administer. All the Germans who had not already left with the evacuating Germans had to leave.

"How long did the trip take to Stettin?"

"This time it didn't take long because we took a direct approach. Let me think it through. All right, my daughter, Idusha, was born in Stettin in May the 13, 1946. Ah-ha! So I came to Stettin in 1946, about a month before, and soon Henya went to the hospital to give birth."

"Where was Danny born? Was he born in a hospital?"

"Yah, yah. In this city what they call it Aravan. Oh, this is the name of the city where all the *kolkhoz* were, Aravan."

Aravan! And Osh, where Josef, Henya, Dov, and Chapka first got off the train after the Separation. Aravan and Osh were stops on the Great Silk Road, an ancient trade route four thousand miles long, dating from the first century BCE and linking China to the Roman Empire. *Aravan* and *Osh*, such exotic sites, and yet the names flow so familiarly out of Josef's working-class Polish-Jewish mouth. It produces in me some cognitive dissonance about the man who grabbed at me on his New Jersey chicken farm.

The market in Osh, where Josef traded in black-market grains and Dov in stolen cotton bags rustled out of Soviet collective factories, was famous along the Silk Road. How did he and the others absorb these fantastical geographies? What are the traces? Completely invisible to me as I grew up with these people. Well, perhaps except for Dov's eyes that were full of distance. When they talked about Aravan and Osh, it was in bread-and-butter terms. Where they lived, where they worked, what they ate, how they survived. Yet they had walked upon the Silk Road as Jews had millennia ago—discarded escapees from the murderous countries of their birth, despised wanderers and traders. Like the Seven, their Jewish kin brought cultural variety wherever they traveled—new music, songs, languages, and ideas. They traded, the Seven and their ancient relations, in material goods and gave away for free the invaluable immaterial.

Josef arrived in Poland in April and reconnected with his brothers shortly before Itzak, Lola, and Dov smuggled into Berlin. He stayed in Stettin.

"And I went there with the black market to make some money."

"You came to Stettin from Osh. What did you have with you to trade?"

"I didn't have nothing to trade. I just started there."

Each place he went, he had to begin again. Again and again, from nothing or next to nothing. At least in Poland he knew the language.

"How was Henya at that time?"

"Well, one of those days, Henya start getting sick. She got a nervous breakdown. She came back to Poland. Maybe things what she heard that all her family got killed and nobody's alive. And those voices came around in her head, you know. And she kept thinking about them. Then was another cause, the Poles themselves there in this town were very anti-Semitists, and they start going over to Jews and killing them. Yah, robberies and murders, and she was very afraid. And this went in her head, and that's how she started.

"And your father a few months later came over also from Berlin with all kinds of things to trade when she got the attack, a *real* attack."

"How did she act?"

"She start talking a lot of nonsense. She heard things and sees things. All kind of things. She was afraid of everything. She was afraid of the people around her. She was afraid that nobody lives from her family, and things like this. Well, there's a lot of things what people getting sick, and we don't know what causes it.

"So the kids, meanwhile, I had to give them away in a home there. Was a Jewish orphanage in Stettin. Your father tried to take Henya and Danny with him to Berlin, but they got caught some place, and they had to go back. And he made another attempt to bring them, but he got caught again, and he went back to Berlin. Later, about in December, I made an attempt to take Henya and the kids and come as a German refugee. We somehow got listed then as German refugees. As a German refugee, they had to let us back into Germany. And we went on a train. And we start going to West Germany. The destination was Frankfurt."

When he got to Frankfurt, he put his young son and daughter, Danny and Idusha, in an UNRRA orphanage and Henya in a hospital.

"What did the doctors say about Henya?"

"Well, they said right away, this is schizophrenia. And they cannot make any promises, prediction how long this is going to take. Sometimes it disappears from the people in a short time. Sometimes it takes a long time, and sometimes it will never go away.

"Well, they give her electric shocks, insulin shots. They using it today. And after a series of shots, you wouldn't recognize her, she was okay. But then, she start dipping down again. The shocks start dissipating. And she was the way she was again. The treatment last two to three days, the most. I took her out many times from the hospital to be with me, then I put back the next day. And things like this. I tried all kind of things. It didn't work. Tried to take her to the children and see the children, and it didn't work."

"What happened when she saw the children?"

"She recognized them. But she didn't show anything that she wanted to be with them. When she was finished with electric shock, she cared for them. But you could see that it's cosmetic, you know? Not real.

"Well, I lived in Frankfurt for a while in a place where all the people what they're coming through from another country, they lived there for a while. It was in the middle of the town in Frankfurt. And they served there meals, and there was enough food."

"So you lived by yourself in a refugee facility, a DP camp?"

"No, not by myself—in a big room with a lot of people together. And then from over there, I find myself a room with German people. A German apartment, yah."

"What did you do?"

"I went up on the black market. And we dealt all kind of black market things."

"What did you think would happen? Your children were in an orphanage, your wife was in the hospital. It must have been pretty terrible then, after the war is over, and all these things happened."

"You didn't have a home. You just struggle from one place to the other, that's all."

Persistence is also a kind of optimism—although Josef's optimism was draining with his youth.

"Why didn't you go to Berlin with Itzak and Dov?"

"I could go to Berlin. But I didn't want to. I made good in Frankfurt. Frankfurt was a more international town than Berlin. Frankfurt was a point where from all European countries they came. First of all, the Americans were there. And they had their big PXs, and it was maybe a hundred thousand Americans there. And this is where the money was. You could do a lot of business."

"When did you get your kids back?"

"The kids stayed there until 1948. And then the orphanages start emptying. And they told me that I have to take them home. And if I don't want to take them home, they going to send them for adoption. You had the discomfort. And when I heard this, I start thinking about it. And I said, what I went through with them, we went through all those things, and now they going to take them away and give them away to adoption. No. I'm not going to do it."

It was through the Germans from whom he rented a room that he met Lina, the German farm girl. She made it possible for him to retrieve his kids from the orphanage. She would be their nanny and bring her own child, Brigit, the product of a liaison with a Mexican-American soldier.

Lina, who married Josef after he was divorced from his institutionalized common-law wife, came to his household with a "brown baby." As historian Brenda Plummer explains it, this term was created by the black press to describe babies born after the war to soldiers of color and European women. Lina's lover had been Mexican American, and her baby was curly-haired and dark-skinned. The soldier left her with promises of marriage and America, which he did not keep. Permission for marriage was at the discretion of commanding officers, who were inclined to deny it. Bizarre practices were attached to these mulatto children. If a soldier came from a state that had made interracial marriage against the law, as a considerable number of states had, permission was denied. Astonishingly, a couple of the racial laws established through the Nazi Nuremburg laws were reinstated by Western powers in divided Germany to deal with these brown babies. To discourage the fraternization resulting in these babies, the US armed forces' newspaper *Stars and Stripes* created a cartoon character named Veronika Dankeschön, who appeared regularly. Her last name translated as "thank you" in German, and her initials reduced to the clear message: VD.

The earliest memory of Josef's older son, Danny, is of the orphanage when he was about four years old. He remembers seeing his younger sister, Idusha, in a sandlot there, and he said that he knew she was his sister. He slept in a big, open room with a lot of other kids, and out the window he could see mountains. He remembers his father coming to see him and his sister in a big black car, but that's all he remembers of his father's visits.

Danny's memories include his biological mother. They are not pretty. He thinks he was four or five when, on one of her visits from the hospital, he was sleeping in the same bed as his mother and he wet it. His mother took him by his feet and hung him out of the second-story window, yelling—this would be in Yiddish, I think—"*Du zolst dos mer nisht ton. Du zolst dos mer nisht ton!*" meaning "Never do that again!" That's his only childhood memory of his mother.

Where did it go? *Where did the love go?* What happened to the love? Some went to madness, some went to starvation and other deprivations, some did not go away but shifted shape, and some went into the pits at Bronnaya Gora, the fetid air of the Warsaw Ghetto, and the smoke of Treblinka.

I taught in Frankfurt as a guest professor. I went there out of curiosity, to walk the streets they had walked, and to deal with my feelings about Germans. I had had a wonderful exchange student from Frankfurt in a US literature class who said to me one day, out of the blue, that in Germany students are taught in detail about the Holocaust. Why did he say that to me? I felt he meant well. He was trying to explain something to me. So when I was invited to Frankfurt, I was interested. The German academics went through a lot of trouble to get me there.

I tended to hang out with a group of graduate students and a couple of professors in American studies. One afternoon after classes, we all went to a beer garden. While we waited for tables, they started talking about where their families came from. The last woman to speak pointed out that no one had given Germany as her origin. She then added, "I guess there are no Germans here." Silence followed her witty irony, and then we were seated and talked about other things. All the women, of course, were German except for me. The witty woman married an undocumented African heroin addict and became addicted herself. The marriage to the African was her revolt against her homeland, which still measured proper German citizenship by bloodlines, as it had done under Hitler with the Nuremburg Laws of 1935. When I was in Frankfurt in the early 1990s, that German history still smarted. But you felt the sting only if you understood the cause, felt historical guilt, like my smart student.

Where did the love go? In this case it went to heroin.

I asked Josef whether it was dangerous for Jews in Frankfurt after the war.

"We had some scuffles and incidents. But it was after the war, and we were young and wild, always have knives, and we always have guns with ourselves."

"Did you?"

"Oh, I always had a knife and also a gun. And the slightest word that a German would tell me, I would kill him today. I wouldn't care what happened."

Danny's first memories of Lina are that she began to raise him and his sister Idusha. Lina lived with Josef beginning about 1948, when she was twenty-two and Josef was thirty-six. Danny remembers the day when all of them went to Giessen, where his biological mother was institutionalized at the time. There he was introduced to his new brother, a baby with a head full of golden curls. Pavel was being carried by his mother, Henya, who had not been cured of her psychosis through his birth as the doctors and Josef had hoped. That was the first Danny had heard of him.

One day, without telling anyone, Danny took Idusha to school with him. He wanted to show her what it was like. Maybe he just wanted her with him. Danny is a protector. He turned out to be a good man, a devoted father and husband. I can just see him at six, toting three-year-old Idusha to school with him.

Even though Josef was never married to Henya, she appeared on all of his papers, so he sued for divorce in the German courts and successfully obtained it. He told me that he could not have brought her to the United States in any case. Her illness precluded immigration.

With Henya, the love may never have been there, so I will not ask where it went. I'm not sure that his love went to Lina either. Or hers to him. It was one of those war compromises. His children needed care, and she needed a last name to give her out-of-wedlock child.

I asked Josef whether his friends also left for the United States.

"Only the Jewish refugees who had a bad record stayed, let's say that they did a lot of black market things or they had arrests. In this time it was black market with cigarettes a lot. You exported them from Switzerland and then sold them duty-free. These people bribed the border police, bought them off them. You know people like this got arrested. So they got a record. Then the United States didn't want them. So those people stayed in Germany. And they all multi-millionaires. Rich like anything, you cannot imagine."

Josef's Shangri-La in the shape of postwar Germany. Although Germans were starving and surrounded by rubble, Josef saw opportunity, especially in hindsight, especially if you were lucky enough to have a criminal record and prevented from leaving. By the spring of 1947, the displaced persons (DP) population in the Western zones of occupied Germany amounted to about two hundred thousand Jewish refugees. They were mainly housed in DP camps administered mainly by UNRRA. Most left to go to Israel. My family chose the United States.

I asked my cousin Danny if he remembered immigrating to the United States.

Danny's memories are specific about the early years in the United States. He spoke no English and was beat up on his way home from school. He remembers the misery of being an immigrant, being "different" in a way that seemed to offend people enough to want to hurt him. I myself remember the bewilderment of not knowing the language when I first attended school in the United States. I was not beat up, but I felt like a freak not knowing the language and later as someone who wore the wrong clothes and ate the wrong food, whose parents had accents and didn't go to the right synagogue. I always felt that to my American friends, when I finally had some, and particularly to their parents, I was a charity case. Being friendly to me was like giving to the poor or to the displaced over there in the old country. Friends with the little immigrant girl? No need to make our annual donation.

Between 1948 and 1952 almost three thousand Holocaust survivors, many of them from Poland, bought chicken farms in South Jersey, including my Uncle Josef. Vineland, deep in the Pine Barrens, was one of the main destinations. It attracted Jewish immigrants for a couple of reasons. First, there had already been two waves of Jewish immigrant farmers to the area. Second, that's how immigration to a certain place happens—by accident and precedent. You have a plan to go to the United States. How do you decide where to go? Close your eyes and put your finger randomly on a spot on the map?

I have a friend who went to a tiny college in the South straight from Nigeria. "How did you even find that place?" I ask. It seems that all the boys from his neighborhood who came to study in the United States went there. Why? One of them had gone some years ago, and the others followed, forming a US satellite of their village.

A neighboring town to Vineland was another such place. In the summers we would go to Alliance Beach in Norma, New Jersey, with other immigrant families. My parents spent their days playing cards, gin rummy. It was a beach carved out of the woods, along the banks of the Maurice River. There was a whitewashed, barnlike structure there with a jukebox and snacks for sale. I loved that place. When I was fourteen, fifteen, sixteen, I would shake my grabbable ass to rock and roll, which kept spinning out of that jukebox at three songs for a quarter. "Sweet Little Sixteen" by Chuck Berry and "Peggy Sue" by Buddy Holly. If I got lucky, some bare-chested hunk would ask me to slow dance to "Who's Sorry Now?" by Connie Francis or "You Send Me" by Sam Cooke.

Alliance was a tiny rural Jewish community that had upwardly mobilized from its immigrant and ideological beginnings. Touch a spot and it bleeds history. The first Jewish settlers were refugees from late-nineteenth-century Russian pogroms. Funded by HIAS (Hebrew Immigrant Aid Society), they formed the Alliance agricultural colony in 1882. Each family got fifteen or forty acres, depending on the source I consulted, to clear for farmland. The ideology was back-to-the-soil self-sufficiency to counter the stereotype of the Jew as crooked moneylender, I think. Of course most of these people had not been farmers so there was no "back to," only forward and up for the lucky ones. The second- and third-generation Jews who lived there in the 1950s and 1960s were lawyers and doctors and business leaders. Their children, my generation, left Alliance, never to return. Their parents are buried in Alliance Cemetery. Josef is buried there.

I asked Josef why he invested in a farm.

"Because you talked with friends what they came here before you, and they said they doing a nice living. You just buy the chickens, you put them in a coop, they laying the eggs, and the bums are collecting the eggs and packing them in cases and selling them to dealers, and doing all the dirty work. And the farmers, they ride around with the cars to Ocean City and Atlantic City. And they enjoy, and this is the way they did. They didn't exaggerate. But I went in with the wrong foot. I got sick chickens, and everything was going sour.

"The chickens, they got cholera. I lost all the money in the first three months when I came here in 1952. I lost the chickens, I lost the feed what I feed them. I lost the medication what I gave them."

Josef also puts blame on my father for this disaster. Throughout our conversations, Josef described him as someone you could not count on, despite his promises. As teenagers they plotted to leave home to escape the tyranny of their father and strike out on their own. But their mother always cajoled Itzak into coming back. Itzak talked Josef into immigrating to the United States and into buying a chicken farm by offering to partner with him but then backed out.

Like Lola and Dov, Josef had his resentments too.

"So I start losing money and borrow more and more and more. The feed men start giving me credit. The hatchery men start giving me for the baby chicks credit. The company who makes equipment start giving me credit. So I went in a hole with everybody up to my neck. And couldn't pay nobody."

Like his father, he put everything on the book, on credit, with his debt only increasing. Josef declared bankruptcy in 1968, and he spent the rest of his life doing tailoring in the garage of a small house he bought with a little money he had hidden from the IRS.

Danny remembers the sudden poverty. He remembers going to school with holes in the soles of his shoes and keeping his feet flat on the ground so no one would see them. He laughed as he told this story. Danny has that salesman's habit of treating misfortune lightly.

In the early 1980s Danny went to visit his biological mother in a small village nursing home in Bavaria. The town is called Wolfratshausen. She didn't accept him as her grown son. She showed him a gold locket with pictures of her children, Daniel and Idusha. Pavel had disappeared. She was too deep in her own head by the time he was born. Time had stopped for her. Her children would always be babies. She died two months later. She left about $3,000 in marks, which she had earned by selling her knitting at local fairs.

When Josef died of a stroke, my father demanded that he be buried in a Jewish cemetery that would not allow Lina to be buried next to him because she wasn't Jewish. My father never owned much real estate, but he kept insisting on the wrong real estate for others.

Lina was buried in a Christian cemetery. At her funeral Danny gave the Disney version. He spoke about how Lina brought two families from different backgrounds together into one family. That did not happen. In one way or another, despite her loveliness and kindness, she was always the stepmother. She saved her heartfelt warmth for her own daughter. For her alone she had unconditional love—hugs and kisses and the nightly piece of chocolate only her own daughter received. There was such ugliness in the crevices of that family. Josef's daughter, Idusha, and Lina's daughter, Brigit, were the same age. When they were teenagers Lina and Josef took a trip to Germany to visit Lina's family. Only Brigit went with them. Lina bought Brigit clothes for the trip, only Brigit.

Imagine being a teenager and watching your stepsister get all the new clothes for a trip to Europe while you were stuck on the farm, working.

My mother loved Lina, despite the favoritism she showed to her own daughter. She admired her uncomplaining hard work on the farm and in the house. She thought Lina had gotten a bad deal with Josef, whom she thought of as mean-spirited and cheap. Danny feels she was a good mother, doing the best she could.

It was his father who was, in Danny's phrase, "old school," tough on them, wanting them to work on the farm. His father told Danny that he was too dumb to go to college. He discouraged him even though Danny was a good student in high school. He wanted him to stay on the farm and work. Lina, on the other hand, encouraged him, told him to go and follow his dreams. No simple bad and good, as in the Cinderella story. She was not the evil stepmother, but she was not a fairy godmother either.

Idusha remembers that we smoked together on those weekends we spent in my apartment when my parents were working at the farmer's market. I invited her to spend weekends more than I invited Brigit, trying in my own way to right the inequities. She remembers that I taught her how to inhale. She told me recently that Brigit would steal her clothes, but Idusha never stole Brigit's. She remembers that her stepmother, Lina, always said that she, Idusha, was a bad kid. I guess Danny told her I was writing a book, and Idusha wanted her secret resentments on record. She told me that she loved me. She breaks my heart. Like her mother, she was diagnosed with schizophrenia decades ago. Times change, though. As far as I know, she has never had electric shock or insulin treatments. She lives in her own place, supported by the state as a resident of New Jersey and a citizen of the United States.

For Josef, as for Dov, his best time was when he was young, really young—before the army, before Brest. Of the three brothers, he took the most photographs from Warsaw. I asked him why he took them, whether he expected he would never be back.

"Oh, I took all those things with me, right away. And they travel with me all the way from Warsaw through Russia and back from Russia and back here to the US. All the way. Photographs were a way to remember by and to show people how Poland looked, how you did in Poland, your friends, what you did."

"You took a picture of Natcha with you. You wanted to remember her."

"You didn't know what's going to happen. I didn't expect nothing. I expect only to take those things what they go from a lifetime, from when I was little until I grow up, to take them with me; they're always with me. I would risk nobody."

I asked Josef in our last interview, "What was your happiest time? When you think back."

"Well, you know, before the war started. This was the best time. Because I was young. I didn't have any responsibilities. I went with my friends always with the bicycles."

"What were some of the places you went to on bicycles?"

"For instance, we went, let's say, from Warsaw to Zakopane in the Carpathian Mountains. It's more than three hundred miles from Warsaw. We also went to Gdansk and Vilna. We went to Brest-Litovsk. And then we made a trip around the border of Poland. This was a trip about two thousand miles. I always took off, took off from home."

On that bicycle he was young and on his own and ready to claim the road. In his memory the bicycle took him away from the grind of work, from the grim poverty of his family life, from the oppression of an alcoholic, spendthrift father, from the seduction of a loving mother who wanted him close. It took him out of his own history to a paradise of carefree freedom. Dov romanticized his war experiences; Josef told a story of his personal victories over brutal, assaulting circumstances, which he saw more clearly than Dov saw his. How, except for in America, time and again, he outwitted fate, and finally how he was chained again to "the book" and his creditors, more than he had been in Poland, and chained to the sewing machine, doing tailoring for pennies and this time stranded without a bicycle. Despite all the miles he covered, and the exotic, punishing lands to which the war brought him, he had traveled no distance at all.

In *Lost Horizon*, before they decide to return to civilization, the Ronald Colman character tells the Jane Wyatt character that even though he's been "kidnapped and brought here" to Shangri-La against his will, he is not angry, that everything feels "somehow familiar." She explains, "You've always been a part of Shangri-La without knowing it." She continues in the optimistic spirit of 1930s movies, saying that "there's a wish for Shangri-La in everyone's heart." All people are "hoping to find a garden spot where there's peace and security, where there's beauty and comfort, where they wouldn't have to be mean and greedy." She wishes that the "whole world" would come there.

The Colman character replies in an offhand way that the audience could take as a joke, "If that were true, it wouldn't be a garden spot for long."

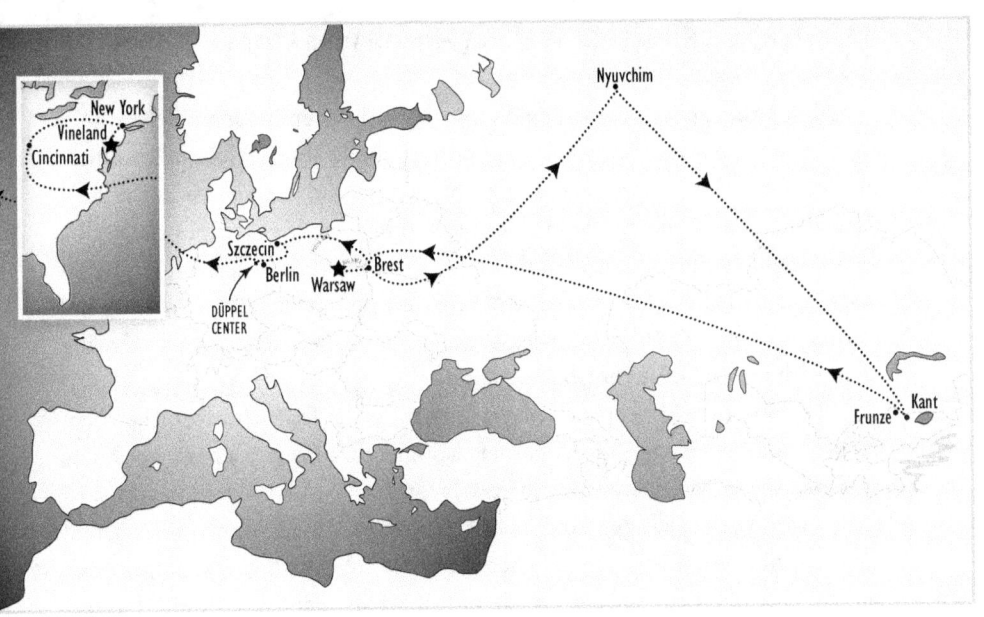

4

Itzak with Lola Interrupting

I have four tapes of my father's voice, but I did not finish taping him. I never interviewed my mother—though on the tapes I have, I can hear them bickering, contradicting one another, finishing one another's sentences, and, from time to time, reaching for the long-ago detail together. I know I wanted to finish taping my father, but I was delayed by a new semester of teaching that began in August. By November my mother had had a heart attack, and everyone's attention turned to that.

My parents were supposed to come from Queens, where they lived, to my house in New Jersey for Thanksgiving dinner. I got the call in the morning, before I put the turkey in the oven. The four of us, my daughters and my husband and I, drove to the hospital in Nassau County where she had a quadruple bypass. She was to live ten more years, but they were filled with illness, dementia, and, in the end, incontinence.

My mother always seemed lonely. No one in her family survived the war—not her father, not her mother, not her brother or her sisters. Not one cousin or aunt or uncle. She told me repeatedly she had no one but me. I was the only living person tied to her by blood. She died within a few days of my birthday. She used to call me after a fight with my father. And then she would not let me do anything to help her. Her deep sense of propriety prevented her from sharing her marital problems with a friend. She dodged shame all her life. Except for sharing them with me, she kept her troubles close.

She took care of people. That was her role. She fed them to make them happy. It was her gift. She could whip up a dinner for fifteen in a matter of hours with her specialties: salmon croquettes, roast chicken or turkey, juicy brisket, carrots with raisins, zucchini and onions, casseroles of cauliflower, broccoli, and potatoes, all covered with melted cheese, noodle kugel with cinnamon, and her famous cheeseless cheesecake—made out of what? Condensed milk, I think. Oh, and also chicken soup with *knadloch*. Sometimes, of course, she made her wonderful *cholent*. After my father died and I went to clean out their apartment, a woman stopped me by the elevator to tell me how much she had loved my mother. This was seventeen years after my mother's death. The woman told me that while she was sick, my mother baked cookies and cakes and brought them to her. My mother knocked on her door almost every day with something new from her oven. Her neighborliness always struck me as odd because it did not seem to interfere with her impenetrable aloneness.

After my mother died, she visited me for a couple of years as I was falling asleep. She floated above me. These—do I call them visitations?—did not scare me. It felt like a silent communing. She looked as she had when she was fifty, with her stiff, hair-sprayed, poufy, beauty-parlored reddish-brown hair, which came to the middle of her ears and rose above her forehead at least four inches. She would stay less than a minute and then leave. She has been the hardest loss.

In the summer I sometimes go to the Delacorte Theater, an outdoor free public theater in Central Park. In August 2006 I saw *Mother Courage* by Bertolt Brecht with Meryl Streep and Kevin Kline. Meryl Streep's performance in *Mother Courage* reminded me of my mother so vividly that I cried. It wasn't the first time Streep brought my mother to me. In the film *Sophie's Choice*, Meryl Streep's Polish accent was my mother's exactly.

Streep's Mother Courage portrayed my mother's character: Like Mother Courage, my mother carried her pots and pans on her refugee travels—from Poland, through the USSR, and then back to Poland and over the border to

Berlin—so that she could cook for her family, for the Seven, then the six, then the two of them, and when I arrived, the three of us. She traded in sugar, flour, watches, and nightgowns—not always scrupulous about her dealings—her eye on survival in wartime, on protecting her flock from hunger, from the danger of starvation. Brusque and pleading to get her way, she fought to be first in line no matter what the occasion—whether to make a dollar or get me an ice cream cone. My own Mother Courage.

Unlike the ragged Brecht character, my mother was in her own way fashionable and hunted a bargain as if she were in battle. I remember going with her to a sale at Philadelphia's Gimbel's department store when I had freshly sprouted breasts. Tables full of sweaters were piled up two feet high, some falling to the floor as women tore through them. She had pushed us to the front of the line, so we would be first through the door when the store opened. Then she elbowed her way to the front of the table where she grabbed the best for us. If anyone complained, she pretended that she could not understand them, that she did not speak English. My mother had a bit of the grifter in her. When I was a teenager, I rebelled and refused to buy anything on sale, but her more lasting legacy is that as an adult I buy on sale. Like her, I don't like to pass up a bargain, whether I need it or not, whether I even like it or not.

My father died March 15, 2011. I spoke at his funeral, as did Danny, and my two daughters, and the young rabbi from the Orthodox synagogue my father attended. My father did not choose Orthodoxy. It was the neighborhood synagogue, and when he first joined, it was a Conservative congregation. It changed later as Orthodox Jews bought up the houses and the coop apartments within walking distance of it. Here is some of what I said:

> I am the only child of Itzak and Lola G. My father was born in Warsaw, Poland, on October 20, 1917. He was one of six children—two sisters and three brothers. As I look out on the people here, I see the grandchildren and nieces who now carry some of the names of his family: Brianna for his mother and Roslyn for his older sister, at least the first letters of their American names. They died either in the Warsaw Ghetto or in Treblinka. My daughter Sonia is named for his younger sister who died at the hands of the *Einsatzgruppen* outside of Brest in what is now Belarus. Now the brothers: Motel, the youngest, stayed in Warsaw with his parents, who didn't want to leave their new mahogany furniture. My grandmother, Brandla, would not let go of Motel. The

other three brothers, Josef, Dov, and Itzak, survived together with my mother, Josef's wife Henya, and Josef's friend Chapka in the Soviet Union. When they were together in the Soviet Union, running from Hitler, they were known as the Seven among the Polish-Jewish exiles there. All seven are now gone. My father was the last of them. He died seven years short of a century.

I knew that the chapel would not have many people beyond my relatives, and so I wanted to present him the way the people sitting in the chapel knew him, only a little bit better:

> My father had a reputation for being tight with money. If he was ever consistently generous, it was with me, his only child. When we lived in Vineland, New Jersey, and I asked him for one dress, I got three. Of course, they weren't from the stores on the main street but from farmer's markets—but I appreciated his generosity.
>
> He was fiercely independent and stubborn. Until he was ninety-three, he lived alone without help. He refused aides, Access-a-Ride, assisted living, and even living with me. Even though he was practically deaf, until about a week before he died he was driving because to be alive meant to him to take care of himself.
>
> Until his late eighties, he would walk up the seven flights to his apartment, after his morning exercise, which consisted of fast-walking for three miles. Before he left for his walk, he would do one hundred pushups. Even after bypass surgery, he continued dancing at the senior citizen center. He demonstrated his spins and twists with me when he was ninety.
>
> In his ninety-second year, he was in the hospital with congestive heart failure. When he got a bit better and the physical therapist wanted him to walk, he got out of his bed—all 105 pounds of him—grabbed his cane, put on his slippers, and with the hospital gown flapping open in the back and his white combover dislodged and flopping behind him, he walked so fast down those narrow hospital hallways that the physical therapist had to chase him.
>
> That was my father.
>
> I will really miss him.

I ended by reading Walt Whitman's poem "After the Supper and Talk." The poem compares a man who is dying to someone reluctantly leaving a dinner party, "postponing" leaving, delaying saying the "last word." The poem ends:

dimmer the forthgoer's visage and form,
Soon to be lost for aye in the darkness—loth, O so loth to depart!
Garrulous to the very last."

My father did like to talk. Particularly, he liked to tell you how to live your life. At the funeral, that's what the rabbi remembered about him, how my father would tell him to exercise more. In the last months, my father prepared for dying. He emptied out his safe-deposit boxes and gave me the contents. He gave me copies of all his accounts and put my name on whatever he could.

My cousin Pavel, Josef's younger son, sent me an email about how he remembers my father. "He always reminded me of who I was, a Jewish boy, although I never did go to any Hebrew school. He always asked me how much money did I make. I was always a little embarrassed, so I said enough (I wonder if it was enough in his eyes)." That's about right. The beginning and end of things for my father was money. Every conversation with him would lead to the stock market and how much a person earned.

Money.

I have some painful memories of his betrayals of me, his only child. The earliest was in Berlin at a lake. I was little, maybe five. I jumped in, even though my father told me not to. The water was above my head, and I was holding on to one of the pillars that held up the wooden ramp leading into the water. My father was close, so I felt brave and let go of the pillar, confident he would not let me sink. He did, though, and I will never forget the feeling of terror as I sank and my head was submerged in the water. Through the water I saw him watching me, not making a move to help me despite my struggles, and I was astonished. I fought my way to the surface and back to the pillar. For me that incident defined the limit of his love. It was less than I expected, and his treachery changed me. Although I now understand his motives, I feel the sting of it even today as I write this. The undependability of parental rescue was shattering knowledge.

The second betrayal came at my wedding. My mother pleaded for a conventional wedding, and I relented since, as an only child, I was her only chance to have one. I was still a student, and my future husband had just started working and had no savings. Without warning, after the Queens wedding factory celebration, which was during a blizzard, my father demanded the gift envelopes. He took all the cash and on the spot, with me still in my wedding gown, had me sign over the checks. Honestly, he grabbed it all, grumbling that it was the groom's portion. My new husband and I went home empty-handed. Itzak got to look like a big spender in front of his immigrant friends and relatives by giving his daughter a proper sendoff and also got to keep the money.

When I cleaned out my father's apartment, his pajamas were neatly folded under his pillow. My parents had the kind of bed that has twin mattresses on top of a king-sized box spring. My mother's side of the bed was neatly made, perhaps untouched for all those years that she had not slept in it. He used only his side. A decorative pillow lay on top of a flowered quilt on her side, and on the pillow was a doll. She loved decorative dolls—porcelain ballerinas with stiff pink tutus, French can-can figurines holding their skirts with a leg in the air caught in mid-twirl, Spanish dancers with lace mantillas, coquettishly carrying open fans. This dark-haired beauty wore a purple, tiered silk dress with a black-velvet vest and a tiny string of miniature pearls around her neck. She was smiling and her eyes, which opened and closed, were open. Unlike my mother's.

When she talked about her prewar life, my mother gave me mainly the honey of it, its sweetness. What made me think of honey? The name of the street, Ulica Miodowa, where her family had a shop, means "honey." The shop, she said, was in a fancy neighborhood—"beautiful" she murmured in a reverie of times past.

These days the internet is a time-space portal. If I had the exact address, I imagine I might find my way to the virtual front door of their shop. Ulica Miodowa threaded its way from Christian Warsaw to the edge of the Jewish ghetto. In the morning Lola and her brother, along with their parents, could walk east to the end of their street, turn right on Pokorna, cross the Plac Muranowski to Nalew, and walk through Krasinski Ogród to reach Miodowa. Then which way would they turn—north or south toward the shop? I can see why she was proud. Even today Miodowa is an elegant, wide boulevard of stately multistoried buildings.

She had a life-long addiction to clothes and shoes. When she died her closet held 103 pairs of shoes, all in their boxes. About half the boxes also had matching purses. Inside each purse was a lipstick, a handkerchief, a cosmetic mirror, and a pair of gloves—I mean every separate purse held these things. My mother never walked out of her apartment dressed casually. She put herself together right down to the matching costume jewelry, which filled several large boxes in her chest of drawers. She was a natural actress and knew how to hold her head and shoulders to communicate dignity. She faced the world as a lady, and when she wasn't elbowing her way to the front of a line, she had a lady's reserve. Her dignified public personae masked, I think, a profound wariness at being at large in the world where anything could happen and had. Once out that door any terror was possible, and she would at least be dressed to meet it.

The degree of her anxiety showed in the tuna fish cans she bought on sale and stored on the top shelf of the small foyer closet. I started to count them after her death. At first I rolled my eyes at them, but by the time I reached three hundred, I felt I was betraying her and I stopped counting. There was other evidence that she was preparing for Armageddon: a mountain of toilet paper ten-packs stacked in the back of a utility closet, a small hill of Ivory soap bars, piles of cornflakes boxes, an entire shelf of powder laundry detergent, and dozens of jars of Sanka and nonfat Cremora. This collection was bought on sale, accumulated week by week, with coupons clipped from circulars. It was also a way to undermine my father while following his miserly principles.

She kept the hoarding secret. I did not see all the stuff crammed into closets, cabinets, and drawers until she died. Hoarding, according to the Mayo Clinic, is a subcategory of Obsessive-Compulsive Disorder. The syndrome is associated more with older people than it is with younger ones, with having had possessions violently taken away, and with trauma suffered in youth. For sure my mother fit the profile, but she was not as extreme as pathological hoarders like the Collyer brothers, famous New York City hoarders. They filled a three-story Harlem mansion with wall-to-wall, floor-to-ceiling stuff. Langley Collyer died in 1947 while attempting to deliver dinner to his immobilized brother, Homer, who then died of starvation. The police excavated more than one hundred tons of stuff from the mansion, including ten grand pianos.

What I know about Lola's family, my maternal grandparents and uncle and aunts, can fill a teaspoon. She loved her father and her brother, did not mention one sister as far as I can recall, and talked about what a pest her younger sister Felusia, was. There's still room in that teaspoon for the rest: Her mother was religious, her best friend's name was Studnia, and her family took summer vacations in the country, in a place called Kazimierz.

Google brought me to a travel website for Kazimierz. Here's what it says:
On the banks of the Vistula River, "Kazimierz Dolny offers a unique charm of pre-war days with cobblestone streets, breath-taking views of the countryside

and other attractions...." Among the "other attractions" is a wall that was created after "World War II with Jewish shards of recovered Jewish headstones that were destroyed by The Germans." Note the emphatic repetition of "Jewish." On another travel site for Poland, Kazimierz is on a list of sites right above Auschwitz.

No matter where you begin in Poland, you always arrive at the Holocaust. Since the thirteenth century, Jews had lived on and off in Kazimierz. As in the rest of Poland, they had been welcomed, and thrived when they were allowed; then they were expelled and, later, tolerated, sort of, again. The town is named for King Casimir the Great, who welcomed Jewish immigration into Poland in the fourteenth century. But for most Jews it finished the same way in Kazimierz and Poland—in a ghetto, a ditch, or the death camps.

It must be like that for certain Europeans thinking about America. The sense of "the horror, the horror" at the center of its history. That "horror" is how Joseph Conrad in *The Heart of Darkness* describes the European colonization of Africa. In the same way, the Holocaust seems inescapable from most things Polish or often, even European—at least for me.

It is a curious phenomenon of the European dissertation mills that their students churn out so many American studies dissertations on race. I have recently been an outside expert on yet another European dissertation on race. This one was on "Whiteness" in the work of an American writer. If you don't know, Whiteness studies are big in academia now. Scholars look at how being perceived as White makes a difference, the unearned privileges it conveys. They also look at what qualities being White entails; how you whiten yourself. Many immigrant ethnic groups took their turns being Black or not White—the Irish, the Italians, the Jews. You get the picture. How do Europeans, though, get a free pass on issues of color? They did the colonizing. Until fairly recently, laws in certain European countries made getting citizenship nearly impossible if you are from, for instance, Africa or Turkey. Europeans, especially Germans, are fascinated with the non-whites of the United States. I will never forget the crowd watching Native Americans perform in the square of Frankfurt's old town while I was a visiting professor at the university there. Three or four of them with braided hair, feathered headdresses, and beads, dancing and chanting, performing the part of the exotic others of America. It shamed and embarrassed me.

Several days before this performance, I was on a train to Berlin. In my car was a graduate student from India who told me that the professor in whose lab he worked as a postgraduate fellow terminated his fellowship and insisted that he go home. The reason was that the graduate student had told his professor that his wife was pregnant. The professor did not want a dark-skinned baby with German citizenship rights. The horror, the horror indeed.

My mother used to sing the chorus of "*Yidl mitn Fidl*," or "A Jew with His Fiddle," a song from the famous 1936 Yiddish film of the same name starring the renowned Yiddish comedian Molly Picon. The plot is about her cross-dressing as a boy in order to travel as a musician. The opening scenes take place in prewar Kazimierz. Lola used to sing the chorus, which is all she knew, in Yiddish: "*Yidl mitn fidl, Arye mitn bas / Dos lebn iz a lidl, / to vozhe zayn in kas. / Yidl, fidl, shmidl, hey, / dos lebn iz a shpas.*" She sang it around the apartment as she cooked and cleaned. The translations I've seen are similar, but the variations in the translation of the last word *shpas* matter:

> Yidl with his fiddle,
> Aryeh with his bass,
> This existence is a song,
> Why should I be upset?
> Yidl, fidl, shmidl—hey—
> This life is a pure fun.

Sometimes *shpas* is translated not as "fun" but as "a joke," but I would translate the last line as "This life is just a game." "Fun" is more lighthearted than the song should be in Yiddish Poland in 1936, and "joke" is too cynical. "Game," I think, conveys just the right idea of luck and strategy for this moment in time.

As I started recording them on tape, Itzak and Lola, my parents, were giggling. They were talking about how they met, their courtship. The tape is chaotic, with my mother and father talking over one another. There was a kind of competitiveness between them, felt more by my father than my mother, I think. He tried to remember better than she did, but she also made him doubt his answers. Sometimes, though, their agreement was so complete that they finished one another's sentences. More than my father, my mother did not want anything in the interview that would tarnish her respectability.

I asked my father what he was doing in 1935.

Itzak: I was in Warsaw. I worked with my father tailoring.

Ellen: What was your typical day like?

> I: Starting from when? In the morning?
>
> E: Yes. You got up in the morning...
>
> I: Was by 8:00. We start working.
>
> E: What did you work on?
>
> Lola: Pants.
>
> I: Well, tailoring.
>
> E: What did you make?
>
> I: Pants. [Laugh.]
>
> L: I went for two years to his house, I know. Day in and day out, I know.
>
> E: You knew each other for two years? Do you remember how you met?

My father gets impatient with my mother's answering the questions I ask and says, "Are you gonna interview her or me?" I tell him that I'm interviewing him, but she answers anyway.

> L: My cousin brought him to my house. And from this moment, he didn't want to leave my house no more.

She laughs and then he laughs.

> I: It's not exactly like this. I knew her cousin. And he said, "You know something? I have a cousin, she lives on the Niska 39; she's a nice-looking girl. Come up, I'll introduce you."
>
> L: And he didn't want to leave me.
>
> E: So what happened?
>
> L: He didn't want to leave no more.
>
> I: You want to talk to her first?

I say to my father, "Talk. I'm listening."

> I: What happened? I came up, I saw her, we talked. And I was with her an hour or so, and I went down on the street. After that I came up

by myself next time I think to where she lived, okay? And we kept talking. Then we start making dates, going out.

L: He didn't want to leave. This was 1936.

I: Wait a minute, we not there yet. I don't know why she . . .

E: It's a little later than we were talking about.

I: Yeah, that's what I said.

E: I think you specialized, no?

L: He told you.

I: Specialize on pants. Making it for officers. For Polish officers. We didn't sell it. We were, my father was a, what you call it?

L: Manufacturer.

I: What's called below that?

E: Contractor?

I: Contractor. Let it be that contractor is right.

E: Were just three of you working? Your father, you, and Josef?

I: My father and my brother. If was busy, my mother was sewing too. By hand.

L: First time I hear this.

I: Josef was sewing by hand, too. Handwork.

E: What was the handwork?

I: The lining. And then the buttonholes. Buttons. And the cuffs. The seams, the part which shouldn't rip out, you know, we did by machine, but the rest by hand. You know before you sew 'em together, the seams, it was a lot of handwork. Okay, then around three or four o'clock, we had by us what's called here supper, but by us was called *mitik*. Yeah, *mitik* means supper. They are the same. Here they eat at six, but by us they eat at three, four o'clock.

E: What did you eat at *mitik*?

I: Well, the average could be potatoes and borscht and meat.

L: Goulash, no?

E: What kind of meat?

I: What kind of meat? Meat was *treyf* (nonkosher). Beef, beef. Okay? Beef. No. Don't say we were not religious, okay?

L: Oh sure, are you kidding? She wouldn't write that.

I: Was not kosher.

L: Do you have to write that?

I: My father was not a religious man so we didn't eat kosher, okay? I got to be honest. Wait a minute. Let me think about the kosher. Wait a minute. I think the meat was kosher because we bought in a kosher...

L: Kosher butcher on Mila Street.

I: In a kosher butcher. But we ourselves didn't keep kosher, but meat was kosher. Okay?

L: It must be. Because your friends were the kosher butchers. His father had a friend what they had a meat store.

I: Yeah, sure. Schmul.

L: He knows.

I: Okay, what is next? Where we at? What meal of the day? Okay, now, for nighttime we could have had some tea with something else. I don't know.

L: Cookies, cake.

I: Never big meals at night, just light.

E: Did you have a bar mitzvah?

I: I was what—bar mitzvahed? In 1935, was over bar mitzvah.

E: I know, but did you ever have a bar mitzvah is the question.

I: Well, the question, if I had a bar mitzvah, no.

E: Because Josef said he had a bar mitzvah, and Dov said he didn't have one himself.

I: I don't know.

L: Didn't you go to Hebrew school? Tell her.

I: Yeah, I went to Hebrew school.

L: They had enough Jewish learning.

E: Where did you go to school? Did you go to the Polish schools?

I No. Just to this place. Josef went to public school, and Dov, too, okay? I went to a private school. A private school.

E: How many years did you go?

I: For six years. And they spoke Yiddish and Polish and taught us Hebrew.

L: That's right. That's why he knows Hebrew.

I: Like here is the Jewish yeshiva. They teach everything there, right?

L: Yeah, yeshiva. That's how he knows Hebrew. He went to a private Jewish school.

I: They all went to public school except me.

E: Okay, so you worked at home.

I: Well, we start eight in the morning and when was busy we used to work until nine, ten o'clock at night even. Six days a week. We used to work on some Saturdays, too, when it was busy. I didn't like it. I didn't like it because most people which we live in the same building, they were all going to *shul* and they looked sideways to us. My mother didn't like it either because my father was not religious.

All his brothers were religious. All were except him. He wasn't religious; he didn't believe in it. That's all. And myself, I felt guilty because of this. Because my mother felt to be religious and my father not. I even sometimes had argument with myself. Not with my father. I thought to myself, "Why does everybody in the building go to the synagogue? Why doesn't my father go? Why is he like this? What is the matter with him?" I couldn't understand why he was like this, which did bother me a lot in this time.

L: The part about not religious not going to be in the book?

E: No.

I: Okay now: In our apartment, in the kitchen, we had a sewing machine. And a big table. Extra-large table for ironing. And there was other table for the hand-sewing, and then behind the table from the hand-sewing was chairs. Sometimes when we were busy, there were sitting three people sewing by hand. And my father was standing by the table, pressing. And I was sewing by the sewing machine.

And the work which we done for the manufacturers, mostly they did not pay.

E: What do you mean they didn't pay?

I: This was written down on a book, this IOU for sewing so many pair of pants. Okay? This was very hard to get the money because my father was too soft. I ask him that he should tell to the manufacturers, "You pay me, or I will stop sewing for you." He would have never said this. He was too good-natured to say this. And because of that, instead of money, we took fabrics. Raw fabrics to make suits. Okay? And if we had a customer for it, we sold to him the goods. To keep us going. I had arguments with him, why he does those things like this. What is the use of the sewing and everybody working hard if he doesn't get paid? Well, he was natured like this, and he couldn't help it. Okay? It was like this since I knew him and until I left him when the war broke out in 1939. We couldn't change him.

A lot of times we were very squeezed for money. We had to take in boarders to keep paying the rent for the apartment. We used to have two bedrooms, but we have to give back to the landlord one bedroom. We couldn't afford to pay it. And then on top of that, after we done this, we have to take in boarders. A couple. To help pay the rent.

I myself, on the weekends I needed some money for a movie or for ice cream or for anything else, I couldn't get it because he didn't have it. So I had to sew my friends' pants which they needed. I kept the money.

Money.

Now my older brother Josef, it was with him a lot of arguments at home, mostly with my father. He did make him very nervous.

L: He didn't want to work.

I: Every four weeks he went on strike. If my father give him two *złotys*, next week he wanted five *złotys*. If he got five, he wanted ten. So was always arguments. My father told my mother, when he comes back, we shouldn't give him food. No food for him.

L: Wasn't so easy like here.

I: But my mother, as a mother, she kept in the oven for him, when he came late back at night. And she gave it to him, without my father knowing it. And a lot of times he—my brother Josef had a bicycle—and he was going on tours in Poland. All over Poland with a bicycle. And when was busy, he took off with his bicycle. And my father got very nervous. One time came to a point my father was so nervous, he went to the window—we lived on the top floor. He wanted to jump out from the window.

He made him so nervous, he was ready to jump if we wouldn't hold him back. Because of Josef.

L: Oy, yoy, yoy. You mean people will read this book?

Suicide. In her last years, my mother made a suicide attempt. It came out of the blue. She was taking an antidepressant because of her worries about her health. My father called, saying she swallowed every pill she had—heart medicine, antidepressants, high blood pressure medication, water pills. She consumed whatever was left in four or five bottles. The ambulance took her to the closest hospital, where they pumped her stomach. I was so angry at her. The emergency doctor on call saw my anger and told me I had to leave until the next day. When I asked my mother why, she said something like, "You know. Sometimes things come into your head." A couple months later, I heard a radio news story about how antidepressants cause suicidal thoughts in the elderly. My anger lessened but did not go away. Although I was a grown woman, I felt abandoned by my mother, and I was hurt.

I: I myself was considered at home the best one from all the kids. I couldn't take the arguments. So I kept always quiet, and I mostly did what my father told me to. I want to please him. But sometimes my brother Josef talk me into go on strike, too, with him. He knew without my support he cannot accomplish anything. The only thing he was thinking, if I go with him, he could accomplish something. Well, a couple of times, he talked me into it, and I went on strike with him. And I thought maybe when I go, my father gonna get smarter. Maybe he's going to ask the people to pay him for the work which he does. But anyway, it did not help. He was like this. Nothing could have changed him. I got sorry for my parents, you know, and I came back home. I went back by myself. I couldn't take because my mother was suffering very much from this. She wants to say that her husband is right, but she knew my father was wrong, too, so she kept it inside.

E: Where did you go when you went on strike?

I: We tried to open up on our own and get work.

L: You did?

I: Before I knew you. I could've seen that it's not going to work out. It wasn't even so easy to get the work, anyhow, okay? I didn't want to go into my father's manufacturers—even if they giving the work, to compete with him, and new accounts was very hard to get, okay?

L: I didn't know this.

I: So I went back home and start working again with parents and I try. And after that, my father did gave me, I remember like five *złotys* a week. When I told him I have a girlfriend, I need money to take her out, something like this, you know. Then even the five *złotys* wasn't enough. I sew for friends, pants, which they paid me. I took all the money for myself.

There were times which my parents saved some money. And every time when they saved up some money, my father always find a friend to borrow the money, and the few *złotys* which we have he always find a friend which was in bad need.

He had friend, this friend was called Yosel. He was a shoemaker. And one time he decided he wants to go to manufacture by himself shoes. So he came to my father for a loan. The loan was that my father will cosign to make good his checks. This was called *weksel* in Polish, you know? It means promissory note to be paid. My father did sign that note. It start out to be good, with my father's friend, with the shoemaker, start out to be good. But after a year or two, my father's friend, which called Yosel, without saying, he didn't pay off the note. He went bankrupt without my father knowing.

And he went with all his family to France. He escaped to France without my father knowing. So all the checks, all the postponed checks which my father signed, he had to make good for it. This was a lot of trouble. And how he got out of it?

Okay. My father has friends. His habits were that after eight, nine at night, he used to go down to a bar. In the bar he met with his friends, which they drank mostly beer. Okay? Maybe they had a snack or two also. Okay? And those friends of his, they were known in Warsaw; everybody was scared for them. They were—how do you say—*shtarke*.

E: Tough.

L: Tough, right. You're right. Tough.

I: Tough, strong people, which everybody was afraid of them, okay? He sent them to the people which he cosigned, that they stay away from my father.

And after his friend Yosel went to France without telling my father; after a year that he was in France, he's back in Warsaw. He came up to our apartment. And he was crying, "I made a mistake that I didn't tell you. And I am broke. I'm back with all my family." His family consisted of two sons and him and his wife. So my father was so good-natured, he took them in, and they all slept by us. And ate by us, too.

He must have came back in 1937. Okay? Imagine so many people in two rooms and an alcove. So after living with us for a while, he finally rented an apartment and he moved out from us.

My father not only had the shoemaker for a friend, he also has friends, very educated people, too, which they were short of money. And he used to borrow them money. They were very smart and educated people. Makes me laugh what they did. One of them was from Vilna. The guy from Vilna, he used to make tricks to cheat people with money. He showed them how you can make from five *zlotys*, five hundred *zlotys*. Like from a dollar to make one hundred dollars.

And he find all these customers which were interested to make money. And he took the money from them and never came back.

He was operator. Means he cheats you. What they call conman. And he cheats you with tricks. Okay? He makes it so fast that your eye cannot catch what he does.

L: Like here on the street. They doing it with the cards.

I: It was not card tricks. It was money tricks.

L: He had a friend like that.

I: Didn't they tell you, Dov or Josef, this? Maybe they forgot all about it.

L: Okay, it's enough already with this.

I: In our apartment used to live a Drexler. He was boarder. He was also a very high, talented guy. He, himself, come from the part of Poland that was in Austria. The town where he was born was named Żelechów. All those people there, mostly Jews, they were very high educated, and he was one of them. He was older. When my sister was sixteen, he could have been thirty-four or thirty-five. They felled in love without my parents knowing it. Living in one apartment. One day my sister came to my mother and said that he wants to marry her. So my parents rejected. They say, "How can you? He is so much older than you. You a kid. You just got out of public school." They wouldn't allow it. So without knowing, one day they moved out, both of them. My parents didn't know where they disappeared. It went by let's say five or six months.

L: They had kids already when I met Itzak.

I: Anyway, we didn't know where they are, where they live. And one day somebody told us. When we did find out, she was already pregnant. She was pregnant, and they did live not far from us. And somehow, after we find out she's already married, my parents got used to the idea. Nothing they could have helped and they forgave—okay, we'll put it that way. They forgave her, okay. And her husband, Drexler, he was a very talented guy.

He used to go in Warsaw in a business street in the window. There was a Polish lottery. Like is here, like is now in New York. He used to stand in this lottery window. He used to stand so you would believe that he's a dummy. He was standing in the window and showing signs. Not talking. "You buy a ticket for a *zloty* and you'll be rich." Showing signs. And people was tempted—maybe fifty, sixty, maybe one hundred people looking. They couldn't believe, they couldn't think what he is. Or alive or is he a dummy? Okay? And he make like this the money he earned for a living. Every now and then he changed his occupation. Other times he was window decorator, to display for merchandise. In the best stores in Warsaw. Which he made a very good living.

L: He made beautiful living.

I: Above middle class.
Anyway, I don't know if I'll mention it or not. . . . He didn't like our manners. The way we behaved. By sitting on the table or eating the food. Or talking, you know?

L: You shouldn't say that.

I: It's true. When I came up to his apartment, I was scared to death. Whatever I did, I thought he doesn't like. I didn't feel comfortable. Let's put it this way. When my sister was home . . .

L: He was very fussy. Fussy.

I: With the two children, I felt okay. But otherwise I didn't feel right to be with him. I didn't feel comfortable. He always looked at me like this. [Furrowing his thick eyebrows, he makes a disapproving face.]

L: He was fussy. Very fussy. He was Litvak.

I: He was very particular and very arrogant, okay?

L: All the Litvaks like this.

All of my childhood I heard summary judgments of my parents' friends and business acquaintances as, "He's a Litvak." That supposedly explained everything. The distinction between Galitzianer Jews, like my parents, and Litvaks, like Rachel's husband, still matters. The Litvaks came from Lithuania and northern Poland. The Galitzianers came from Galicia, in southern Poland or the Ukraine. Bill Gladstone of the San Francisco e-zine *J Weekly* describes it as the "gefilte fish line." Galitzianers put sugar in their gefilte fish. They liked things sweet, while the Litvaks ate their fish with lots of pepper. Litvaks considered the Galitzianers irrational and uneducated, and Galitzianers found Litvaks cold control freaks. My mother put sugar in everything—meatballs, chicken soup, vegetables, and, of course, gefilte fish. She had a sweet tooth and cultivated the sweet tooth in the rest of us. She was a true Galitzianer.

E: Which brother were you closest to?

I: [Laughs.] Which one I didn't like him? Josef I didn't like.

L: *Aargh*. You! Boy, you shouldn't tell.

I: I'm going to tell them. I'm not afraid. Because all the problems he gave, all the aggravation my parents had because of him. I don't mention my brother Dov, because he still was a baby. In those days he still went to public school.

E: When was Motel born?

L: Seven years old he was in 1939, because my sister Felusia was the same age.

I: Now I remember exactly, okay? Now my sister Rachel and my mother was pregnant at the same time. Yeah, my mother was already forty-two years old when she had Motel. Yes, I was ashamed.

L: No, who was ashamed?

E: You were ashamed, why?

I: Because a woman in this time and with a baby wasn't—don't write this, come on. This means in this generation was pretty old to have a baby. Okay?

I gave birth when I was twenty-one and twenty-three. My own daughters did not marry and have children until their thirties. My youngest grandchild was born to my daughter within months of her fortieth birthday. She already had gray hair, and in the hyper-beauty culture of Miami Beach, where she lived and where women have facelifts and boob jobs by the time they are thirty-five, she was sometimes mistaken for her daughter's grandmother. They couldn't have looked at her closely because she has the sweetest face, the face of a kid, with startling green eyes.

Experts say that after age twenty-two, a woman's fertility declines, so I thank my grandmother Brandla for the good egg genes she passed on to my two daughters. They had healthy pregnancies. One daughter, like me, even enjoyed being pregnant, while the other one felt as if an alien had taken possession of her body. I understand that but I did not feel it myself.

I: Okay, when mine brother Josef went away to the army, was drafted to the army, he left his bicycle home. And he told me not to touch it till he comes back. But eventually, I didn't listen to him. I kept riding it and riding it, and I went in also on the bike to some races, bicycle races. I used to go to different towns from Warsaw with the bike. I went to Brest-Litovsk with my bike to mine family and cousins. This was the time I seen them all what they looked like. How they lived.

Okay, now when I was not out with the bicycle in the evenings, when I wasn't out of town. Okay? In Warsaw, I was seeing Lola for dates.

L: [Laughing.]

I: [Also laughing.] Wait a minute, okay? I'll tell you what. One time I was walking with her on the street. Okay? You should write it down, was called, the street was called Zamenhof. We intended to go there to a movies. Meanwhile, passed by a boyfriend of hers. He came up to us. And he was mad at me why I was with her.

L: This was already in 1938.

I: And he was mad at me why I go on dates with her. So almost came to a fight between the two of us. I said to him, "This is not up to me; this is up to her. If she wants to go with you, I have nothing I can do about it." This is up to her. So he realized what I said made sense. And he walked away.

L: He was nice-looking boy. In Russia he sent me a letter. Why I went.

I: And he tried several times to see her; he came up to her apartment.

L: Leon. In Germany I threw away his picture and his letters. I threw away his letters. I was stupid. He [meaning my father] start to be jealous, you know. He, Leon, was crying. He loved me so much.

I: She's going to interview you. Why don't you leave it alone? Okay?

E: Where did you go on dates?

L: We went a lot to movies.

I: Buck Jones. Harold Lloyd movies. Do you remember Harry Lloyd movies, the one with the glasses, like comedy? Funny, funny movies. We went to dances, too, okay? Dancing.

L: Oh yes, I liked it so much.

I asked if they remembered the names of clubs where they went dancing, but the names were lost to them. Dov remembered the Rendezvous, but hard as I tried, I could not find it. The twenties and thirties in Poland was an era of jazz, the kind you danced to. YouTube has wonderful old recordings of famous jazz singers and bands doing Polish tangos. One 1930s club is called *Oaza*, meaning "oasis," and another is in the Hotel Bristol, but in contrast to my parents, the patrons look well-to-do, with furs, tuxes, and monocles. My mother had a fur coat, but none of the photos of her or, of course, my father displays the affluence that is so obvious with these patrons. The Bristol is still open, taken over by a hotel chain.

With their few *złotys* my parents no doubt went to more downscale clubs and dancehalls, and in summer, to the dance pavilions in parks, where they may have swayed to the plaintive sounds of Stanisław Ferszko, a Polish-Jewish composer of smooth, stylish tangos. He left Warsaw for Palestine in 1938, moved to the United States in 1952 to conduct the New York Symphony Orchestra, and died in Miami in 1990 at the age of seventy-six.

I remember so well my parents doing the tango. My mother elegant and graceful as she bent her body to the music. Just as when I was a kid and she would grab me and twirl me around the living room, I danced with my daughters, spinning them until we were dizzy and laughing. Now we are cautious even in touching one another. How does that happen? They suckle at your breast and wrap themselves around your body as tightly as they can until, exhausted, you peel them off you with a kiss. Then when you'd love a hug from them as adults, there's a hesitation. Freud wrote about the desire for universal oneness, the craving to be one with your mother as you were in the womb, the unconscious wish not to be separate and autonomous. He believed we all yearn for that impossible unity. I ask you, whose desire is that? If Freud was right, this desire must also include with it a fear of the desire being fulfilled, a fear that we will regress to an untenable dependency, like when we were infants. I remember stroking my mother's hair as I wheeled her around the hospital, but by that time she was already well on her way to another world. How she would have loved my stroking ten years earlier. I have my own betrayals to answer for.

Whether he was dancing to Tony Bennett or Elvis, my father's feet followed an identical pattern. The only concession he made to the particular music was to adjust the tempo of his moves. Although his feet had found a working formula, the creativity was in the improvisations above the feet—letting go of my mother for a few beats and then reconnecting with a spin. He danced smiling and did not take up a lot of space, like some people do. His dancing was contained, tutored no doubt by the crowded dance floors of prewar Warsaw.

I: Yeah, I was joined in a club. I joined a Jewish Club. Maccabi for sports. I was not a plain bicyclist. I was very good at it.

L: I had a lot of friends in Maccabi what they playing ball.

Unlike his brothers, my father did not join a youth group attached to a political party. He tells me about the sports club's richer members.

Money.

I: Maccabi used to be a club from the upper-class Jewish people. They were an organization also for Israel, but for the upper class. Okay. Not a proletariat class, but for the upper class. I joined anyway because I like this club. Okay?

Once I started with this club in a race of 210 kilometers, which was joined by Polish gentiles.

L: What a ride. Wow, wow.

I: Which was maybe five, six Jews and maybe forty, fifty gentiles in this race. Okay? When I was together with a gentile, he didn't let me ride behind him because the main thing is if somebody cuts for you the wind, you don't have to work so hard. If he cuts the wind for you and you stay behind him, the behind cyclist has easier to pedal, to bike. Every time I sit on him, go behind him, he wanted to knock me off. They couldn't take it that a Jew was so good. Okay? They couldn't take it. Or he tell me to go out in front of him, and he would sit all the time behind me to get me tired out. You understand? I was cutting the wind for him. So he stayed so close on my rear wheel, so I cut the wind for him. So anyway, it wasn't so easy with them. Okay? And when we came back to Warsaw, I was anyhow the first one of the Jewish bikers and the second best in the race. I could have won the race if they wouldn't force me to cut the wind for them.

L: Tell her.

I: If they didn't take the advantage—how you call it?—*oysnitsn*.

E: If they didn't use you.

L: Yeah, right.

I: Yeah, if they wouldn't use me, I would have won the race.

E: Your father once got ready to emigrate?

I: Oh, you said you start in 1935. Now, this this comes much before that. We can tell some stories from this, too. Okay, I'm gonna start from me, okay? It's better. I was born in Warsaw on the—write it like I said.

E: Okay.

I: I was born in Warsaw in 1917 on the Świętojerska 19. On the first floor. The whole building contained only one floor. This building was in the upper-class Jewish neighborhood. And the apartment was a large apartment with a bath in it, with electricity, and with all the modern stuff in this generation. My father then was furrier. And we used to live there till 1922, the year they did close the immigration for the Jews to come to the United States. Okay. And our windows from this apartment went out to a park. To a public park which called Krasinski Ogród. And under our windows was a restaurant which they served coffees. From the windows you could see tables and chairs. People were sitting and eating, okay?

When I was three or four years old, I can remember, I went to the park with a three-wheeler, bicycle. And I went all the way down the hill with the bicycle, with the three-wheeler.

And all of a sudden my father decided to go to the United States. So what he did, he sold the apartment there on the Świętojerska. He sold whatever he could from furrier business. He took in enough money to pay passage for the ship to take us all across the ocean.

> When he sold this apartment, came out a new law, that we need special visas, right?

L: A visa.

I: To travel you need a visa, permission. We didn't get it. And we couldn't go anymore.

Congress enacted two laws to restrict the immigration of Jews in the early 1920s. The Immigration Acts of 1921 and 1924 imposed quotas—allowing entry only to a certain percentage of applicants from specific ethnic groups—that mainly restricted Jews from Poland and Russia, where severe pogroms raged, spurring immigration to the United States. The quotas were deliberately based on the 1890s census rather than a later census because 1890 preceded the influx of Jews fleeing persecution. Thus although the law did not specifically name Jews, Jews were the intended target.

E: As I recall, your parents met in jail?

I: I remember I heard them talking that my father was in jail because he was a PPS. PPS means Polish Socialist Party. Okay, he was caught.

E: What was he doing?

I: Because they were against probably the tsar, which they didn't like him. And they got them in jail. And it was the same jail like Józef Piłsudski. My father was with him together in jail.

My father does not know the year this took place, but it must have been long before the 1917 Russian Communist Revolution since he mentions the tsar, and also before Polish independence from Russia, which finally succeeded in 1918 under the leadership of Józef Piłsudski. Assuming my grandparents were already married when Josef, the eldest child, was born in 1912, they must have met before that, perhaps by 1910. My grandfather Chaim was probably jailed as an insurgent by the Russians for working toward an independent Poland. The Polish independence movement was in full swing then. The progressive Polish Socialist Party (Polska Partia Socjalistyczna, or PPS), also headed by Piłsudski, promoted a democratic agenda that was friendly to Jews—with equal pay and equal rights for all, though the historian Joseph Marcus is skeptical about the good intentions for Jews.

I like having a revolutionary grandfather who served jail time for his beliefs. Perhaps it was his politics that helped to make him a soft touch. He may have believed that money was secondary to camaraderie. Perhaps it was hope rather than inertia that kept him anchored to Warsaw in 1939. Hope rather than his mahogany furniture. It is nice to think of him as an impractical, generous dreamer, an idealist. I also must admit, though, that it was my grandfather's profligacy that may have helped to make my father miserly.

I: My mother was visiting in the same jail her brother who later was sent to Russia. We never could find out where he was. So that's how my mother and father got to know each other.

E: Do you remember 1939?

I: Yeah. Wait a minute. You want to write on this? Okay. In 1938 Nazi Germany began really heavy on Poland on the pressure. They want back their land that they thought belong to them. And Poland had a slogan: "We won't even give them a button." They wouldn't give a button or a *guzik*.

L: Not a button!

I: In the first of September 1939, I was sitting working on the sewing machine. I saw through the window a whole fleet of German airplanes coming through the skies. The next day the planes came and they throw bombs on Warsaw. I think in a few days they took all Poland. Everything was in a chaos, the whole city. You know, chaos. People grabbed everything they can get their hands on. There were landlords who they would give a building for a loaf of bread. They didn't have what to eat. From the bombardment, a lot of horses got killed. So people used to skin the horses for meat. For horsemeat. To survive. Yeah, I had some horsemeat too.

I sat by the window doing my work and I saw the bombers coming. I saw the Nazi cross on the planes. I thought any second I'm going to be dead because the bombs, they were dropping them. Buildings went just like that. A lot of people got killed on the streets, walking on the street. You heard *brrree boom boom*. Every second. They didn't let up. Nobody knew if he's going to be alive in the next two seconds. Okay? A lot of people got hit with shrapnels. A lot of people died. Big buildings from two, three hundred families in it collapsed. And on the streets nobody was safe either. I saw them right in front of me, they got killed. Right in front of me, while I was walking from our street to her street. I wanted to see what's happening there by Lola. So you could have seen people lying dead. Between Muranowska and Niska, it was maybe a seven minutes' walk. Okay?

When the Germans marched into Warsaw, still was no water, was no bread, was no food, was nothing. And after a few days, the bakeries start producing bread, so people went in a line to get bread. And I got in line for bread. So a German soldier was holding order so people should stay in line. Meanwhile goes by a gentile, a Polish Christian. He saw a Jew standing in the line. He couldn't speak German. He said to the German in Polish language that this is a Jew. The German couldn't understand him. He was talking to him for maybe a half hour. He still couldn't understand what he means. And he wouldn't go away till he makes sure that he does understand what he's saying.

In mine opinion, the German couldn't care less who took the bread. Jews or no Jews. But some of the Polish people were so bad, a hundred times worster than the Germans.

The politics of blame. Who's at fault and how much? My father put Poles above Germans in the hierarchy of perpetrators, as did his brothers.

In giving a Presidential Medal of Freedom to the Polish freedom fighter Jan Karski in May 2012, Barack Obama used the phrase "Polish death camps" in explaining Karski's heroism. He meant death camps run by the Germans and located in Poland, as he carefully explained after Poles and Polish Americans exploded in rage at this characterization. *The New York Times*, the *Wall Street Journal*, and the Associated Press banned the phrase "Polish death camps" from their stylebooks, which they had all used before.

Polish anti-Semitism is palpable even today. When I was visiting the geographies of this book, I went to Warsaw. As I checked into a three-star hotel with my married name, "Friedman," the woman at the desk exchanged a knowing look with her colleague. I understood that look as a comment on my Jewish name. Walking the streets of Krakow, I saw two fortyish Polish men, who by their clothes appeared working class, showing no self-consciousness as they pointed and laughed at a Hasid they saw on the street, with his defining side curls and black hat and long black coat. Polish anti-Semitism. How can it be weighed against German atrocities? Jan Gross, the scholar of postwar Polish anti-Semitism, explains and explains it. The death camps were German, not

Polish—no argument—but Polish anti-Semitism seems to persist even though Jews have virtually disappeared from Poland. The only help for it is the rule of law—control it through law. Let national ethics trump individual prejudice. Let the law represent our best selves.

I: The first few days when Germans come in, they didn't do nothing special. The first few days. After two weeks, they start grabbing people in Jewish neighborhoods on the street, putting them to work. One which they grabbed was my sister Sonia.

So after this, they came to every building and demanded a certain amount of people, every day should be put to work. And at this time, there was no water. We had to go to a big river, which called Vistula, and get here water. This was maybe back and forth about six miles. Also there was no food to get. The only way you can get food is on the black market.

Meanwhile one of my father's manufacturers sent somebody which he shall get back those pants we finished sewing, which he never paid for the work even before the war. Was on the book. I saw my father wanted to give the pants. I stopped him. I said, "If you're going to give him that pants, he didn't pay you anyhow. Now the money isn't worth it much. At least what was worth something was the pants. If you sell on the black market, we can get some food." So he realized with this I was right. With this we can have food meanwhile to survive.

When the war started, my brother Josef was drafted to the Polish army because he was a soldier. A trained soldier. So we didn't know if he's dead or alive. After few weeks, somebody came from Brest-Litovsk and told us he is okay, that he is there by our family. Okay? And the man also said over there is nice. There's life, there's food, there's everything normal. Because this part took the Russians. The Russians took over this part of Poland. After I heard this from the man, I said to my father, "Why sit here?" I said to him, "You have an apartment there ready to move in. Let's take the sewing machine, everything we need, put it onto a horse and buggy, and get there."

He said to me, "You want to go, go. I'm not going nowheres." So I saw there is nothing I can do. And the pressure was every day from the Germans. Taking Jewish people to work, demanding more Jewish people to work. I didn't like that.

So I took a bicycle from Warsaw, and I went to Brest-Litovsk. I couldn't do much miles because the German army were marching on the road. I had to go by the side of the road to let them through. And they were going toward Warsaw. So the first day I made about ninety kilometers from Warsaw. Then I slept over, and the town was called Siedlce. And I was staying overnight. I had an address from somebody. Just in case. Okay? In the morning I went on the bike again, and I went to the Russian-German border.

I went straight to the bridge, which crosses the river Bug. So there was a German soldier keep watching. I went straight in, and I told him I want to cross the bridge. He asked me why I want to cross the bridge. I said all my relatives are there. I want to go to them. He said to me, "I'll let you go, but . . ." Then he pointed with his finger that the Russian man on the other side won't let me in. A lot of people tried. They don't let nobody in. Anyway the bridge was collapsed anyhow. In the middle it was collapsed, the bridge.

Meanwhile I met a few other Jewish people, and they said that there's a Polish guy, a farmer, which has a horse and buggy, that he knows a place where the water was not deep. If we'll pay him, he will take us over the other side. Okay, I went to the guy. I settled for a price. He said, "Now it's too late. We gonna go early, very early in the morning." Okay, I was in his home till the next early hours of the morning. He took this horse and the buggy, and we went through the water. In middle of the river, the horse got loose [laughs], and he went on the other side. And the buggy was stuck in the water. So he said to us, "We have no choice. We got to hurry up because the Russians can spot us." He said to us, "You just go straight and you come to the other side." I took my bike on the shoulders, I went into the water [laughing], and I walked to the other side. He also said, "When you gonna come to the other side, just go straight till you hit a town. Till you gonna come to the town." Every time I went away straight from the water, I came back to the water. This was three times I tried. And I came back to the same spot. And then I figured out myself, if I go straight, I come back again. So this means I got to go different now. I went on an angle. Okay? Not straight. And this was the right direction.

Meanwhile, came a Polish farmer with a red armband. And he said, "Where are you going?" I said, "I want to go to Warsaw." Special. I told him the opposite side where I want to go. He said, "This is not true, you coming from there," he said to me. I know he could see I was wet. He knew that I crossed the river. He said, "I'm going to take you to the commandant." To the Russians. Meanwhile, while I was walking with him, I had a heavy sweater. This was a special bicycle sweater. I said, "You know something? I'll give you this sweater and let's forget the whole thing. Okay?" He asked me where I lived. I told him my family's address. Bialostoskaja 19, Brest. I tell him the address because I knew the address. Well, he didn't know what to make of me. If I was telling him the truth or not. The address was correct. Anyway, he took the sweater and let me go. And he even gave me direction how to go to the Brest-Litovsk. Finally I came into the outskirt of Brest-Litovsk. I thought I was in seventh heaven. I saw lights, I saw water for drinking, I saw people working, not afraid. Like normal. Normal times again.

I didn't know where the street exactly was. I asked directions, and people told me till I got there. Finally I got there. Everybody came to me, and I tell them exactly what happened. I was so happy. I gained so much weight there. I was a like a barrel.

So after eight days, people came arriving to my uncle through my father's recommendation from Warsaw.

E: Who?

I: People from our building, some other people. To everybody he knew he said, "Go there. You're gonna have a home. Tell them that I sent you."

My uncle's apartment had one bedroom, a little foyer, and large living room. In the living room was a big table, a square table, a double bed, and a couch. The place in a couple weeks got so crowded.

So my father keeps sending everybody he knew to my uncle. Mine uncle was also a very good-natured man. He couldn't say no if it was sent from my father. He accepted everybody, too. We were sleeping on the table, under the table.

L: On the floor.

I: I cannot figure out until now how we all managed that. I think at least fifteen people in one time.

Okay. We were there and meanwhile our cousin used to have in Brest-Litovsk a clothing store. So he picked me to sell his suits on the black market. The Russian soldiers were the buyers. He gave me a price. Whenever I take more, I can keep it for myself. So I was selling suits for him. And I came into money.

Meanwhile, I was by myself without Lola there. I did send a special friend of mine, which he was going back and forth from Brest-Litovsk to Warsaw. I tell him I'm going to pay him. He knew Lola anyhow. I tell him, "I pay you whatever the price is. Just bring her." Okay? In a matter of three weeks later, Lola came with her cousin.

L: My cousin Lodja.

I: She was stuck on the border. She was sitting maybe how long? Two weeks?

L: Yeah.

I: On the border. They wouldn't let you go through. They wouldn't let her through. It was already harder. Every day it was harder to cross. It was more patrols.

I: The brother came a few days later. Listen what I am telling you. Okay? Okay, eight, ten days, your brother arrived, too. Lola's brother, Natan.

L: Ellen, we could made a whole story. I gonna tell you.

I: She gonna tell you, you going interview her too? Okay, she's going to tell you. So anyway, being there in Brest-Litovsk, I used to go on the black market and make money. Josef probably did that too. And Dov, we had an uncle which he put old books together. What do you call it?

E: A bookbinder.

I: A bookbinder. Dov was sitting by him and reading books. That's all he did—nothing. Didn't interest him a thing. Just sitting there and reading and reading books. Nothing else. I told several times why don't he take the advantage to do something, to make something of himself. It didn't bother him.

We all had a good time. We went always, it was still warm; it was sunny, and out we all went to the beach. By a river there near the Bug. Cousins and me and Josef and everybody went.

E: Did you hear anything from Warsaw?

L: Yeah, they killing people.

I: And in 1940 there was a German embassy in Brest-Litovsk. A friend of mine which used to live by my uncle too, myself too, and Lola—we all went to get permission with a lot of other people to go back. So a German officer came out and he told us, "Why do you want to go back, you people? You have it here so good. Why do you want to leave here? Why do you want to go back there?" He pleads with us not to go back. So we thought, "Look at him. He works for the Russians probably; he doesn't want us to go back." Because nobody could believe what's going to happen in the future. But he was honest. He was right. A few of my friends went back, and they are dead. Killed.

L: My brother went back.

I: Everybody wanted to go back to their family. To be together. A lot, a lot of people which were from the other side, in spite they had freedom, but they didn't have where to sleep and where to get food. And no bed. They had freedom all right, but a lot of people were sleeping in synagogues and some other places. They didn't have what to eat. We were lucky because we had family.

So this was only for a day or two, this registration to go back. Okay? After registration was closed, it was still a lot of people that wanted to go back. So one day, Lola's brother went back with her cousin. Then after her brother left, a week or two, in the morning, early in the morning . . .

L: I wanted to leave him.

I: She left, too. I caught her up on the street. My uncle came to me.

L: No by the door. By the door.

ITZAK WITH LOLA INTERRUPTING

I: "Lola's going, Lola put her coat on," he said. "She probably wants to go back, too."

L: By the door he caught me.

I: So I caught her and I didn't let her go. I stopped her. And after that, a week or two, she still was crying, why I didn't let her go back home.

L: Now start with Russia a couple weeks later.

I: In 1940, the Russians came out with it's not healthy for us refugees to live in the border towns. So one day in 1940, this must have been in June, the Russians arrested every refugee that they were living within a hundred kilometers of the border. So they came to my uncle. They knew that we are by our uncle. I don't know how they knew, but they knew everybody who was living with him. So we hid in the attic until they left.

Meanwhile, my sister Sonia got in contact with a boyfriend which was living next door. In the next building. He was a plumber. His father was also a tailor. They also had their own building.

L: Yeah. Leibel was his name. Nice, good-looking boy, Ellen.

I: Average, okay? He was a plumber working for the Russian army, okay? Anyway, we had a meeting between us Seven, and we had to decide what to do. What is the use staying here? We won't be able to get out on the street. We gonna get caught. So we decided, we have to go, too. We hired a cab. We packed our few things which we had. And we all went to the station and got on the train. And during the night, we start moving.

L: A Russian boy want to marry Sonia. When she was with us. Before she went back. Oh, what a nice-looking man. Nice-looking.

My mother's mind has shifted to Nyuvchim. She is stuck on Sonia's love life. Leibel in Brest and the Russian officer in Nyuvchim. In the midst of the story that cost her her family and home, my mother wants to think about romance, about lovely Sonia with her suitors. Sonia the songbird who, along with Dov, gave European popular music to backwater Komi SSR. In the formal black-and-white photo I have of my father's family, Sonia is placed next to Dov, who is probably standing on a riser because he looks tall. Her long, dark hair is styled with finger waves on top and on the side and then, given what I can see—I am guessing—the back of her hair is rolled at the base of her neck in the style of the time. Her eyes are fixed on something outside the frame of the photograph, already disconnected from the family, or so it seems to me. Her ears are not pierced as my mother's are in this era, and she is not wearing a string of pearls around her neck like her sister, Rachel, pearls perhaps given to her by Simon Drexler, who could afford them. Sonia, the Juliet of this Jewish history, though the analogy falls apart as soon as I try to make it. Literature, unlike life, is carved by the writer for a purpose. In Shakespeare's play the dispute between families is paid for with the lovers' suicides. Then their tragedy is redeemed by the cosmic understanding and healing the shock of their deaths inspires. Peace, tranquility, and a world that makes more sense follows. The heartbreaking love story of my poor Juliet, Sonia, brought no enlightenment. She was consumed, as were so many, by the extravagant malady that was Nazi Germany, the consequences and lessons of which we are still puzzling over.

Her murder and that of millions of others has deepened our understanding of the absurd, has made it more present. In the late twentieth and early twenty-first centuries, the absurd is our constant. That is not a restorative lesson, as in Shakespeare where tragedies lead to the return of equilibrium. The sea change produced by the Nazi horror transformed what it means to be human. Against the break the Nazis wrought, the West and the people in it are changed. The recovery from tragedy depicted by artists such as Shakespeare is a reminder that art is not life. Art and literature have limits that history does not. My mother understood that and wanted to remember the honey, to suck out the little bit of it that was there and savor it. Sonia and her lovers. My mother and the beaus of her youth. They are precious drops of sweetness in a bitter world.

> I: Well, anyway, there was very little food on this train given to us. We were dirty. Filthy. When the train stopped, people need to relieve themselves. Was no shame. Everybody was under the wagons and doing what they have to do. There was no shame between men and woman. And when we stopped in a big station, and I knew that the train gonna be staying at least for twenty-four hours, I went in the town with the black market to see what I can sell for food. Okay? They gave us, but wasn't enough. A lot of times I came back with food, but I missed the train. The train was gone. I knew every train had a number so, okay, if I missed the train, I asked the dispatcher there from the station which way the train went. So he told me. And

so I got on a passenger train till I caught up with our train. This was happening a lot of times like that.

On the tape I hear my mother doing scat to the tune of *Carmen's* "Habanera" song as my father tells this story. This move is very familiar. She used it to criticize my father without actually saying anything. Scatting over his words when she did not like what he was saying, such as the business with dirt and no toilets. She would get loud to drown him out if he began to yell. She would roll her eyes, and then to really unnerve him, she would start dancing around their apartment to her scat to let him know that he did not exist for her. My father kept his cool this time and continued his story.

I: Finally we arrived to our place which was called Nyuvchim. We was given a big room which had a big stove. And around the walls were beds. All around, all the way around. In the middle was a table.

L: Was sixteen people there.

I: Our commandant himself was a Russian, not local. He was also sent there for not good behavior. All which was there, they were people what the Russians called "enemy of the Russian Socialist Republic," okay?

When we got there, we were assigned to work. Everybody who has no little children has to work. We were assigned to work in the forest.

Challenging Lola to remember the sixteen people in their barrack, Itzak says to her, "Tell me the names. I know every name. I know every name."

I: Okay, in our own family was seven. They called us *di Zibn*, the Seven.

L: Was a blondie.

I: *Di zibn*, the Seven. Okay? So after us seven, next was the blondie called Figa, with Ersel. They slept together, an old guy.

L: She married him later. Yeah. Next to them were two crazy people.

I: And next to Figa and Ersel was Berel from Lodz, with the beauty, the tall one. He would straighten her valise.

L: Yeah, everybody was laughing. We had a good time. He was crazy for her.

I: He was married to her. He lived in our room. When he got nervous, he took out her valise. She wasn't so handy. She got mad because he took out her belongings. She wasn't so handy in putting things straight.

L: No, not handy. She was a slob. He put away her panties nicely.

I: Her shirts, her underwear.

L: So he put her panties nicely. And everyone was laughing.

I: Her underwear—everything.

L: We had a good time laughing. She was called Selena.

I: No, not Selena.

L: Stasha?

I: No, you're just saying all the Polish names.

L: Stasha.

I: No.

L: She was Stasha.

I: No.

L: Yeah.

I: After them was a family, Koslovski. Three people.

L: Regina and her husband and his brother. This was Dov's best friend. And that's all. So how many people you have there?

I: Wait a minute, not yet. There's two more. Okay, so you have Berel and his wife and who else?

L: The Litvak.

I: Rose?

L: Rosie.

I: And him?

L: I don't know. So many years, who can remember? Rosie and Yankel. [Laugh.] Rosie and Yankel.

I: She's making it up. I can't think of the name. So okay, we were assigned to work in the forest to cut down the trees. Lola was working on bricks. Making bricks. Right?

L: I was *Stakhanovite*, very fast worker. The fastest worker.

The Soviet Stakhanovite movement was named for Aleksey Stakhanov, a model Soviet worker in the 1930s who out-produced everyone else in the mine where he worked. Thereafter, those workers named Stakhanovites were rewarded with more pay and privileges. Stakhanovism lasted only until the end of the war, when it became clear the work produced inferior products. As for my mother, she was a Stakhanovite because she was fast. She did everything fast—work, walk, clean, cook. The war had taught her that being first had advantages. But quickness had its down side.

Until she learned English well enough, she was a pieceworker in a clothing factory, a member of the Ladies Garment Union. In piecework, you get paid according to the number of items you finish. She sewed sleeves onto clothes. She would come home crowing about the compliments the factory floor supervisor gave her for her productivity. From time to time she also came home with bandaged fingers because she pushed the garments through the sewing machine so fast that the needle caught her finger. These were industrial sewing machines. Nails and flesh moved through as easily as silk.

I: We working on those trees for maybe six months or so, and after this they opened up a tailoring shop. I went working for the tailor shop, so we worked for the army—pants and jackets. We were working on clothes which are especially for wintertime. It was cotton and quilted. Belonged to the government, was government factory. They always promoted to work fast, to produce. Which worker produced a lot, they used to give special privileges, like a reward of money or more food to be given to him. So I was one of them. Reward for fast and good work.

I was called up in a social club. They made a dance, and I was called up to the stage. And they said to everybody that Itzak Chaimowitz of G.—this is my Russian name; Chaim from my father's name. This the way it goes. Itzak, son of Chaim of G., produce so much and so much work. He was a Stakhanovite. And I got for it some kind of reward with money. Rubles.

Money.

I: While we were in Nyuvchim, my sister Sonia was working in one of those places which give bread for ration coupons to everybody. She got the job through the commandant because he liked her. And naturally we went to get our ration, too. Then we came home, we put our bread away and the other things we got for the rations, and then with an eraser we crossed out on the card. And we took again. We went several times. Everybody went back to get some more food. We dried the bread. We did dry the bread to last longer. You know, for storage.

And when we came home, all the women which they lived with us, everybody was rushing home to grab a space on the kitchen stove. Because was only I think four holes, four of those holes to cook. And there were maybe five families. So Lola [laughing] always was the first one to grab in the kitchen a place to cook.

The summer there had the white nights. This mean daylight all night long. In the winter was dark. All the way dark. No light. Okay, now, sometimes when we had off, like a Sunday, we went to the forest for blueberries. What we saw, as we looked up in the sky, we saw the sky and forest. That's all we saw. Nothing else all around you.

And this was the everyday living till one day, Sonia's boyfriend, which he lived in Brest-Litovsk, made papers for her to return back. Everybody was very jealous that she can go back, and we have to stay—all the refugees. Of course we were glad she was going back to a real normal life.

Wait, what was her name? Her name was Wanda Wasilewska which freed us, was Wanda Wasilewska. She was a communist Polish leader which she works with the Russian government, and she freed all Polish citizen in USSR. The reason for it was to take all Polish people to form a Polish army and go fight against the Nazi Germany.

E: Why didn't you go?

I: Why I didn't go? Why we didn't go? A lot of us thought that we gonna go to fight for her, Wanda. Actually there were two Polish governments then. Was Wanda Wasilewska and was another one, General Anders, which used to stay in England. He was an anti-Semite.

So I didn't join the army because, first of all, if I did want to go to fight for Wanda Wasilewska, I knew that she was a communist. Nobody, nobody joined. None of our people joined.

For my father, it was Wanda Wasilewska rather than General Anders who was responsible for setting free the exiled Poles in Soviet gulags after the German invasion.

In her book *Caviar and Ashes*, Yale historian Marci Shore describes Wasilewska's role, and thus helped me to understand my father's idea that he owed his freedom to her. Wanda Wasilewska, a Polish communist and a polemical poet, was thrilled when the Germans invaded the Soviet Union. She offered herself to the Lvov Communist Party and wound up a propagandist on the radio. She was the founder of the Union of Polish Patriots and an officer in the Soviet army. She appealed to exiled Poles to "liquidate all Germans." Imagine the Seven's hopeful hearts when they heard her rousing speeches blaring from Nyuvchim's communal loudspeakers and thought of Sonia and their parents' possible liberation. My father's heart must have beat faster when he heard her message to "have no mercy on the wild beast drinking our blood" and connected her to the promise of a normal future at home in Poland. Also, Wanda Wasilewska's father, Leon, was a follower of Józef Piłsudski. This connection was positive for many Jews in the Soviet gulags.

For Poles, however, she is a traitor to Polish independence, a lackey of Stalin.

When the time came, Stalin took advantage of the large population of Polish Jews who had survived in the Soviet Union, using them to help make Poland a communist state. Josef's friend Chapka, the only man of the Seven not related by blood, stayed in Poland after the war and became a minor communist boss and politician, helping to administer Soviet rule. And so was another myth reinforced. Poles could blame the commie Jew for Stalin's subjugation of Poland.

My parents' version of the Separation is different from that of Dov or Josef, who dismissed it.

I: Wanda freed us from Nyuvchim. We all decided to go where it is warm. We made our way from Nyuvchim to Syktyvkar. And there was waiting for us a freight train. A number of people, I don't exactly remember how many, were assigned to each car. And somehow Josef and Dov and Henya and Chapka got into one car.

E: That was later, that was in Samarkand, no?

I: No, this was here.

E: You took the whole trip by yourself?

I: Write the way I said it, okay? Because this was there. From there we went to Kyrgyzstan. And that's why we got separated.

E: In Syktyvkar?

I: Listen to me what I'm telling you, okay? You're not listening. Somehow, in Syktyvkar Josef got in a different car. And I got in a different car. I came to his to get in, and somehow I couldn't get in. There was no room for us. Josef said there was no room for me and Lola. So I got in a different car. Which was also a guy of Warsaw was in there. He asked me from what town I am. I said was Warsaw. He said since we are from Warsaw, come in, I'll take you. By the way, he was somebody, a big shot. He took over the whole thing; he was boss over the car. And every car was like this. Every car had a boss. So I went into his car.

And with his explanation, I finally understood that they were in separate cars almost the whole trip to Asia. My mother added the detail that the three brothers avoided and that must have defined the trip.

L: Was not like this. We got mad because he did not want to give us food. Josef had food and he would not give us, so we went in to another car. You not gonna write this?

For the entire time of the trip, with its circling around and delays due to troop and military transport needs, the resentments must have festered.

I: Again she interrupts. Write like I say.

So finally, we start after a day or two, we start moving toward the direction of Samarkand. The voyage was filthy and dirty. The war was going on. Was not much food to eat. And every station where the freight train stopped, I got to go into the city in the black market, try to buy some food.

Food was the main element over which grudges gathered, and resentments were harbored at this time. Dov rebelled against his brother Josef over food. Josef denied Lola and Itzak entry to his cattle car, according to my mother, over food. And Itzak's friend Asher Dorn, who in the 1980s had a thriving Fifth Avenue antiques business and with whom my father talked daily about the stock market when they were both safely in Queens, New York, betrayed him over food. At one of the stops on the way to Kyrgyzstan, my father came back to the train empty-handed from the black market, without food, while Asher Dorn had done well. Dorn had bartered for more than enough food for himself, the story goes, but he refused to share it with my parents or even to sell it to them, despite their pact to help one another and despite the fact that they had come from the same neighborhood in Warsaw and the families knew one another.

When Asher and his wife left our apartment in Queens after one of Lola's spectacular dinners, after my father closed the door, it was the first thing out of my mother's mouth. Despite the laughter and the memories shared over *schnapps* and the promises for another get together soon, that memory was the silent companion of the evening.

The glue of secret resentments.

I: We bought something in one town and then next town, the prices is much higher for the same thing. Okay? We knew how to get along, how to speculate, how to survive in other words, okay?

One day, when I got out of the train, I looked at the name of the station. What was it?

L: I don't remember.

I: Was Samarkand. I remember now. I looked where the half of the train is got lost overnight. It's not there anymore. My brother Josef and Dov was on it. They were gone. I did ask the dispatcher, "Where?" He couldn't tell. He didn't know. I didn't see them again for a long time.

Over there it was warm, was always warm. Like Florida, you know. Anyway, what was left from our train went to Frunze, and years later we found out, they went to Osh. From Frunze, we went to Kant and from Kant came a horse and buggy and took us to a small village, which was very small village for farmers. And me and another friend from our wagon, they gave us a small house. The house contained one room. Was made of manure.

L: And we were sitting all four of us on something like that, too. Us and another couple. Tiny room. One little room.

I: One little room. Also from the same thing what the hut was built, was built high for a bed.

L: And all four were sleeping like that.

I: Like this. You know on the end of the world it was built like this.

L: Wasn't a bed. Was made the same way. From manure.

I: Nothing else was there. Okay? Just that. We didn't sleep. How could we sleep in this condition? The next morning we got up, we were hungry. We didn't have no food. We went out to the small village there. Anyway, we got to sell from us what we have. To survive with some food. We didn't have much to sell, so during the night, we went out on the fields from the farmers. What we find . . .

L: Frozen onions.

I: Onions, the ground was so hard, like frozen. We ate them. There was nothing else. During the night, nobody should see us. Wasn't allowed to do it.

So while we were in this little village, I met a refugee like I am from Warsaw.

L: Who was this?

I: So he said to me, "What you doing here? Why do you stay here? Is nothing in here." I ask him, "What you doing here?" He said he's coming to buy *tabac*. *Tabac* means tobacco. For cigarettes.

L: This was Heniak.

ITZAK WITH LOLA INTERRUPTING

> I: Yeah, I know it was Heniak. He said, "You know what? You go at nighttime on the fields..."
>
> L: Stealing.
>
> I: *Ach*, if we all gonna talk, how she going to record it? No good this way.
>
> L: I don't gonna to say nothing.
>
> I: Heniak said, "Take and steal those *tabacs*. And I'm going to pay you money, so you can buy food for it." He sold it to the Russians. So me and my other friend which we lived together went in the nights. For a few weeks we used to steal those tobacco from the fields. And Heniak came once or twice a week, and he took it and he paid out money.

Stealing, finagling, bartering until they gained some purchase in this strange new land.

> I: After two weeks, a lot of our people which came to this little village, they start getting sick. Of typhus. A lot of them died. After a while, I caught it, too.
>
> L: Very dangerous.
>
> I: Typhus. And I went to the hospital in this little village. My typhus occurred in such bad condition. And I knew myself, I felt it in myself. The nurse said to me—I ask her—and she said she don't know if I'm going to make it or not. She said to me, if I'm going to make it this night, I will survive. And I did fight for it to stay alive. I remember it very well. I fight for it. I knew my condition, and I did fight to stay alive. And somehow I got through it. And the final fever was broken. And I got better day by day, but still there was no food.
>
> She came to me and brought me food. She sold something from our belongings. And brought me what—butter, right?
>
> L: And got a piece of bread. Little bit rice.
>
> I: A little bit rice.
>
> L: And that's why he survived.

The day my mother had her first major heart attack, she was walking in her neighborhood for exercise. She had chest pains, and they became so intense that she collapsed on someone's lawn. Cars stopped, but she refused their help. She got home somehow and told my father. They arranged to go to the hospital, but before she would leave, she insisted on cooking him food for a few days—her estimation of her hospital stay. So she cooked for a couple of dangerous hours before she left for the hospital. That was my mother.

I: After I made it out of the hospital, then Lola got sick from typhus. She went into the hospital. Her typhus wasn't as severe as mine. She probably became sick because she was coming to me. To visit me. After a couple of weeks, she got out of the hospital.

L: You forgot how thin I was.

I: She was so lightweight I could . . .

L: Carry me out . . .

I: On my arm. She was so skinny. There was nothing to her.

L: Yeah. Tell her, after I got better . . .

I: Well, then I pick her up. I took her out of the hospital. I had a suit from Warsaw. A blue suit.

L: With stripes.

I: Suit with stripes. This was very dear to me because this was from Warsaw still. I never wanted to part with it. I did have no choice. I had to sell it for food. And I was thinking, it's no use staying in this little place, Pashka, so we went to Kant.

Where did we sleep the first night in Kant?

L: They gave us. They gave this house to us.

I: This house? They gave to us?

L: Yeah, was six, seven people, Ellen. Yeah, they gave us. The government. Was seven people. I remember everything, Ellen. He [meaning my father] bought once a melon. And one of them stole our melon. So they start fighting. It was a *royter*, a redhead, who took it.

I: I was mad at the guy.

L: They were hungry. They stole our melon. So they got a fight. I remember everything, Ellen.

I: And since the fight, I moved away. I couldn't take it no more. Then I bought a house, and I moved out from there. A house also from manure.

E: What did they put you to work doing?

I: They put me to work in a factory which produced sugar. From the sugar came out is a dark, sweet liquid.

L: Like honey, something like. They called *patika*. Like condensed milk but this was dark brown.

I: I was given barrels on a buggy, two big barrels. And they didn't give me horses. They give me two big steers.

L: Right.

I: Yeah, steers right. Two steers. I had a stick. I had to hit them they shall go.

L: To go.

I: If I wanted they shall go right, I had to say, "*Sop, sop.*" And left I had to say, "*Sipa.*" "*Sop*" and "*sipa.*" Okay. And she was waiting, Lola was waiting outside. She knew the route which I was going daily. I stopped and she was waiting with …

L: A bucket. Wasn't easy.

I: She came with a bucket. She was waiting for me. And I open from the barrel like you open Champagne. Pull out the cork. So drip out this *patika*, which is sweet sugar, okay? Sometimes one bucket and sometimes times two buckets of it. And she went with it on the market.

L: On the market. And sell it.

I: On the black market, five rubles for a glass of this liquid. Of this sweet liquid. And after a while we saved up money. With this money, we start buying meat, fruit. Also on the black market. With this money, we start living well.

L: Well? *Okh un vey.*

Lola's Yiddish phrase for contesting my father's idea of "living well." It means something like "alas and alack."

E: I thought Mom sold bags of sugar?

I: Yes, she did. The native people, the farmers, the Kyrgyzians. Okay? They give the factory the sugarcanes, and the factory did give them some sugar for it, okay? White sugar.

L: I was buying from them. And I went to Frunze and sell it.

I: And there was a Russian woman on the scale, there. I remember everything.

L: A man, too.

I: A man and a woman, okay. On the scale to weigh the sugar. Would you listen to me? It went by the kilo, okay? How many kilos you had. Russian people working. Not the native people.

L: Big shots. Yeah.

I: They were in charge of the scale on the market. So every time they saw Lola with sugar coming, they knew how to weigh the sugar.

L: So they knew already.

I: They knew already to say less. Let's say it was ten kilos. They would say seven or six.

L: This is the way they made money. But I made money, too.

I: And later Lola made good with them. She pay them; she pay them money.

Money.

L: And I went to Frunze and sold the sugar to people who came from Moscow.

I: She never let finish.

L: Okay, goodbye.

I: So after she started this business with sugar, there were other refugees which they did the same thing.

L: They saw me and they copy.

I: Okay? And she went on the train from Kant to Frunze, which was a local train, which was but a half hour ride. When all our refugee people got off the train with the sugar, everybody want to be first.

L: So they can make more money.

I: In Frunze on the market to sell for a better price because there were waiting Russians to buy the sugar.

L: From Moscow they came to buy.

I: So everybody tried to be first.

L: I was the first one.

I: Lola was always the first one with the sugar on the market. She got always a better price.

L: When the other refugees came, I had sold already my sugar, was sold. I was very fast. *Got, mayn got.* Everybody was so jealous.

I: So we had to do it to survive. Okay? From this we bought our own house in Kant. The street was called Kantovskia.

L: Made from the same *dreck*.

I: It was made of the same manure. If there was a heavy rain, the ceiling collapsed. There went the half of it.

L: So half house is gone. When was raining, you couldn't go out.

I: When you put your foot out the door, you lost your shoe. Was stuck in the mud.

Then after a while, I went and did business with the Russians what came back from the front. A lot wounded. And they always brought something back—suits or yard goods. I start buying it from them. And then I sold it again. So I made money on it.

And every time, it was coming more and more wounded, and when Russian army went out of their borders, they used to bring goods from Europe, Western-style things. They took it away from the Germans. Mink coats, all kind things.

And out came from the Russian government some kind of order. The whole Polish citizens which lived there, must take passports.

So when the order came, almost every refugee there refuse to take Russian citizenship. Because we thought we take Russian citizen, we never can get home.

L: No. We didn't take it.

I: So they start arresting our people. Some was put in the jail for a week or two and still refusing. A lot of people gave in and took those passports. I myself was stubborn and didn't take one. We were hiding out, okay? We hide in some homes. When we saw them coming, we went out from the house, and we went to a different house, okay?

L: The Russian people were nice. They let us in.

I: One time she was running. She saw the police coming, and she wants to run. So I took right after her, and she got bit by a big dog, a German Shepherd on her thigh. Everybody had a dog there. Very wild, very big dog. She had a very bad wound. She couldn't walk for a long time.

L: That's how they didn't took me. They didn't touch me. I had so many stitches! *Oy, yoy, yoy*! And needles. So many needles, *ach*!

I: So after a while I was called in to the police station. He asked me if I'm going to take a passport. I refused. He told me to sign something and he took mine . . .

L: From the hand.

I: My fingerprint. He didn't tell me anything. He let me go. After a four or five weeks, I received a noncitizen passport. A non-Russian citizen passport.

I read in Katherine Jolluck's *Exile and Identity* that such Polish refugees who refused Soviet passports were called *bezhentsy*. Their official status was "special settlers—refugees" who were supervised by the NKVD.

L: After us, a lot of people they took like this.

I: Around this time your mother met Josef in the market where she sold the sugar.

L: I was pregnant. When Josef came to Frunze, I was pregnant.

I: Are you sure?

L: A hundred percent. Not ninety-nine. A hundred. I give him the bed where I was sleeping, and I was sleeping on the floor. Finish your story.

I: I can't... You keep interrupting.

E: Josef said that when you met him, the first thing that you did was to shove some *kielbasa* in his mouth.

L: Was salami. Yeah, I was so excited. He was dirty. Yuck! He was dirty. Lice and everything.

I: The first thing she put a piece of *kiel*—I mean salami, yeah.

L: Salami in his mouth.

You may know the joke here. My parents are cueing one another for the correct vocabulary. My mother could not admit to *kielbasa* because it is usually a pork product, therefore *treyf*, an injury to the image she keeps wanting to get on the record. They have corrected the sausage Lola shoved in Josef's mouth to a beef product that has Jewish credentials—salami.

I: And after a day, he got sick from malaria. You know what malaria is? He was trembling. Everything we put, blankets and all that, he was still shaking. This took, I don't know, maybe eight days like this.

Henya, and Chapka, they all were there in Osh and a lot of other people which we knew, too. They were with him in this Osh. Dov, he told, was taken to labor front. Nobody knew where, so now we knew where everyone but Dov was.

Then I had some connections by the commandant. We needed it false papers for Josef to travel back. So I made some. I got it for him. You need a transfer, a special transfer to travel the train. Otherwise they wouldn't let you. They wouldn't sell you even the ticket without this.

I had this connection because I got job with NKVD what I was responsible for the goods they put in a freight car.

L: Like vodka.

I: The goods for the NKVD.

L: The military. Big shots.

I: This was Russians. Everything belonged to the government. They gave me one freight car. And in the freight car, everything, all contents was weighed and measured. And I signed for it.

L: From Kant to Moscow, even.

I: *Tabac* to make cigarettes. And there was wine. Would be three, four barrels, big ones. And then could be dry grapes. And there were dry peaches. Some other things which I don't remember no more. Yeah and watermelons. What do you call the other one? The yellow ones, like the watermelons.

E: Cantaloupes?

I: Cantaloupes, yeah. All this stuff grew in Kyrgyzstan. Okay? I signed for it. I had to take it to Chelyabinsk, which is in the Urals already.

My father's memory of finding Dov differs from that of Dov himself. Itzak's regular route was through Chelyabinsk, and one time the refugee network connected him to Dov. Someone in the labor front near Chelyabinsk, a Polish-Jewish exile who knew Itzak and Dov from Nyuvchim as belonging to the Seven, saw my father at the train station or the black market and told him about Dov. The details of this reunion, unlike that of Josef with Lola and Itzak, are vague in both accounts. Although Dov thought he saw his brother, Itzak does not remember actually meeting. But they each now knew where the others were and how to reach them, the connection restitched, at least for six of the Seven.

I: And wherever the train stopped, I sold maybe some wine or whatever I had.

L: A little bit, you know?

I: And I filled it back with plain water, just so be the same amount. And then I sold the dry fruit, dry peaches, too. I did on every station, where the train stopped.

E: How did you replace the peaches? The dried peaches?

I: You put water on it. So it's wet. It's more weight.

L: It's heavy. A little bit, you know.

I: So a little. What difference does it make? I had to do it because the reason I went is to take in money in those big towns.

Money.

I: I went through Moscow one time on the way back from Chelyabinsk. How I got to Moscow? In those times if you wanted to go to a train, you couldn't get because so many people traveling—soldiers, everybody. You couldn't get on the train. It was impossible. Just was impossible. Sometimes I had to wait to catch a train, three or four days. Sleeping in the station. Not only me. *All* stations were overcrowded. There were only so many trains to take the people. I took train to Moscow because we got to wait for right train so long. I was miserable, so I took first train I could take no matter where it goes. So I wound up in Moscow.

I only went one time to that Moscow. The only time I went, when I got into Moscow, was the day of celebration.

He must have been in Moscow in July 1944 because this trip is associated with my birth. My mother tells the story of how he left right before I was born. The NKVD called him and he had to go. In Moscow he saw the fruits of Operation Bagration, in which the German forces were overcome by the better-armed Soviet military. Fifty-seven thousand German POWs were marched through Moscow on July 17. There were photos in the Soviet papers. My father was there.

I: I saw the Russian people, they were happy. They were dancing. Was a happy day there in Moscow. Very happy there. They knew they were chasing the Germans already.

I wanted to go to the marketplace in Moscow. So I went in the underground to get there. I was amazed. How was it human possible? The underground, it looked like palaces. Clean.

L: Yeah, I remember he told me.

I: Palaces. Was out of human imagination that could look so beautiful and nice. Everything on the wall looked hand-painted. Beautiful. I never seen in my life anything like it. I was so surprised, I hate to go out from the underground. I never seen anything like it in my life.

Suddenly, my mother remembers one of her missions for today's interview, to make sure a story of their marriage gets recorded.

L: He forgot to say the whole story. When we got married. He forgot the whole story. Was a candy man. He married us. He marry us.

Now my father gets on board to make sure I include a marriage event in the story about them. Not only one, but two marriage stories.

I: This was the second time.

L: This was for the second time.

E: What's a candy man?

I: We were married before that.

L: Yeah, it was the second time.

I: I'll tell you. After we bought this house in Kant, we had a neighbor, a very Orthodox Jewish family. His family contains two sons and a father. He was a very religious man. He married us. He did marry us.

L: We decided to have a baby.

I: What was the day then? What year was it?

L: 1942, May 31.

I: May 31, 1942.

L: Yeah, but we were married before. When we coming into Russia, you know. You're supposed to get married.

I: He was making candy, the guy who married us.

L: Yeah, you can write down.

Thanks, Mom. I'll let everyone know that this is the Lola-approved version of the story: The candy man married you. I just can't suppress the "Candy Man" song from *Willy Wonka and the Chocolate Factory* because this film's excessive fantasy matches that of my mother's marriage story:

Who can take tomorrow

And dip it in a dream

Separate the sorrow

And collect up all the cream . . .

The Candy Man can

'Cause he mixes it with love

And makes the world taste good

I: He was from small town in Poland. Okay? Candy-makers, they were good off. They make so much money.

Money.

Somehow money legitimizes the story of candy-makers marrying them. I don't believe a candy-maker married them in Kyrgyzstan, but there must be a reason they fastened on this story, something that happened so that this story makes sense to them as a story to tell me for the record. But the reason remains a mystery.

L: Yeah. The two sons of his, they married two sisters. Two sisters married to two brothers. They were all candy-makers.

I: Yeah.

And that's the end of their account of their marriages. They were married twice. Once by a very religious candy-maker. And once before because when you leave home with a guy, you're supposed to. Although the candy-maker element of the story is subsequently dropped, my mother would announce periodically, "A very religious man married us." This theme became more and more insistent until she declared that her fiftieth wedding anniversary was coming up and what was I going to do about it? Fifty years from May 31, 1942, would make it 1992, and I threw them an anniversary party, playing out this charade to my mother's dignity. My father went along with propriety as long as it did not cost him dignity or, of course, money. Although many people there knew the anniversary was a fiction, they played it straight. Everyone brought my parents presents, about which my parents complained. "Junk," was my mother's summary judgment. She died two years later.

> I: And what else do we have to tell about?
>
> E: I was born there. How about that?
>
> I: One day, the twenty-second of July, 1944.
>
> L: He supposed to go to Moscow. Don't write down what I say, listen to him. I gonna say my own story.
>
> E: Is it different?
>
> I: My daughter was born. My daughter, Ellen, was born, okay?
>
> E: What about my name?
>
> I: Olga Izaakovna. Every child wears his father's first name, okay? So after, I don't how many days after I left, she was born . . . Do you remember?
>
> L: Four days, five days after he left.
>
> E: Who was I named after?
>
> L: After my aunt—it's called *Elke* in Polish—because I didn't know then if my parents are alive or not.
>
> I: Yeah. We couldn't give you another name because we didn't know what happened to our parents. So she did give you a name from aunt she knew she was dead. *Olga* was the Russian of *Elke*. According to Jewish law you name baby after dead family member.
>
> L: When I came home from hospital, he was on trip. One month or more. Weeks and weeks.
>
> I: Who remembers? Maybe four weeks it took because they put always my train on the side to let the troop trains go. Every supervisor from

a big station knew what I'm carrying because he had the papers. They said to me, "I want something from you, then I'm going to ship you." Otherwise he kept me there for eight days if I wouldn't give him anything.

They gave you allowance for a little drying by the time you get there. That's how; they give you a little allowance. There were no complaints. If there would be complaints, a guy that was checking could be bought, too. The whole Russian system was just like that.

Okay, after the war ended, we were free to go back—all Polish people could go back to Poland. All the refugees.

We were traveling back to Poland, and every station I came, I met a lot of other refugees on the way back to Poland, I ask them from what part of Russia they are coming. I was asking if some train came from Chelyabinsk because I knew Dov was there. So on one of those stations, they told me their train come from Chelyabinsk. And somehow they took me to this train. And then finally, this is how I met Dov.

E: Just like that? By accident?

I: By asking people coming from there. Our people, okay? Just like this. He was on the same station. He tell me his life story. He tell me that he had a bathroom in Chelyabinsk. He had girl. He had a Russian girlfriend there. Emma. You know the story. He was taken good care of, and it wasn't so bad for him. So I took him to mine car of the train. And since then, we traveled already together. Okay? Finally, we came to Brest-Litovsk.

E: What did you expect to find?

I: I expect to find somebody alive. I went straight to the street where my uncle lived. Bialostoskaja 19. When I got there . . .

L: Everybody was dead.

I: We were both sad, me and Dov. We were very sad. We thought there is no use staying there because not even one Jew was alive in the whole town. So we went back to our train.

Soon as we crossed the border, we were hearing stones banging on our train.

L: They was throwing stones.

I: There were a lot of gentile people, Poles, which was traveling with the same train. They were hanging out in front by the window their Jesus Christ or Mary. They drew crosses on the cars where they were. They said here in this car is traveling Christians which you shouldn't throw stones on it.

I felt very bad. Every Jew felt so bad. After what happened to the Poles and to the Jews. I felt so bad, I was sorry that I returned to Poland. I couldn't believe it. Everybody felt the same thing. We couldn't believe it.

Then the train took us to a part of Poland which used to belong to Germany.

L: Stettin.

E: Why didn't you go to Warsaw to see what happened?

I: What would I go?

L: In Stettin they tell us everything what happened. We knew there everything.

I: We came to Stettin, there was Jewish organization there. They took care meanwhile of the refugees were coming from Russia, okay? They give food or something like this, but we needed quarters to sleep. I wanted to obtain a decent place. The places they give us, I didn't like. So what I did, I had left some valuable things which I sold. I had some gold pieces. I had also a fur coat. I saw an apartment which I could obtain. I think the apartment was on Jana Żupańskiego 8.

L: Yeah. And we sold almost everything. We took Dov, too. He live with us.

E: Dov didn't bring anything with him?

L: No. Not a thing, not a thing.

I: He brought love from Emma. [Laugh.] The apartment in Stettin was the most beautiful apartment I ever saw in my life.

L: Yeah, I know.

I: This was taken away probably . . .

L: From Germans.

I: Probably from a German family. Everything was furnished in there. Everything was clean.

L: The Germans live beautiful.

I: I think was a bathroom and . . .

L: Everything, yeah.

Germans were clean. Germans were efficient. Germans would have been better communists than the Russians. Germans were less anti-Semitic than Poles.

I: When we came to Stettin, we were told what happened to our families. People which lived through the camps. We met a lot of people which lived through—Jewish people—which lived through the concentration camps. Which was liberated from the concentration camps. The way they looked was horrible.

L: Like skeletons.

I: They looked like skeletons.

L: Bones, just bones. They couldn't walk even.

I: They told us the stories. The horrors. What they lived through, I thought that we were in palaces in Russia. According to them, I didn't have nothing to say.

Many of the Polish-Jewish survivors of the Soviet gulags must have felt that way as they encountered camp survivors and heard the stories of the murdered. *Droit de parole*, the right to speak, is a blood sport. The closer to the black hole of the gas chambers, the greater one's right to speak, some have argued. My parents were silenced, as were so many others, their stories dwarfed by the astonishingly mad brutality of concentration camps. What was left for the remnants of Jewish Poland and of the Seven to say—that they were, as one scholar of this population writes, in a "little paradise" of hell? It was a silence enforced by their lesser suffering and also a silence they owed to their own dead.

Coming out the other end of history, well fed and in the United States, money in the bank, a gin rummy game on Saturday night, his kid a college graduate and married, the American dream in his fist, my father looked back at his time during the war with some generosity when he did speak. *La vie en rose*, as Edith Piaf sang. Dov was the one with regrets, who looked backward. Not my father, who is the most materially focused of the brothers, dogged and single-minded in his pursuit of money. But his appetite for it was not large, just persistent. He did not like to risk what he already had, so his gains were small but steady. He accrued his fortune, whatever it was, dollar by dollar. He was always small time. Even in Berlin when he had some wealth, he was less rich than Jews who had elaborate black-market operations.

One of the things that he gave me before he died was the gold fillings from his teeth. He kept them when he had a bridge made. His plan was to go to the jewelry district on 47th Street in New York City and sell them. Through the years, he repeatedly asked me to go with him on this task, and I refused. Then months before his death, he gave me an envelope and told me to open it when I got home. It was the gold fillings.

The Germans had slave laborers, often Jews, who mined the tangled bodies in the gas chambers. Body orifices were searched for valuables, hair shorn and sent to make stockings or stuff pillows, and gold fillings extracted, collected, and melted, the origins disguised, into gold ingots for the Reichsbank. In Treblinka, as Tim Snyder writes, Jewish prisoners cynically called dentists would extract the gold from the dead. The victims' mouths were examined before they entered the gas chambers and, so that they could be more easily located when they were dead, their bodies marked with an "X" if they had gold fillings.

Every time my father brought up the fillings, I thought of that. In truth, there was no connection except a poetic one. My father was never in a concentration camp. His gold fillings were acquired in Berlin after the war. In physical terms, they had nothing to do with the Germans. Yet I think many people could not resist the association. But he did not even have to resist it because the connection never occurred to him. Gold was gold.

Money!

To survive, they were thieves and liars and grifters, my parents. They knew they had been luckier—my father would say "smarter"—than others. They saw themselves as doing what was necessary. I am proud and ashamed of them.

I: I would say, thank God that the Russians saved us.

L: Tell her, tell her.

I: By sending us away so far, what they did to us was seventh heaven.

L: They give them small piece soaps. To make believe they going to take a bath.

I: She doesn't have to know this, okay? How they got killed. And which way they got killed.

L: Oh, yeah. You're right.

I love them for still trying to protect me from this knowledge as if I were ten years old. I also appreciate that this knowledge they had did not come from books.

I: So of all my misery and all what other people told us was done to them—it was still not an end. Every day on the market in Stettin, the Polish people which were there used to kill Jews.

L: Yeah.

I: Every day in Stettin we heard, "There was killed two Jews, three Jews," without any reason whatsoever. I thought to myself, for all the money in the world, I'm not going to stay here. Meanwhile, Josef came into Stettin. When he arrived, I was ready to leave Stettin already. I was thinking of going to Berlin.

L: We give our apartment.

I: I think I must have said to Josef, "Don't buy anything. I'm going to give you mine apartment. I'm going to leave. I don't want to stay here." I said, "If you be smart, you would leave together with me."

L: He didn't want it.

I: He said, "No. I'm not going to leave now." I told him I don't want to stay here anymore and live with those barbarians. So I took Dov with me to go to Berlin.

E: Why Berlin?

I: Yeah, because people came back and said in Berlin was the UNRRA, you know what it means?

UNRRA, the United Nations Relief and Rehabilitation Administration, was organized in 1943 to help those areas liberated by the Allies. Fifty-two countries contributed 2 percent of their national income in that year to fund the organization. Following this rule, the United States contributed more than half of the approximately four billion dollars spent. For the one million refugees who did not want to be repatriated, including my family, UNRRA funded displaced persons camps.

UNRRA, the Joint Distribution Committee, and also the Haganah, an Israeli paramilitary group formed when Palestine was a British mandate, saved Jews. The Haganah played many roles, among them to smuggle Jews who were passing as Christians out of Poland. A friend from Vineland is the daughter of a Polish gangster, a Catholic, who got false identity papers for his Jewish girlfriend, my friend's mother, and the two kids they had together. They passed as Christians, and he got rich smuggling. The romance ended when the mother refused to convert, and he became increasingly violent and alcoholic. The Haganah smuggled the mother and her two small children, my friend and her baby brother, from Poland to the West. They wound up in a DP camp somewhere in Europe and then, like us, immigrated to New York City. Without a man to provide for her, the mother struggled in the projects, neighborhoods that hardened my friend. Her mother eventually married an older kosher butcher and moved to Vineland, where they had a chicken farm, like Josef and Dov. My friend claims that from the time in the projects, she always carried a knife, even in high school. Even in rural Vineland.

Picture a lovely, soft-spoken, slender, blue-eyed blonde. She was the prom queen in high school. As a stepfather, the kosher butcher was short-tempered, always threatening her and her brother with the belt. But Sabina was fearless. When she was fed up with her stepfather's threats at the age of eight, she told him to stop waving the belt. Laughing, he asked her, "Or what will you do?" She looked him straight in the eye, fingered a kitchen knife, and said, "You have to sleep." According to her, he never threatened them again.

The kosher butcher, it turns out, had been a partisan, fighting in the Polish forests and rescuing Jews, some of them living in Vineland. Sabina learned about his heroism after his death.

Would that have made a difference? Could they have met on kinder ground if he had revealed his history and she had heard it?

> I: They wanted like, I don't know, 25,000 *złotys* per person to cross the border, okay? In a car. And I still had a coat made of silver fox, a

three-quarter coat. I wanted to sell this to get enough money to be able to pay for the trip to Berlin. Anyway, I went to Lodz and I sold it. It was 1946, weather was warm.

L: In Berlin we start to live.

I: We had a lot of packages. Which was impossible to carry. We had to leave behind a lot of it. What we took is the important things. She wouldn't part with the pots and pans.

L: Pots and pans I brought. Yeah. Just to cook a little. To cook for her.

I: She was always worried about food. Have to eat, have to survive.

L I had a baby.

I: So we came to the American side of UNRRA, to the *lager*, the camp.

L: Schlachtensee *lager*.

I: Okay, this guy Mische was in the same camp as us in Berlin. After a while he told us that he was a smuggler. And he told us the story of his life. He came from Galicia part of Poland. And so, when the war started, he was about ten-, twelve-year-old boy. Imagine. He was much younger than me. He told me he survived by being in the forest. He was with the partisans in Poland most of the time. He was fighting against the Germans. When he was young, he was like wild. He didn't care whether he lived or died. That's the way he was.

In the *lager* he belonged to a group of people which they were all involved in dealing with the Russians. The Russians used to sell them cigarettes. And for the cigarettes, they had to deliver gold and silver and diamonds.

E: How did they get the gold, silver, and diamonds?

I: From the Germans for the cigarettes. Black market. They opened up in East Berlin warehouses.

L: Was very big ones.

I: Russians gave them cigarettes, and they have to pay not in German marks but in gold, silver, valuable things to the Russians for this. The Russians with Mische were the first ones to start with it. Later the other refugees start doing the same thing. So the Russians did give two, three, four people in a group, they gave them in the East Germany a couple of towns—some they gave a big town, some they gave a small town, to go and do the same thing. I was given also with two other refugees. Don't you remember? Of course. I was given.

L: When you was given?

I: You forgot they gave me towns. You don't remember nothing, okay? Was in Eastern Germany. Three small towns. To go there to take from the Germans the gold and silver for the cigarettes. For the *tabac*.

My mother and her convenient memory would like to eliminate this chapter from the official record. My father, a *goodfella*. He had his illegal territory, and he reported to higher-up international gangsters. The story had shifted from Steven Spielberg to Martin Scorsese. My father owned a long, black leather trench coat in that era, which he wore belted. He also wore a fedora like they do in Mafia movies.

He and his partners in crime gained enough assets to open up two jewelry and antique stores from those black-market deals. One was on Alexanderplatz. I remember the velvet-lined jewelry cases and clear-glass shelves. My mother and I would sweep into the store, and she would grab anything that caught her eye. That's how I'm stuck with all the crap now. Broken figurines of lords and ladies. Intricate crystal vases, bowls, ashtrays. Silver trays and a silver tea set. Eighteenth-century Meissen porcelain with hand-painted lovers dancing and chasing one another around coffee cups and cake plates, as in Keats's poem "Ode on a Grecian Urn":

What men or gods are these? What maidens loath?

What mad pursuit? What struggle to escape?

What pipes and timbrels? What wild ecstasy?

For Keats the figures on the urn represent immortality because they were not subject to death. They chased one another on the urn forever. The figures also represent the anticipation of happiness though they never achieved it. They were static and could not reach one another but, unlike human beings, they would never be disappointed or betrayed. Keats did not concern himself with how the urn was acquired or what its provenance was. The immortal nature of art itself is what obsessed him. Whenever I look at that Meissen, though, I think about who had it before my father. I wonder whether they ever used the coffee and tea set for twelve. I want to know what desperation led them to sell it. Were they hungry?

Photographs from Berlin confirm our affluence. My father behind the wheel of a Mercedes-Benz, his fedora still on his head. My mother positioned by the other window and me in the middle. Whoever is photographing us is outside the car because the windshield is in the shot. Lola's hair is elaborately coiffed. Her dark hair is pulled back on the right side, and on the left, her hair is a grove of carefully planted corkscrew curls. Around her neck she wears a triple strand of pearls. Her matching pearl earrings sit in diamond flowers that echo the flower print of her dress, which has the thick shoulder pads stylish then. In another photo, one of my five-year-old self, I am wearing a white fur coat, perhaps rabbit, that extends below my knees. My hands are hidden in a matching muff. On my head is a white woolen pom-pom hat that must have been hand-knitted. I know the coat was custom-made for me. Dressing a five-year-old in white—white fur no less—makes a statement way beyond the utilitarian. It is about the means of the child's family. After the Jewish ghetto in Warsaw, living "on the book," the deprivations of Komi and Kyrgyzstan, and the humiliations of postwar Poland, conspicuous consumption, especially at the expense of Germans, must have felt like righteous comeuppance. I know I had a German nanny. What weird reversals of history and what tangled emotions must have woven through those relationships on all sides.

When I was in Berlin to give a lecture at the university, I took a look at Alexanderplatz. Still today it's a big commercial square, in my father's time dominated by a train station and department store. It took quite a hit during the war but is now a big pedestrian mall, as well as a train station. Beginning there, I walked almost six miles along Kurfürstendamm, known as Ku'damm, the most famous boulevard in Berlin, until I reached 132A, where we had our apartment on the first floor. Kurfürstendamm is Berlin's Park Avenue or Champs-Élysées. We lived in one of the more elegant neighborhoods in postwar Berlin. I was so excited to finally reach the building marked 132A after a two-hour walk. As I looked up at the front door, I had a moment of déjà vu. I knew what was behind me without turning my head. I had played in the park behind me as a kid. I knew it was there. I turned around and there it was. My heart was pounding as images out of memory competed with one another for my attention. I remembered the bakery in the basement of my building where I used to wander in, drawn by the aroma of freshly baked bread and cookies. I stopped going, though, when a woman behind the counter told me that I had better be careful because there was a demon who ate fat little girls who were alone.

Fuck those Germans who sold their Meissen. It sits in my living room. I can break every dish if I want to.

There's no more bakery there. It's been replaced by a bar.

On moral grounds, my mother insisted on leaving Germany to immigrate to the United States. My mother boxed up her Meissen, crystal, and silver and took it on the ship with her. They turned their assets into diamonds, which they sewed into the linings of their coats. Upon landing, we were shepherded to the Bronx by our sponsors, the sister of my grandmother on my father's side. I remember my parents carefully removing the lining stitches to extract the jewels in the small bedroom we were allotted in her apartment. My parents never lived as if they were rich again. I don't think they were ever poor, but the lesson of not spending was delivered daily. They lived an immigrant's working-class life.

My father did not believe that there are things money can't buy. In his old age he hated to spend anything. He would finger every coin, massage every dollar he parted with. He would go out of his way to save pennies, even when he was barely able to walk. When I took him grocery-shopping in Queens, I had to drive him from one impossibly crowded store to another where the broccoli was a few pennies cheaper per pound. I would fight my way into the first parking lot and then fight my way out and then in again to the equally crowded neighboring parking lot of the other grocery store. He was too weak to walk the short distance between them but still insisted on going to both stores. He would bring home dozens of napkins he had secreted from the synagogue's senior citizen lunches, as well as piles of mustard and artificial sweetener packs.

Unlike Dov and Josef, he never grew tired of life. His pursuit of money kept him focused forward on the future, on acquiring the next dollar. I wonder if it is something like what the economist John Maynard Keynes meant when he wrote, "Money in its significant attributes is, above all, a subtle device for linking the present to the future." Money in your possession is, after all, a promise that can be kept only tomorrow, when you can exchange it for something that will get you through the meal, the day, the week, the month, the year. It is a credit redeemable in a time to come. If there is an upside to my father's tight-fistedness, it is that his fixation on money tied him to the future, to the belief that it would come, and he could greet it protected by his bank account, his stocks, his T-notes.

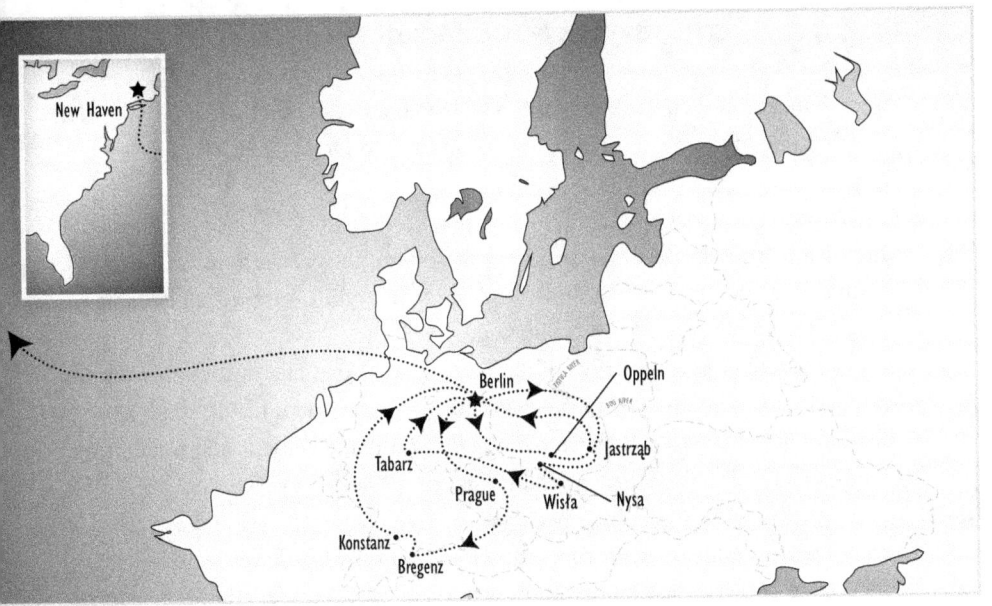

5

Eva

My mother always thought of Dov's first wife, Eva, as the *daytshe*, the German. After all that Germany had done to the Jews, he married a German. What a *dummkopf*. He got what he deserved.

My daughter asked why Eva and Katja, Dov's two wives, have sections in this book about the Seven. Until she asked, an incongruity had not occurred to me. The group called the Seven in the prison camp lasted only from the time they quit their wooden-legged uncle in Brest until Sonia left the camp for her lover—about a year, maybe less. "The Seven" is more than a number or a name, though; in the technical language of my field, it is a trope that points beyond itself. It includes not only their particular exile in the USSR but also the incalculable legacy of this time and experience even beyond the prison settlements. My Seven and yours. My cherished Seven swept up others who entered their aura and changed it. Such were Eva and Katja, who are also exiles of World War II. Neither one of them would have ever connected to Dov otherwise.

Eva was a teenager when Dov met her. From his first sight of her sunbathing on a balcony in Berlin wearing a white bikini, he was smitten. A toss of her shoulder-length blonde hair and the flash of her white-toothed smile, and he couldn't keep his eyes off her. So he said.

I remember her from my childhood. She was gorgeous. Although we were not all dark and olive-skinned—my cousins Danny and Idusha had blonde hair and green eyes—her carriage distinguished her, confident and unfaltering. Unlike the square-jawed blondes in Nazi propaganda posters, her face was a rounder oval with high, pink cheekbones. Her eyes were hazel and her teeth, a row of perfect Chiclets, were so white, whiter than any I had ever seen in real life. Of course, this was way before tooth-whiteners occupied dental-supply shelves at CVS. Her teeth seemed to sparkle with their whiteness, making me think of the old Pepsodent toothpaste ads. Perhaps you are old enough to remember: "You wonder where the yellow went, when you brush your teeth with Pepsodent." Everyone I talked to who remembered her remembered her white teeth.

She had natural blonde hair that was thick and almost straight, styled simply with a side part and held in place with a barrette. It flipped up at the bottom, First Lady Jacqueline Kennedy–style. She was a bit taller than the men in the family, maybe a little under five-six. Not tall enough to be described as "tall," but with enough height so that the brothers, including Dov, had to raise their eyes slightly when they spoke to her. Being with her felt something like having the "it" girl from high school in your family. Unlike Dov's second wife, Katja, who was clothes- and jewelry-conscious, she dressed simply. I remember straight wool skirts with jewel-necked sweaters in pastel colors and flats—preppy and understated. She had a charming, European-accented English. They all had accents and some of them were attractive, such as Dov's, but hers was a superstar European English. It sounded sophisticated to me instead of screaming "immigrant."

Eva was aware of her difference, I think. Her address to us was just a bit aloof. Coolness was the way she faced anyone—everyone, I think, not just us. There was a sense of self-containment about her, even inaccessibility. She was crisp and adamant. I think we all watched her both for the sheer pleasure of it and to see what she would do or say. I think my mother watched her with suspicion, for the hidden *Sieg heil!* in her demeanor. Eva could be sharp and cutting in her responses. She had a definite sense that children had their place—outside the adult circle. I cannot remember my mother shooing us outside so that she could talk to the other adults. Also unlike my mother, who cared about propriety, Eva's boundaries had to do with her mood. My mother may have been disapproving, but she was rarely impatient with me or my cousins. Eva was often impatient, though she was so graceful and nice to look at that, except for my mother, we pretty much forgave her.

While Lola thought Eva was cold, my father admired her penny-pinching ways. Why waste the ketchup at the very bottom of the bottle? Turn it upside down and eventually the last of the ketchup will make its way to the opening. Money doesn't grow on trees. A penny saved is a penny earned. She paid attention to the cost of things, the dollar and cents of them. What a bad match with Dov, who was incorrigibly profligate. He saved nothing. Spend, discard, and spend again. Why bother washing it yourself? Just send it to the cleaners. No need to fix the handle on that pot. Throw it away, for God's sake, and buy a new one.

When I saw her for this interview after more than fifty years, I recognized her immediately. She still sparkled with that Eva smile. Her hair was short and now not a natural blonde. Her body had thickened, but I really would have known her anywhere. She lived in a modest condo in a gated community in a Southern state that fought on the side of Lincoln during the Civil War.

Her compact living room was neat and undistinguished. Couch, two armchairs with an outsized, square coffee table in the middle of the room. On the table was some cognac in a crystal decanter. Maybe some nuts in a bowl—I have forgotten, but not much food. You know the old saying, the *goyim* always serve liquor and the Jews always serve food. I remember thinking that as I organized my tape recorder and note pad.

I could see she was ambivalent about the interview and wary. She had made some decisions about what she would say and what she would not. If a family book was being written, she felt she owed it to Dov to relate her role in his life—but was reluctant to talk about her life before and after. I did get more out of her, though. I think the cognac helped, and I can be hard to resist. Her reluctance is understandable. After all, she was not a good girl. She had an affair while she was married to Dov, and taking their daughter, she left him for her lover, whom she also discarded or who discarded her. She would not say. She was cautious, and I think she told me some lies. Or maybe that's just the way she remembered things or chose to.

What is the relationship between remembering and forgetting, anyway? What memories do you let go and what memories do you keep so that you can get on with your life and with yourself? How did Germans live with themselves once ordinary morality was recovered after the war? What pacts, silent or otherwise, did they make with themselves and with one another? In marrying a Jew, a Holocaust survivor, was Eva atoning for herself as a member of Bund Deutscher Mädel, or BDM, the girls' arm of Hitler Youth, for her father, her brother, and brother-in-law who were soldiers, for the songs and marches to Hitler, for the anti-Semitic textbooks she must have studied? Or was she just hungry, as were most postwar Berliners? And Dov, who worked for the American army, was a solid meal ticket. Was she a little bit in love with the idea of the exotic other, which Jews must have been at that time, an adolescent flirtation with the forbidden? Did he win her over with the very generosity and easy-spending ways that later seemed to her self-defeating?

The 1949 East German film *Rotation* by Wolfgang Staudte offers some ideas of the German postwar mindset, of coping with the fact that one's country lost a war fought in the name of heinous ideas. The film traces the pressures on an ordinary German worker, Hans, to join the Nazi Party, even though he is against it, in order to keep his job. Hans's brother-in-law is a communist hiding from the SS. When Hans's son Helmut, a Hitler Youth member, denounces his parents for harboring the commie, the father is jailed and the mother is killed. At the end of the war, Helmut visits his father to apologize, and Hans forgives him because Helmut is his son. It's a story that on the face of it skirts blame—all Hans wanted to do was feed his family, after all. If he had to become a Nazi to do so, who can blame him? As an ordinary worker, what did he have to do with ideology? It also grants the perpetrators forgiveness if they are sorry for their crimes. How can the Fatherland not forgive the sons who fought for it? So proposes this film. Truth and reconciliation. The problem, though, is truth and the next problem is reconciliation. Both are necessary gestures of impossibility.

Me: I don't think I've seen you in fifty years.

Eva: That's correct. More. We saw you when we arrived here in 1951. But I don't think much more often later.

"I'd like to ask a few background questions first. What year were you born, may I ask?"

"Nineteen twenty-nine, in Berlin."

"Who were your parents?"

"Now, you know what? That does not need to all be in the book, for heaven's sake."

"We're just filling in a little background. If there's something you don't want to talk about, you don't have to."

"Well, I cannot see the connection."

"Just locating you in space and time."

"Locating in Berlin. You need to tell me what kind of book you're writing."

"Okay. I'm going to turn this [tape machine] off."

I don't know what I said to her, but subsequently she answered most of my questions on tape until I asked about her leaving Dov.

"I was ten when the war started. And I was sixteen when the war was over. And I had no teenage-hood whatsoever. None. And it did not get any better when the war was over. Here we were, you know, 1945. Met Dov, I think, '46 or '47. He was twenty-seven. He's ten years older than I. The years of *my* war were not of course comparable to the heartaches yours were."

My heartaches? I can see that Eva has decided on a strategy of sympathy for the Jews during this time. She is tuned in to mainstream American attitudes toward the Holocaust and knows what attitude she should take. But she does not keep to that attitude. She is a confident woman, and she sees herself in sympathetic terms, something that comes out in the interview. She also will not excuse her betrayal of Dov. She does not show guilt or regret. By virtue of her own suffering during the war, I imagine that she feels she does not have to answer to me or to anyone. I like that about her.

"You had your own heartaches."

"I had my own heartaches. It is a very long, difficult story."

"I would like to hear it. That's why I was asking about your background, to get a sense of situating you in a family, in a place, in a moment in time."

"Situated in Berlin."

"Berlin, good. Do you have sisters and brothers?"

"I have one sister, one brother. But my sister was fourteen years older than I am. And my brother was ten years older than I am. I was the baby. *Ja.* I was supposed to save a marriage, but I didn't."

"So your parents were divorced when you met Dov?"

"Yeah. My parents divorced in 1937. Unheard of! Unheard of. Even in Berlin. I remember I was caught doing something in school, and my teacher said, 'Oh, your mother and your father have to sign this.' And when I came home, I was all bent out of shape because there was no father to sign it, so my mother had to sign her name with the word 'divorced' behind it. She was just devastated. It was tough to deal with.

"The school system in Berlin at that time was such—we're talking 1939—that when you were ten years old, you went to high school. But you only went to high school if your parents could pay for it. It was twenty marks a month. And that is just about like twenty dollars because at that time, probably a dollar and a mark was all about the same. Maybe the pound was always a little bit higher than the other currencies. So my parents paid for me to go to the First Bismarck Lyceum for Girls. And I went there when I was ten."

By 1939, German schools were affected by the many racial laws aimed at Jews. As early as 1933, the number of Jewish children attending school was restricted. An online archive kept by the Jewish Museum of Berlin and the Leo Baeck Institute shows the letter the parents of Honoria Plesch, another Bismarck student, received. Because of a new law in effect, called the Law to Prevent the Overcrowding of German Schools, the principal sent a letter to Honoria's parents to determine her Aryan credentials. The law was aimed not at overcrowding, but at limiting the number of Jewish children in the school. Honoria's family, which was Jewish, saw the things likely to come and moved to England.

About the time Eva began the Bismarck Lyceum in Berlin in 1939, Dov and the rest of the Seven left German-occupied Warsaw for exile in the Soviet Union.

"Was the school a *gymnasium*?"

"Mine was called *lyceum*. *Gymnasium* were also. But ours was *lyceum*. Guess it cost a little more. I don't know. That was probably the reason."

"Do you remember air raids while you were in Berlin?"

"In Berlin, we had a cellar in the house, and when the sirens would go off or in case of a bomb raid, we would go down into the cellar and sit there until it was all clear.

"Before I left Berlin we would always have tests in the first two periods. You know, so you're well-slept and well-rested. And so we always were hoping that we have an air raid, you know, so we're not going to have the test tomorrow because when that happened, we would go to school two hours later, so we wouldn't start until ten. So no test.

"And on the way to school, we would collect all the shrapnel, and then we would compare who got the biggest piece of shrapnel. Can you believe it? And I had a little sack where I put them in. I wish I had those; it would have been really interesting to still have them.

"My God. We were youngsters. I was eleven! That was before I left for the KLV camp.

"Dr. Goebbels had a plan. He called it *Kinderlandverschickung* [KLV]. He wanted for the youngsters to get out of Berlin. And then you ultimately lived in a setting that is very much like a—I like to call it like a boarding school. We got fed there. We had our beds there. We ate our food there. We did our homework. We had our instructions in the morning. We took walks and played games and had this and that. I mean, I loved it! I always loved it because I did not have any brothers and sisters at home. My sister had already a job. My brother was in the war. And there was just my mother and I, and she was old. She was forty when I was born. She was fifty-two when I was sent away because, now we are talking, I'm twelve. I was always in the way.

"I was supposed to save the marriage. I didn't. And now my mother has a grown daughter and this little snot-nosed young one. And I felt it every day. Because she had her life, and I was in the way. She went to the theater, so do I now. I mean it's delightful. I'm not complaining that she went to theater, but she had that life. And I was a youngster and in her way. Well, I was seven when they divorced."

Beginning in 1940, more than two million German kids participated in *Kinderlandverschickung*, including Eva. In August 1943 Reichsminister Goebbels addressed a letter "To the Parents of Berlin's Schoolchildren," making the program mandatory:

> Concern for German youths, their health and their lives demand extraordinary measures.... Effective immediately all Berlin schools ... will be evacuated.... Your cooperation will ensure that the evacuation takes place smoothly and that your children will be protected from the consequences of the enemy.

Unlike in Britain, where kids were sent away from areas vulnerable to bombing, to be hosted by volunteer families in less-populated areas, German children were mostly sent to *lagers* or camps, numbering about nine thousand. Here they had academic instruction for about four hours in the morning, and exercise, paramilitary, and indoctrination activities after lunch. KLV students traveled to these camps accompanied by their own teachers, as well as with members of Hitler Youth (HJ), who oversaw the camps.

Eva emphasizes the ordinary and rigorous curriculum she had at KLV. But it was not ordinary at all. All teachers were forced to swear loyalty to Hitler and to join the Nazi Teachers' League. A new curriculum was created that emphasized

German racist and nationalistic propaganda. The curriculum also stressed physical fitness to produce good soldiers and healthy child-bearers. Every academic subject was revised to reflect the new ideology. Biology emphasized Darwinian survival of the fittest and a eugenics that taught the superiority of the Aryan race and inferiority of the Jews and disabled. Here are two math problems from German textbooks of that era that use an appeal to self-interest to justify policies against the mentally ill:

1. The construction of a lunatic asylum costs 6 million *RM* [Reichsmark]. How many houses at 15,000 *RM* each could have been built for that amount?

2. To keep a mentally ill person costs approx. 4 *RM* per day, a cripple 5.50 *RM*, a criminal 3.50 *RM*. Many civil servants receive only 4 *RM* per day, white-collar employees barely 3.50 *RM*, unskilled workers not even 2 *RM* per head for their families. (a) Illustrate these figures with a diagram. According to conservative estimates there are 300,000 mentally ill, epileptics, etc. in care. (b) How much do these people cost to keep in total, at a cost of 4 *RM* per head? (c) How many marriage loans at 1000 *RM* each ... could be granted from this money?

KLV camps were officially governed by a sixty-page manual that directed their activities. The manual emphasized military training and military language. Children wore uniforms, and their days were strictly regulated: rise and shine at 6:30, flag salute at 7:30, academic classes from 8 AM to noon. The afternoons were devoted to Hitler Youth activities.

"So the KLV was, you know, like a godsend. I liked to just get away from my mother, really. So I was ready to go. And we went first with the KLV to Oppeln.

"And we were all there, and now started the homesickness of some of the girls. My God, they sniffled and they cried until they couldn't look out of their eyes.

"I was a happy girl. All of a sudden I have playmates. We played Mikado and rummy. We played dice and all sorts of stuff. Wonderful. But we slept on straw sacks. And the fleas were biting bad. I got horrible hay fever and have always had hay fever. But nobody had ever identified it as such back then.

"But I never cried. I never cried that I was homesick. I was *not* homesick. And some people couldn't stand it for other reasons. You know, probably food as well. I always enjoyed everything that they served. It was wonderful. Delicious.

"And then we moved as group from there to Jastrząb. That was Upper Silesia. But you know Upper Silesia was in the Polish Corridor. And the Polish Corridor went to Germany and then went to Poland. And then went to Germany and then went to Poland. And these towns they had the names that were very Polish, but at that time, it was not through occupation we were there. Anyhow, we were there probably three years or more."

Clarification: Jastrząb may have been in Silesia, but the Germans did occupy it when Eva was there. The Polish Corridor refers to a strip of land dividing the main part of Germany from eastern Prussia. It was returned to Poland in the 1919 Treaty of Versailles, which set the terms at the end of World War I, giving Poland access to the Baltic Sea. Despite the corridor's Polish majority, Germany resented Poland's control of it, and Hitler made it the pretext for invading Poland on September 1, 1939.

In his 1933 novel *The Shape of Things to Come*, the British writer H. G. Wells predicted this rationale for World War II. Believe it or not, Wells anticipated that Polish-German disagreement over this corridor would be the excuse for a second world war. This science-fiction tale, which begins in 1929 and ends in 2106, has Wells making numerous predictions, many of them wrong, including:

- Poland is well-matched militarily with Nazi Germany.
- The British stay neutral.
- The United States does not get involved on the European front.
- The war lasts until 1950 but no one wins.
- English becomes the universal language.
- All religion is made illegal.
- The world becomes a single utopian state, and each and every one of its citizens is more brilliant in all subjects than any genius in history.

Wells envisions a perfect world order in the new millennium, something that is probably no longer possible to even imagine. Postmodern philosophers no longer see history as a story of continuing improvement, as a story of incremental progress toward a utopian end. Some, like Jean-François Lyotard, attribute the disappearance of this optimistic view of history to Auschwitz, which Lyotard believes created a moral break in Western civilization from which we have not recovered. We no longer have the expectation that things, on the large scale, get better and better as time goes on. How can they, he reasons, if Auschwitz is part of our world?

"And then my sister got married," Eva continues.

"During the war?"

"Well, yeah, he was a career soldier."

A career soldier? Is she implying that he did not sign up to fight for Hitler and Aryan purity, but was already in the army, soldiering being his profession? He chose a profession rather than an ideology.

Although it is unfair to Eva, I am reminded of Aleksandr Solzhenitsyn's novel *The First Circle* about the Russian gulags for political dissidents. He describes the distinction between the language of "apparent clarity" used by totalitarian regimes to disguise their actions and the language of truth or "utter clarity." The language of apparent clarity uses vague vocabulary and the passive voice to disguise meaning, as in the statement that seems not to be about human beings at all: "The undesirable elements were eliminated," when you really mean, "The secret police shot the dissidents."

She may be evasive, but Eva is willing to talk. Postwar, accounts of the war are difficult if you are German and related to soldiers.

"I was supposed to be coming home for the wedding. And I did. This was 1941."

In the year Eva celebrated her sister's marriage, Dov, and those who remained of the Seven, left the prison settlement in Nyuvchim with great hope only to become separated and starve on a *kolkhoz* in Kyrgyzstan.

"And while I was home, my mother said, 'I have arranged it that you can stay at home.' And I said, 'I don't want to stay home.' So I went back. My mother realized that I was a happy girl there, you know. She was glad to not have me around. So it worked out very nicely.

"So from Jastrząb we were moved as group because the war was getting closer.

"This is now 1942 and the war, I guess that must have been the time when we were, when Germany was fighting in Russia. And we were on the east side of Germany, you know, and we were getting awfully close to all this fighting and what was going on. We did see of course the enormous airplanes going always over us toward Berlin and Hamburg and Dresden and all those cities, and I will never forget that sound."

"Did you have any sort of war propaganda in your school?"

"None. None whatsoever. We were just First Bismarck *schule*. Getting up, getting breakfast, classes, lunch, nap, study time, evening time. That was it."

"There was a lot of propaganda in the US about the war. Certainly, a lot of it in the schools."

"No. Good Lord, we were little, we were twelve-, thirteen-year-old children. No."

No propaganda in Germany! I vividly remember the scary Cold War propaganda as an American elementary-school student. Public service films put out by the US Civil Defense Administration warned that Russian atomic bombs were pointed at US targets, so BE PREPARED. "Bert the Turtle" from posters and civil defense films sent the message to "duck and cover" if you wanted to save your hide in case of an enemy attack.

They played propaganda clips on television and before the feature film in movie theaters that ratcheted up the fear. In one of them, called "Let's Face It," two young men at urinals with their backs to the camera are pictured hearing the air-raid siren in midstream. Properly, they crouch right there and put their arms over their heads. Can't waste a second when those Ruskie bombs are on their way. Frequent air-raid drills in elementary school provided drama and encouraged our terror of the "red scare," communism. When the siren sounded, we would duck beneath our desks with our eyes closed. We wore dog tags—a metal identity necklace similar to those worn in the military. Bodies would have to be identified in case the worst happened.

I remember one frightening afternoon trip to the library. My parents had dropped me off in town so I could pick out some books. I must have been about eleven. As I am walking down the street, sirens sound, and out of portable loudspeakers, an ominous male voice directs people off the main street of Vineland. This same voice instructed us not to look at what was coming down this wide boulevard. Brazenly, I looked anyway and, terrified, watched a very long, somber parade of military vehicles and weapons—tanks, canons, armed soldiers in trucks, one after the other after the other—all in camouflage colors. It went on for almost an hour.

There was no logic to these theatrics. "Duck and cover" as a strategy against atomic bombs? Every town had its bunkers filled with supplies in case we had to wait out nuclear fallout. But there was room only for the very few. As I daydreamed through elementary school days, I played out scenes in which I and whomever in my family I favored that day would be saved.

"The girls had groups A and B. I was in A. And there was this very typical thing that we didn't like B, and B didn't like A. And it was everywhere the same way. And you know something very interesting? The B class, they loved lipstick and rouge and powder. We didn't even possess such things. So we were always thinking, 'My God, who needs to be standing there in front of the mirror putting that awful stuff on?' You know, we were just German girls. It was really all very good."

Eva's self-presentation is a careful narrative of normal girlhood in strange times, the telling of which must have been practiced with others over the years. These children's camps were training grounds for future German citizens. Children were indoctrinated, not educated.

"Then from Jastrząb we went to Neisse, and we stayed in a convent there with the same group of girls."

"Did you know why they were moving you?"

"Further away from the front.

"So we were in Neisse, but Neisse was not the right place for us to be. It was a nun's convent. And then in Neisse when we all went to the washroom—we were the As, remember? We did not use the powder and makeup. So when we go in the washroom, we would just sort of like jump around naked and wash ourselves anywhere that needed to be washed, you know. And Mother Superior would come in her big outfit, I mean in the big habit and everything, and was appalled that we should be jumping around like naked little monkeys in there, you know. And then she spritzed us with a little water to calm us down."

"Was your family Catholic?"

"No! All in the whole school nobody was. All Protestant."

"A particular Protestant sect?"

"No. You're either Catholic or Protestant, or Jewish. And I think there was maybe Jehovah's Witnesses."

"They also got put into the concentration camps."

"Well, you know that name was mentioned in those years. I was aware of that."

Huh? By abstracting "Jehovah's Witnesses" as "that name" and "put into concentration camps" as "was mentioned" and the "Third Reich" as "in those years," Eva again makes use of the language of "apparent" clarity, a language of disguise.

"We had this little ball and we would throw it to the wall and catch it, and then I throw it again, and run and catch it, you know. All to left and right of the crucifix. And then Mother Superior comes in and she says, 'What are you doing?' Well, we are playing ball. And it was of course to her disrespectful. We never hit the crucifix. We hit the wall right and left. And the crucifix was in the middle.

"So the nuns thought we were a discipline problem. And so we moved to Weichsel. That was a fun place, too. There was big river in Weichsel. We walked across the river on these stones. you know, and ran into the woods. We played there every Sunday I think. And we went to a movie there that I remember very well, and the movie was called *Willy Birgel Reitet für Deutschland* [Willy Birgel Rides for Germany]. Willy Birgel was a very famous film star.

"There were all of these riders. There was one riding for France. There was one for the United States. And there was Willy riding for Germany. If I would find that movie, that would be fun to watch.

"It was not a propaganda of any kind. It was a real nice, you know, film. It was just a horse, and he was a jockey in the movie."

Our self-delusions can be astounding, and the repressive processes of our psyches very efficient. The film seems to be a fictional redress of the 1936 Olympics, which took place in Berlin. In these summer Olympics, Hitler's racial policies were directly assaulted by Jesse Owens, the African-American runner who won gold in the 100- and 200-meter races, as well as the long jump and as a member of the 4 x 100–meter relay team. Although Owens was accommodated with white athletes in Nazi Germany, he was segregated in the democratic United States even after his ticker-tape parade down Fifth Avenue. He was banned from the passenger elevator at the Waldorf Astoria because he was black and had to ride the freight elevator to a reception in his honor.

In *Reitet für Deutschland*, released in 1941, Willy Birgel wins an international horse-race competition for Germany. This super-patriotic, nationalistic film is an allegorical drama about the rise of Germany after World War I. It has anti-Semitic content and was banned in the United States. Its director was also banned. The film follows a captain's iron-willed recovery from a paralyzing war wound, after which he rides to victory over US and European competitors.

"After Weichsel we moved to Tabarz, and my Papa wanted to visit me there. But there was some kind of an incident. The teachers thought that since my parents are divorced, why would your father come to visit? And they called actually my mother at home. I still know that number, too—5947. They called my mother and said to her, 'Are you aware that your husband is going to visit Eva?' 'Yeah, of course he is. Yes. Yes. Yes. They going to take a little vacation together.'

"And so we were sitting in the room, and we were doing our homework, and I was reprimanded that I was doing something wrong—either I was talking or laughing or cutting-up or doing something else.

"And the teacher in charge said, 'Well, you're going to have restricted outings.'

"And I said, 'But my Papa is coming tomorrow.'

" 'Well, that's too bad because you have restricted outings.'

"When Papa came, he was downstairs and was asked to go into this little waiting room, and one of my classmates came running upstairs, and said 'Eva, Eva, Eva, your Papa is down there!' And I ran down there with my house shoes on, and I said, 'Papa! I cannot go with you. I have restricted outings. I was caught yesterday doing so and so.' So my father took me by the hand, and he absolutely abducted me right out of that house and went to his hotel. We decided we were going to Berlin. And he packed his whole suitcase full of shirts and underwear and socks. He just closed that suitcase up. He went downstairs, paid his bill, and we went to Berlin. Now that was a big deal, see, because even though it was my school and my teachers and all of my classmates, the ultimate umbrella was Dr. Goebbels from Berlin. And you don't just leave.

"So it was tough.

"So in the meantime, my sister had a baby. And I was now Aunt Eva. So my mother went to some kind of an authority and said, 'My other daughter has in-laws in Konstanz, and if we go to Konstanz, we will be taking Eva out of Berlin.' And they approved it. They agreed. So we went to Konstanz with my mother and my sister and the baby, Iris. And that was 1943. And I went to school there for a year."

As Eva went to school in Konstanz that year, Dov was drafted into the *arbet* force and sent to Chelyabinsk, where he found romance with Emma, helped build a dam, and learned to drive.

"And then I rejoined my First Bismarck *schule* in the KLV, and they were now in Czechoslovakia. So I took the train, and I carried my suitcase and got there. Everybody said, 'Hello, hello, hello.' We are all back together again. Was fun. Now it was 1944. And we were fifteen. And we were really a little bit more bored. 'My God, we are having nothing to do, nothing to do, you know. Nothing ever going on.'

"And we had a very good director, Dr. Guzinski. The only thing that he could really do for us that would be out of the ordinary and would be fun for us to do, he let us go to the movie. So we went always downtown to the movie. And we always walked home. It was so cold. Oh, God, was it cold.

"We were in a nice school there. It was probably once upon a time a real boarding school. *We* were in it, not the people from the town. But I don't recall that there was any problem."

When you are in a group of privilege, when you have unearned privilege, it does not register to yourself—only to those who do not have it. As a member of the occupier nation, she may not have noted a problem, but I'll bet that the Czech kids displaced by the KLV students in the school saw a problem.

"We were always going to town. Couldn't buy anything good. We bought onions. We bought onions and mustard. That's what we put on the bread. Onions and mustard and an extra piece of bread."

When Eva said that, I remembered that my mother had dug onions out of the hard ground in Kyrgyzstan. But Lola ate her stolen onions without bread.

In 1944, as Eva and her KLV friends experienced adolescent ennui, the Seven, except for Sonia, found one another again.

"And then my mother was sending me money, and my mother was sending me food and travel ration cards. Little rations for fat and for meat. And she wrote letters that said, 'Keep them together and keep them in a good place.' And so one day, now we are in 1945, Dr. Guzinski calls me down, and he says, 'I have here a telegram from your mother that she is very sick, and you need to go and take care of her.'"

What Eva is doing is blinking to let me know that it was a phony telegram. This is April 1945 and the war is just about over. Guzinski is telling her she should make her way home. He makes sure she knows where her mother is at the moment, which is in Konstanz, and that she has enough money and rations to get her there.

"So he said, 'Well, pack your things and go.' And he released me. And I went to Prague to buy myself a ticket to go to Konstanz. And I went to the ticket counter in Prague and asked for a ticket to Konstanz. The man there said, 'You cannot have a ticket to Konstanz because they're already occupied by the Allied forces.' And I said, 'Well, not according to my mother.'"

Eva is told she needs written permission from the KLV to keep going.

"And I asked him where is KLV located, and he told me that they are in Katedrála svatého Víta in Prague. It is a very gorgeous, enormous cathedral. And they had offices in there. So I went over there, rode the streetcar, and got over there. I was staying in the, you know, in the YMCA in Prague, and we pronounced it "IMCA." And I took the streetcar to go to the cathedral and find the person in charge that can give me a permit to get a ticket. And I went from room to room to room to room. Everywhere I told the same story over and over. And I gave up. I just broke absolutely down. I could not repeat one more time my story about why I need to have this permit to go. So I finally I found him, and he did have on one of those typical uniforms—brown with the armband for the Hitler Youth, you know. He was in charge of the Hitler *Jugend*.

"He was actually a very nice young man. But God, I was fifteen years old. I told him that I've got to have this ticket. And he said, 'I cannot give that to you. That is impossible. Because there is occupation there already.' And I said, 'On my and my mother's own responsibility. You have nothing to do with it. Just let me have a ticket, and let me see how far I get.'

"And he said that he had to check that out with Dr. Guzinski.

"I said, 'Well, why don't you?'

"And an air-raid siren came. Bombing raid. So then there's nothing doing. You can't make any phone calls, you can't do anything. And he said, 'Oh, for God's sake, I cannot take you with me into my air-raid cellar, and I would have to go with you to some kind of shelter for the public.'

"So he said, 'All right.' And as the sirens wailed, he scribbled something and gave it to me. And I was out of there. And I did go where I was supposed to go during the alarm, to a public shelter. And it was then not long. I mean bombs didn't hit. The planes were maybe just flying over or something, you know.

"And I went back to the train station and I got my ticket. And they said be there tomorrow morning at six for the train, and I was there and the YMCA gave me one sandwich. One sandwich. And so I took my sandwich and I went to the train and got into the train, and we traveled toward Konstanz. I have to change several times, but I don't remember the stations.

"I did get off the train when the train was diverted. And then I was walking through the people, people lying there and sitting there with no place to go. They were all just sitting there in these train stations. It was horrible. I did have some place to go. And therefore I did push on. There's this survival instinct that I had. So I went to someone in uniform who had a shield that meant he was 'in charge.' I mean, it said, 'Ask me. I can help.' Of course, he was not there for me, but for the soldiers. So I approached him.

"And I said, 'I need to get going, you know, and I have a ticket.'

"And just as I was standing there talking with him, he told me, 'There is no way. This is a Red Cross train. There is no way'—here come these three wounded soldiers. One with the arm hanging like in a sling. And the other one with big bandage around his head with a little red bloodstain. And the next one limping.

"And they said, 'Oh *there* is our nurse. Would you please hold on to this man here because he does not have a cane yet, and he cannot walk without her.' And they just grabbed me and let this man in charge stand there, and he did not interfere. And we just walked right into this Red Cross train. And we got one compartment. Four people, three young boys and I.

"As soon as I put my body on this seat, I was gone. I fell asleep. There's no telling how long I slept. Until they said, 'You've got to get up now because we are going now to so and so and you want to go to so and so.' So they woke me up. Can you imagine? I mean, anything could have happened. But it didn't. You know? That was the beauty of it. It did not. And so there I was. And so I got out again and got another train. Actually a train was coming that said it was going to Salzburg, a town in Austria. I got in there and then all of a sudden, big commotion, everybody off the train. They have bombed the train station. The train cannot go any farther. Tracks are torn up. Just walk.

"So here I have this little suitcase and this little carryall, and I lug them. I have to really keep up with all these people because these people knew where they were going. I needed to stay with them, so it was tough.

"And there was one young man, and he said, 'Looks like you are having a hard time carrying your suitcase.'

"Why I did not just let this suitcase go? But the only two dresses that I have were in there, you know? And I just loved that damn suitcase.

"And I said to him. 'Yeah, it's heavy.'

"And he said, 'Well, what I'm carrying I got when I walked by a big field of tobacco, and I helped myself to as much as I could put in this tarpaulin. It is fairly easy carrying. Now if you want to carry it, I will carry your suitcase; we can switch.' I was reluctant.

"He said, 'Now let me tell you something. If you run away with my tobacco, I'll keep your stuff. If I run away with your stuff, you can keep my tobacco.' I mean we are having some very comparable merchandise here you know. Okay. He did carry my suitcase. We got into the middle of Innsbruck to a collection point; it was now about twelve midnight. Dark. Not a light on anywhere. Everything was destroyed, not a light on in the town and rubble on both sides."

"Did you have any thoughts about the war while you were doing this?"
"No. No."
"About your future?"
"None. None. None, whatsoever. Survival. Only survival. So I come in there with this young man. He gives me back my suitcase, and he takes his tobacco. And he's all done and leaves me with, 'Bye, see you.'

"So I found the man there in charge of this place and he said, 'You cannot stay here. There is no way.' I said, 'Well, what am I gonna to do?' And he walked me to an enormous map of Innsbruck. He said, 'You are right here.' And he showed me.

"And then he said, 'The east train station is not destroyed. The main train station was destroyed. That's why you have to walk to the east station. And he showed me where the east train station was. 'If you walk along this street for twelve blocks and take a left, that's where the train station is.'

"It was midnight. So I take my damn little suitcase and my little carryall, and it was still cold, even it was April, and I started walking. Not a soul. I didn't even hear rats. But of course I was breathing so hard because I was never putting my suitcase down, you know. I was not stopping for nothing. And I counted. And here's block number twelve but no train station. I am thinking, thinking, thinking. I mean, you couldn't even sit somewhere without falling into rubble. It was all rubble. And nobody lived there anymore. And there was, thank God, nobody out there luring me in. I mean, I was fortunate. Unbelievably fortunate.

"So I thought, 'Well, the only thing I can think of is that I miscounted.' So I walked that whole damn street back to the beginning. And I began to think that maybe I did count a driveway as a street, and therefore, it could be one farther. I decided to take a chance that I miscounted something as a street which wasn't a street, so I walked one beyond twelve the second time. And lo and behold, there's the train station. With only one little bulb giving light to the station and lots of people who didn't have no place to go.

"It was raining, so I had a rain hat and poncho and hung this around me, and I sat down with my feet on my suitcase, and I fell asleep. Soon an officer came over to me. I have no idea what branch.

"He asked me, 'Where are you going?'

"I said, 'I try to go Bregenz. It's on the other side of Lake Konstanz.'

"He said, 'Oh, good. I'm going not to Bregenz, but I go to a town right before Bregenz.'

"He said, 'I don't want to lug my briefcase the whole time I'm scouting. Would you watch it for me?'

"I said, 'Yeah. I'll watch it.' What am I going to do with it? Where am I going to go? I mean, I was as safe as a safe. So I watched it, and he was gone. I, of course, didn't dare fall asleep now because I needed to watch that damn little thing here.

"And he came back and he said, 'Now don't say anything. Just take your stuff and follow me. I found a train. It will be coming into the train station not until eight in the morning.' By now it was maybe like five in the morning. 'But

I know on which track it is. And we can go and get a seat there. But don't talk, just follow me.'

"Which I did. And I think he actually carried my little suitcase, and I just had my satchel. And I walked and he said, 'Don't step on those tracks because they are switching, you know; you could have your leg caught right in between.' So I was careful. I stepped over. And we walked, and we walked. I mean more luck than sense I had.

"And we got there to this train, and he said, 'This is the one. Do you have second-class ticket?'

"I said, 'No, I don't. I have third class.' Well, when the man comes, 'Tell him right away you will pay. You have money?'

"I said, 'Yes, I have money.'

"He said, 'We are going to second class.' Which is soft seats, not hard seats, you know, and we went in there, and he took seat there and I took a seat there. And put my suitcase in the overhead luggage bin.

"And he said, 'At eight, we will be rolling into the station, and there will be pandemonium. The people will be rushing in here, but keep your seat. You don't have to get up. Just keep your seat.'

"And just as he said, exactly it was. And that train filled up. And then by eight, sure enough, it really left the station, all through the little ups and downs of Austria. And the conductor came, and I said, 'I have third class, but I want to pay,' and I had my money already out and everything, you know. Really, I was not dumb when I was fifteen years old. I was on the ball. I had already in my hand the money, you know? And he give me a ticket, took the money, and I had a valid, second-class ticket. Everything was good.

"And we chug along and it stopped in every little here and there, and the officer said, 'This is where I get off. This is my town. My hometown.' He had sort of deserted his unit. He was on his way home. We are talking now the twentieth of April of 1945.

"So he got off and now I was sitting there, and a big old fat lady with a little dog on her lap, she got the seat that this officer vacated. And so she took out this little sandwich, and she started eating her sandwich, and she gave always a little bite to her dog.

"And you know, my eyes must have given me away because she said to me, 'Would you like a sandwich?'

" 'Yes.' And she gave it to me. You think I ate it? No. I only ate half. There was no telling how long I'm going to be without anything to eat, you know. I cannot just wolf this all down. I'm going to put half in the pocket.

"And sure enough we arrived in Bregenz. And I did not go to the telephone, did not call anybody. I went straight into the restaurant.

"I said, 'I would like an apple juice, please.'

" 'You want something else?'

"I said, 'Yes, I do, but I've got to have an apple juice. I haven't had anything to drink probably, I don't know, for the whole two and half or so days. No water, no nothing. Nothing! Nothing!'

"And so this lady said, 'Well, this apple juice takes two sugar coupons.'

"I said, 'I've got it.' So I gave them to her, and then I drank it down.

"And then she came back, and I said, whispering, 'I would like another.'

"She said, 'You are not allowed another one but just wait. Sit still.'

"So she took my glass away, and she took the little bottle away, and she went, and all of sudden, here she comes with another bottle and another glass. And I ordered something to eat, and I'm not sure what it was because it was apple juice that was the surviving thing. And then I went and called my mother.

"And she could not believe it.

"And she said, 'Where are you?' and I said, 'In Bregenz.'

"She said, 'I cannot believe it.'

"And then, they have these big ships that go across the lake. And so I went from Bregenz to Konstanz.

"So I got there. And now it was the twentieth of April, and I heard that they have not had occupation, but that the occupation is like two villages down. And there were the Moroccans in that part of the South. Konstanz was occupied by the Moroccans. They were black with turbans.

"And so everybody that had a barrel of wine in the basement, they actually let it run down the sidewalk because they were afraid that it would create more problems. They are all so black and from the Moroccan desert. And here are these blonde girls.

"And then on the twenty-fifth, they all came in with the tanks rolling right down the street, the Moroccans right into Konstanz. But not a shot was fired. And they came with their tanks, and of course we were all just nosey. You know, we're all looking out the window, and my sister had dark hair like yours. But I have hair like this [blonde] and so I'm looking out the window, and there is a Moroccan guy marching past our house who points his machine gun at us. And my mother had just about a conniption because she thought, he will remember this house; he saw you, she said to me. You cannot look out the window. I mean she really could hardly stand it that I did that. I didn't do anything, I did not know I did anything, but I realized immediately what I had done after I looked out."

If you are a film buff, you will know Vittorio De Sica's 1960 film *Two Women*, in which the plot hinges on the gang rape of a mother and daughter by Moroccan soldiers in Italy after the Allied liberation. Rapes by the Goumiers, as these black soldiers were called, are well documented, especially in Italy, where the raped women received government compensation. A French colony, Morocco was controlled by the fascist Vichy government until the Allies invaded it in 1942. Morocco was promised independence within ten years if they joined the Allied cause, a promise on which France later reneged.

Moroccan troops also fought in the south of Germany, where Eva was, toward the end of the war, beginning in March 1945. A *New York Times* August 11, 1945, article, "Rape Story Dispute Grows in Stuttgart," gives the Stuttgart mayor's account of almost twelve hundred women reported raped by these soldiers. Rape has always been a part of war. Humiliating the enemy, seen as male, by polluting the women who reproduce the nation is an ancient military strategy—sometimes a formal strategy and sometimes, as in this case, informal. Rape is a crime of power, not of sex. The authorities just turn a blind eye. You attack the enemy psychologically at the same time that you invade their gene pool. Rape is more likely, more frequent, more violent if the enemy is culturally different, according to Keith Lowe, a historian. Imagine, after all the German propaganda about *Untermenschen* (inferior races), the extreme attitudes of the Goumiers, as well as the Russians, who were brutal toward German women, whether eight or eighty years old.

American soldiers were not exempt from this form of victors' tribute. In a book called *What Soldiers Do*, Mary Louise Roberts reveals this side of GI conduct, long kept underground. Another book, *An Unpatriotic History of the Second World War* by James Heartfield, quotes an American general reporting that: "In the regions occupied by the Americans, women no longer dare go to milk the cows without being accompanied by a man. Even the presence of a man does not protect them. In the Manche a priest has been killed trying to protect two young girls attacked by American soldiers. These young girls were raped."

The ironies of history are truly depraved: While GIs across ethnicities and races raped French, German, and British women, the GIs prosecuted for these crimes were largely black.

I asked Eva whether there were problems with the Moroccan troops.

"Yeah, yeah. Was a lot of that, unfortunately. And there were several horrific murders, ritual murders, where there was no blood left in the corpse. I mean I have no idea what kind ritual it was, but they warned us. There was the warning that there is some kind of a holiday, Moroccan holiday approaching, not to go, not to violate a curfew. Stay in your house. And there were awful things that happened."

This ritual murder story is a variation of the blood libel myth usually targeting Jews. From the Middle Ages on, Jews have been accused of using the blood of murdered Christian children to bake matzo on Passover. Eva's Nazi indoctrination seems unwitting and totally unconscious—Jews, blacks, all the inferior people melted into one homogenous group.

"How did you get back to Berlin?"

"And so we are there now in Konstanz, and our apartment in Berlin is occupied by somebody. A family of squatters."

"Did you own that apartment?"

"No, and there were squatter's rights. You found this apartment empty and stayed there until the end of the war. With our furniture in it. And my Aunt Renate, my mother's sister, she was living in the east sector of Berlin. But at that time there was no wall separating East from West Berlin. You could go back and forth with S-Bahn, the metro. And she would go periodically to see if the squatters had left.

"In 1946, January, she told us they have moved, and if you want your apartment back, you have to come now. Would you believe my mother and I got on the train without papers? I mean, you paid your ticket, but without a paper to go back to Berlin? Crazy! And my mother, when the conductor came, and she needed to show her papers, she showed the ticket, and he said, 'Papers, too, you know.' She had a pocketbook and she just pretended to be busy finding the papers, and she sort of looked up a couple of times when the conductor was looking away, and she was giving me the sign to 'move away' to a seat he had already finished with. And she was just digging. And that conductor let her dig and left the compartment. And we were able to go back to Berlin. And then that was winter of 1946, the hardest winter in fifty years in Berlin. You can find that in your history books, the coldest winter in fifty years. And we were without glass in the windows in that apartment."

"What did you do? Did you start to burn the furniture?"

"Well, actually the squatters burned our table, but that's the only thing that burned. They left the rest. And now we are freezing our butts off."

Around January 1946 Dov and my parents were probably back in Poland, in Stettin, occupying the apartment of expelled or fleeing Germans.

"And so what are you all thinking about the larger context, the end of the war? What is the conversation?"

"Do you know what? No. We were numb. Defeated. Numb. Hardship. And happy to have gotten away as well as we had."

My mother Lola's words about the move to Berlin that spring while Eva and her mother faced hunger, scarcity, fear, and the humiliation of Germany's defeat form a strange counterpoint: "In Berlin we start to live," said Lola. The contradictions and reversals of horizontal history.

"Your father, where is he?"

"He is in Russian prisoner of war camp."

"Was he in the Eastern front?"

"No! He was in Berlin the whole time. In 1945, he was fifty-five. He fought in World War I. He was a veteran. And one with a life-long injury. They shot him in the belly and he wore a corselet all his life, which had like a packet to hold everything in there."

"How did he become a POW?"

"Well, he was supposed to guard the street, and so he comes out of his house with his rifle when he sees a Russian tank in the middle of the street. So then of course they took him, you know. And he went to this prisoner of war camp. And he was always a very big man. He was always in like the two-hundred-pound range. He was six foot, two or so. He went during the war down to maybe one-eighty, which was still pretty big, you know. And then he went all the way down to maybe ninety pounds when he was a prisoner of war. You didn't get but soup and then you got diarrhea. You know, it was awful. He told me one time that he traded his piece of bread for a book because he wanted to have some paper. He couldn't stand it that he had no paper, you know, for his bathroom visit. He rather not have the bread. That was what he was like.

"So now I go again to First Bismarck *schule*, but all my classmates are one grade ahead of me. Oh, my God. So I was wondering, I don't think I want to do this. You know? Now I'm seventeen, and I feel too old for this.

"So my mother said, 'Now why don't you enroll yourself into the Berlitz School?'

"Now I have had English for six years in high school. In all the time, wherever we were, we had English, French, Latin, physics, chemistry, mathematics. It was big time, very, very academic, like a junior college.

"And so I enrolled in this Berlitz School and we went there every day. And I met Marlene and Ursula in my class. They were two friends; each of them had an American 'friend.' And they asked me, 'You have a boyfriend?' I said, 'No, God.'

My brother is still a prisoner of war; my brother-in-law is still a prisoner of war. My father, too."

"Where did your brother fight?"

"My brother fought in the front of Stalingrad. But then he got wounded. When he got well, then he fought in Normandy, and he was a prisoner of war in England."

"So I have a brother and brother-in-law and father, all of them are still in prisoners-of-war camps, and there is something about my school, the Bismarck. We were a little bit snobs in that school.

"You just don't fraternize with the occupation forces because you know we're the losers here. And this is, you know, I mean, there is a little bit of honor left.

"You know, I mean, we are young, we had nothing to do with anything, and we felt pretty innocent.

"But when Marlene and Ursula said, 'We gonna have a party on such and such a date. Why don't you just come?' Well, I thought to myself, I can certainly go to a party, you know? I would like to eat something.

"They bring sometimes little Hershey bars to school."

"From the Americans?"

On a website of old magazine articles, I found an article from a July 1945 issue of *Yank*, "The Look of Berlin," by Sgt. Merle Miller. About halfway down the first column of the article, Miller writes, "The prettiest young girls are in the handful of bars and night clubs now open.... Their love is very reasonable compared to the French and English variety, however. Five cigarettes is the standard rate of exchange."

"From their boyfriends, yes. And so they always ate that. And I probably one day was really sort of like pissed that they never offered me the first piece. I mean there are little ridges in it. You can break them. You know? And you can give me one little square maybe? Oh, no. Well, I didn't really make a judgment about their boyfriends, but I was miffed nevertheless. And I probably said one day that I sure would like to have a piece of their chocolate. And from that day on, they actually shared it with me.

"I did make it perfectly clear I was not interested in a boyfriend—in an American boyfriend. And she said to come to the party anyway. It may have been something of a Fourth of July, I don't know. It was not our holiday. It was their holiday. I took the S-Bahn. And I walked down the street, and I found the number. And I walked in and there was, you know, a *beautiful* Boxer dog."

"Whose apartment was this?"

"This was the apartment of Ursula with her friend Murphy. Now he was actually an American occupation administrator. I don't know if Murphy was his last name or first name; he was always just Murphy. He was much older than she was. But they had this gorgeous Boxer dog. So she goes in the kitchen and opens this can of salmon. And gives it to the dog. And I just died. Right there I wanted to say, 'Move over, dog.'

"However, there were things to eat, plenty, and it was nice. There were lots of people there. And so I don't even remember if we played cards or danced, or had just music, or just talked, or whatever it was. But anyhow, we were all happy, was a very pleasant day.

"And here comes this man and says, 'Murphy, do you want to go somewhere?'

"And Murphy said, 'No. I think I'm just going to stay here. Why don't you have a seat, Dov? Just have a seat; stay here, too. We're having a party.'

" 'Oh, thank you,' he says. So Dov, Murphy's driver, also sat down and also was a guest in the party."

"Did you have a white bikini on? Because that's how Dov remembers first seeing you—with a white bikini, a blonde with a white bikini on a balcony."

"Oh, really? I had forgotten that. I remember him, however, saying, 'My God, you have white teeth?' And then, 'You're so tall.' He didn't say anything about the blonde hair, I don't think. It's now not my very own blonde, but it was then."

"What was your first impression of Dov?"

"Of Dov? He was shy and so unsure of himself. I felt for him sort of sorry because I felt like he was the driver for this man, and yet he was not one of them, you know? I have no idea how this arrangement was money-wise. I don't know by whom he got paid, never did find out, never really. But he was nice enough. And he was probably attentive and probably got me a drink when my glass was empty. And I do remember something. He had too much to drink, and we had to put him to bed. And when I took his jacket off, it was difficult, you know? And I had it sort of upside down, and a condom fell out of his pocket."

"And you knew what that was?"

"Yeah. Because the S-Bahn had it in machines. So it always said, '*Danke schön*, VD is not what you want.'

"But I think he probably did ask me out. And I remember we went somewhere, and we drank a little chocolate liqueur. Or something similar to what we now have, Bailey's, you know. *Very* delicious. And my God, was it good! 'I would like another one, please.' And I did get another one, and then I think Dov wanted to order even a third one, and the owner—it was just a little-bitty old place—he said, 'Not for this girl. She has had two; she doesn't need anymore,' you know? And I remember that little liqueur every time I drink a Bailey because that richness of cream and chocolate. You know? Oh. Delicious."

"So we're now at the courtship of Dov and Eva."

"Oh. The courtship of Dov and Eva. Oh. Let's see. Well, bad luck followed him around everywhere. And it was exasperating. Really, how can anybody always be that unlucky with everything?"

"How was he unlucky? You're just dating now, and he was unlucky even then?"

"Yeah, because he came to me with this car from Murphy, and he parked the car in the front. And when he came down, the car was stolen. And it was stolen by someone who conned him. This man had bought a license for Dov for the car so that Dov could drive it, and Dov paid the man for the license. And then this very same man came and took the car and said, 'It's my car,' even though it wasn't. So Dov lost that car and it was, I guess, Murphy's car.

"Okay, our courtship. Dov had a friend, Simon. He had a girlfriend whose name was Margot. And we used to hang out together on Saturday nights. It was nice enough. It was good."

Margot is now in her nineties and, like Dov's second wife, Katja, has Parkinson's disease. Unlike Katja, who lives in a nursing home, Margot lives in a house in Long Beach. Her daughter and son-in-law, who live in New York City, visit her every weekend. She has a very gentle caretaker and neighbors who check up on her. Her account of those times is much sunnier than Eva's. She loved talking about her youth, about her romance with Simon, the Polish-Jewish refugee from the Schlachtensee DP camp who, after immigrating to the United States, came back to Berlin and married her because he could not live without her. They left Berlin in 1951 as a married couple on the SS *Washington*, a former troop transport. Her family was Protestant; they owned a barbershop and, she said, were anti-Nazi. She was a few years older than Eva and a hairdresser in those times.

At the age of eleven, Margot was chosen to carry the Olympic flag in the 1936 Olympics in Berlin because she was a good student and she was tall. She knows Hitler was there, although she does not remember seeing him. In a trick of memory, she does recall seeing Pavlova—Anna Pavlova, the sublime Russian prima ballerina—dance on the Olympic lawn. I could not find a reference to Pavlova at the 1936 Olympics anywhere, and what she may be remembering is Sonja Henie, the Norwegian figure skater who had studied with Pavlova. Henie won the 1936 figure-skating Olympic gold medal with her "Dying Swan" performance, modeled on Pavlova's most famous dance, *The Dying Swan*, and performed to the music of the Saint-Saëns cello concerto. Henie lost some public favor when a picture of her shaking hands with the Führer at the games was published.

Simon helped organize a DP camp soccer team, which included Dov, and they became so good that they played a match with the British soccer team in the Berlin Olympic stadium. I cannot get enough of these ironies of history. Here they fall out as comeuppance. When they are not punitive, the gods must laugh at us.

I asked Margot about all these now-orphaned Jewish boys romancing German girls after the war. She did not know what the Jewish boys thought about their being German. Simon and the others did not say anything about it. She said the children who grew up during the war were victims, too. Traumatic victims, she said, needed someone to hold them and support them. If they could find a little happiness, they took it. She was talking about those like her and those like Simon, too.

Once she married Simon, she converted to Judaism. They raised their daughter in the Jewish faith, and Margot covered her head, as did my mother, and lit candles every Friday night to welcome the Sabbath. After lighting the Sabbath candles, my mother would recite the prayer with her eyes closed. *Barukh atah Adonai Eloheinu, melekh ha'olam, asher kid'shanu b'mitzvotav v'tzivanu l'hadlik ner shel Shabbat.*

Committed to the man, Margot converted. Simon, Margot said, would never have converted from Judaism, even though the Holocaust experience made him doubt God. "Where was God?," the familiar cry of Holocaust victims and survivors, was also Simon's. She said he slowly came back to religion.

But those Saturday nights with Margot, Eva, Simon, Dov, and others at the Orangerie, a small Berlin nightclub on the Hauptstrasse, offered a bit of postwar glamour. An old postcard pictures it with a vaulted ceiling and double rows of table-clothed, round tables lining each side of the narrow "dance café," as the postcard calls it. A fussy rug runs down the long center of the room. It is here that the couples would dance. They danced, said Margot, "*die ganze Nacht*"—all night long—until 4 AM. In those days there was a telephone on each table, and if you liked the look of someone, you could call them up and ask to come over for a drink or a waltz.

I once had a beer delivered to me in a dancehall in Louisville, Kentucky. I have used the incident in the teaching of semiotics, the study of signs and symbols. I was at a conference with a good friend of mine, and we heard of a place for live country music. It turned out to be an enormous barnlike venue with locals in cowboy hats and boots and leather belts with elaborate buckles—both men and women. Signs directed people entering the hall to surrender their guns until they left. They danced the two-step in a big circle around the perimeter of the dance space. I have never seen anything like it. A swirl of blue jeans doing intricate swings and turns as they glided so smoothly around the dance floor that they could have been ice skating. During the musicians' breaks, an enormous screen dropped from the ceiling, and on it was a two-stepping armadillo.

None in my group dared try to dance. The three of us sat at a square table drinking beer on tap and also drinking in the scene. The empty chair had its back to the dance floor. Next to it sat my girlfriend's male colleague, and she sat next to him. Then me, between my girlfriend and the empty chair. As a way of introducing semiotics, I ask my class in literary theory to guess to whom the beer was sent. The answer requires them to read the signs of the situation: boy, girl, girl. Who gets the beer from the stranger? They usually get it and ask if it really happened. Once, a smart-assed student said that the guy got the beer. Everyone laughed, including me. This venue, though, was exclusively hetero; the guy would not have been gifted the beer or swept onto the dance floor. The semiotics of giving and receiving beer in this case had little flexibility. That's what the guns are about, no? Although they may be surrendered at the door, they still police behavior. At the Orangerie there also must have been protocols regarding the phone calls made from one table to another, protocols shaped by the Allied occupation.

Margot tells the story of how Dov did the driving when the couples went out. He always had a full car. Once there were so many people that an axle broke. Like his father, Dov could not say no. His generosity was untempered by common sense, and he was young and in love.

"And then we had, of course, we had the airlift. And if we didn't succumb before, we almost succumbed then.

"It was so hard. Well, the Berlin airlift succeeded because there was a very interesting rationing of things, including electricity. And every household in Berlin was rationed, with the exception of the occupying forces, who had all the time electricity. We had only two hours every day for us. And every week, the hours would change. So this week we would have electricity from eight to ten in the morning. Next week ten to twelve. Next week twelve to two. On, on, on, and on, until you got into the midnight sessions. And we would wake up at two in the morning just to turn on the light, and do a little ironing, and do a little this and do a little that—listen to the radio and do stuff. And then at four o'clock, it went off. And there was no light until tomorrow. For a whole week we had between two and four in the middle of night.

"So when one would take the S-Bahn and go into Tempelhof, where the Americans were located, there were lights from this end to that end. There was not one person, it seems like, that turned off a light even in the bathroom. Because the whole building from top to bottom, every light was on. There was not one damn bit of consideration, probably did not even know, that we didn't have any."

Tempelhof Airport was the center of the Berlin airlift. Stalin turned it over to the US army in July 1945 as part of the American zone of Berlin. The Potsdam Agreement, a month later, formalized the division of the city of Berlin into four occupation zones—Soviet, American, French, and British.

Berlin, though, was in Soviet-controlled Germany, which was itself divided into four Allied occupation sectors. In 1948, in an effort to put all of Berlin within his purview, Stalin decided to blockade all land and water access to the Berlin zones that were controlled by Western powers, thus halting the supply of food, fuel, and other essentials to the city.

The Western Allies successfully resisted this strategy by launching an airlift, in which US and British forces joined with those from Australia, Canada, and even New Zealand and South Africa to provide for the Berliners. The blockade created hardships, which Eva describes, but the airlift succeeded in keeping the West in Berlin. During the blockade, my father moved us from Berlin to Frankfurt, so we did not suffer. The Western Allies became increasingly efficient at delivering supplies, so Stalin lifted the blockade about a year after it began. Afterward, Berlin, as well as Germany as a whole, was split into East and West until German reunification in 1990.

So Tempelhof was a happening place during that time—the center for Operation Vittles, the American nickname for the airlift. Children gathered by the airport fence to wait for the Candy Bomber or, in German, *der Rosinenbomber*, Gail Halvorsen, a Utah-born air force pilot who would parachute candy to them before he landed.

"Now I have to admit it was glorious and it was unbelievable that these planes flew every five minutes! And they also shipped in everything that we ate because we did not really grow anything there.

"They shipped food in big burlap sacks. And when it arrived, somebody told us to use our ration card, the coupon that says 'A.' Use that coupon 'A' to get one pound of what looked like dried carrots. And we went to the store with our coupon 'A' and bought two pounds for Mother and me. And we came home, and we cooked it like one cooks carrots in water, right? We had to hold on, so we were determined to make it work. Well, it was, gosh, it was absolutely awful. Your morale is already taxed with the blockade. And add to that that we are getting something to eat that is not eatable. What are they sending us? Is it like pig food or something like this?

"You know what they shipped us? They shipped us dried sweet potatoes, which is beautiful if you know what that is. And you can make with it like a mashed potato, and they would be sweet, and it would be nourishing. It would be delicious.

"We did not know how to salvage it because once you strain the water off, it's nothing but mush. You don't know what to do with it.

"Then we had a couple of more incidents like that. On your coupon 'B' you can get a pound of what we thought was dried pea soup. And we have in Germany a pea soup that is actually more or less like an instant pea soup. It looks yellow. So we thought we're gonna get pea soup. A pound each. And we go home, and we do it again. Well, it was impossible.

"And guess what it was? Cornmeal. Nobody in Germany has ever heard of or eaten cornmeal or sweet potato. Nobody paid any attention to what people are accustomed to eating and what people are accustomed to cooking."

"Dov remembers that when he met you, you were starving. And your family was starving."

"We sure were. Absolutely. And we were cold. At that time I was going to school at Berlitz, and once there were these people milling about. And I said, 'What's going on here?' And there was one man, some entrepreneur, who had gotten from the Charité, a very famous hospital in Berlin, he had gotten hold of all of the old X-rays in the hospital and with his little chemicals is taking off all the pictures on the X-rays, and now he has clear see-through plastic. And I bought two for the windows in our house.

"But then they froze over and were thick with ice.

"And then we got a stove, and we hooked that up into the big chimney, tapped into it, but we had nothing to burn in that stove.

"So we went down and we bought at some place, where they were selling, sawdust. And we put that sawdust in the stove, and all we had in our apartment was smoke. And then on these connections into the chimney, they all leaked with little brown drops—right on our carpet.

"So what we decided, we just going to go to bed, and my mother went actually into the cellar and got the old featherbeds out of the old container down there. And we laid under the featherbeds, and we just read and didn't get up and didn't do much.

"And then one day my mother said, 'Well, we can go to the bakery today and get our new ration cards, and with it some bread, if we go and get the ration cards.' And I said, 'I'm not going.' I was so hungry. I had no energy. I was not interested. I just slept. You know, dying of hunger is a very nice death. Does not hurt. It really is. And I kept saying, 'I'm not going.' And she said, 'Yeah, we have to go.' We had not even water in the house.

"And we hadn't eaten probably in, I would say, three days. We had in our cabinet the cornmeal, and we had in our cabinet those dried sweet potatoes. Didn't know what to do with them. And it was so cold, and you had only this damn sawdust that we went with this old baby carriage to pick up.

"And it was again a very cold winter, the winter of 1948–49. So she went and got the ration cards, and then on her way home she went to the bakery and she got rolls, and she had them in this little net. No bag, just the rolls, and when she came into the room where my bed was, and she just held those little rolls to show me that they smelled good. I had no appetite. I'm not hungry. And she insisted somehow that I eat one. And of course as soon as you do that, if you do get that down, then you want to eat all ten. Then you feel your hunger again. And so it was so terribly tough."

"So it was in that context that you met Dov."

"That's right. And that's why it was so terrible that I saw that this dog was fed a tin of salmon. And that hunger, you never forget it either. You probably know, your mother knew that hunger."

"My mother knew it very well."

"Once you have hunger, you will never forget it."

"Yes. So that was your situation when you and Dov met."

"So we dated probably a year or so, and then the big thing was that your father and Dov and Lola, they wanted to go to Israel. And so, I said, well if that's what we are going to have to do, that's what we are going to have to do. Because it was not getting any better in Berlin. And then when I said that I would be going, then everybody changed their mind and said, 'No. We're not going to do that. We're going to go to America.'

"And then I told my father, and he said, 'Now, my dear girl. All you want to do is eat better. And I think you need to just stay right here and things will get better.'

"But you know, when we are young, we always know better. But he did have it right. It took me ten years to realize that what he said was really true. And he also said another very true word, which was, 'People who immigrate put forth an enormous effort to succeed. If they would apply that same effort in this country, they would succeed even more.' He was right. I was so young then. So dumb I did not know."

"Are you saying you married Dov to eat better?"

"No, we wanted to immigrate to eat better."

"Why did you marry Dov?"

"Why did I marry Dov? Well, that's a very good question that lots of people asked me, especially my family. He was shorter than I was. He was ten years older than I was. He was of a different religion. From a different country.

"I don't know; there was sort of a soft spot. I felt really so bad for him. I felt a lot of ill had been done to him by the German government to his life. He could not find his parents. He could not find his youngest brother. It all really bothered me a great deal. And really, I needed to do something for this man to make it better. And he was so pursued by bad happenings. I could not imagine how anybody all the time had that bad luck. Always. All the time!"

According to Eva, he never got the money for the stolen sewing machines that he illegally transported, an escapade that landed him in prison as a spy. His so-called contacts not only stole the sewing machines but also the truck they came in. When he finally returned to Berlin, he had to face Murphy, who somehow got him off the hook. Had he had the money, he might have been able to bribe his own way out of the mess.

"He was very much in love with you."

"Well, it was probably very flattering, you know. And then we got married.

"We married the fifth of November 1949; the airlift was over. And we had Lara in 1950. You and your parents greeted us in New York there when we arrived.

"Dov was so damn sick on the ship. He would not come up for air. And I was there with a child, and I was of course lucky enough to be in this officer quarters. What was done for the first time when we immigrated, troops were always shipped into Europe and Germany. And the troop ships were always sent home empty. So somebody in higher echelon said to let these people who want to immigrate go back on these empty troop ships. We were the first ones that did that.

"And we arrived on the Labor Day, Pier 62, I think, and they were not working on Labor Day. So they left us out there looking onto New York with all the cars, and I said, 'Where are all these people going? It's two in the morning. And they're still running back and forth.'"

"How old was Lara?"

"She was ten months old. She was born in Schweinfurt because we were at this immigration camp. I lived for about the last three months with my sister and the child. And Dov would come and visit on the weekends because he was working in Frankfurt."

"Doing what?"

"Still driving. A Miss Deutsch, I think. Heavyset lady. Yeah, we were not pregnant when we said we wanted to go America. And by the time we got here, she was ten months old. See, we really had to do everything twice. When we were first approved, I was pregnant. And then when she was born, now we are three. So you had to start all over again. And now we had a child who had to have a passport. Had to have all of these shots. So we were delayed very much by that.

"But I had a dry birth. At the immigration camp, we were in this room; we were probably five couples, ten people. All husbands and wives in one room. So we all did go to bed and by three AM I knew that I was in labor. And this enormous American truck, I mean it was, like an eighteen-wheeler, I had to step in there. Dov was there too, though. And we drove to the hospital. And we got there a little after three in the morning, and it was the third of December. So this was Sunday, early Sunday morning.

"And when we came in there, and the nurse looked at me, she said, 'Well, it is not going to be a Sunday child.' So they put me in the delivery room and just left me there. So there I was in this cold room on this gurney.

"And I said, 'I like to have an aspirin, please. Can I please have something?'

" 'No, nothing. Why?'

" 'Because I'm hurting. I don't care to hurt like this.'

"They gave me nothing. So they just left me there, and then comes the cleaning woman at seven in the morning. And you know these delivery rooms are tile and have all these little step stools and bedpans, and everything that's down there is all on the tile floor. And when she mopped, she pushed everything with the loudest of noises. This way, you know, and that way.

"I said, 'I don't want to do this anymore. I don't care what's going to happen. I don't want to do this anymore. I don't care what's gonna happen. I don't want to do this anymore.'

"Nobody paid any attention. And then, finally, comes in the midwife. And I said, 'I want to have something, please.'

"'We're gonna be just fine.'

"I said, 'I am not fine.'

"I couldn't win. Didn't give me nothing. So I had a dry, natural birth and that took care of my childbearing.

"I ain't gonna do that again. So that was that. But when I left there, when I left the hospital, I wore the same skirt that I wear before I got pregnant.

"I only had one skirt. And I knit two tops. One in green and one in red. All I had.

"So I went to America with a ten-month-old baby, and I had a very nice cabin with another lady with two little boys.

"Lara was the smallest on the ship. And there was nothing for her to eat. So I went to the kitchen, and most of those cooks were black in the kitchen, and I ask one if he would cook some rolled oats. And I said, I can deal very nicely with some milk on it, and I had some powder for a bottle. And he always cooked me oats and actually found some kind of jars of little baby food of some sort. And she ate that and enjoyed that.

"One day when I went up there to the cook to get Lara's food, I said, 'My husband is so sick down there; what am I going to do?'

"And he said, 'I can give you a lemon.'

"And I went down there in the bowels of that ship where Dov was in a big room with other men. And everybody was hanging over this barrel, and I said, 'What are you doing here? You're getting only sicker.' I mean I got sick just being there.

"I said, 'Come on; get some fresh air, and sit in the cold wind. Put on your coat and just have some fresh air in your lungs. And here is a lemon and just move it.' I was not leaving him.

"'Just go in front of me upstairs.' And he did.

"And I, the one that always got car sick, I was not sick. But I had to take care of Lara, see. Always mind over matter, you know? If I would have been sick, who would have taken care of her? And Dov hanging down there over that big barrel.

"And we were on the high seas for five days and arrived on Labor Day."

"Who was on the boat?"

"They are other displaced persons from the DP camp. All immigrants, and some war brides and other people. Displaced persons."

"Did you feel like a displaced person?"

"No, but I had a very hard experience in that respect, and my family really never wanted to forgive me. When I married Dov, I lost my citizenship."

"Your German citizenship?"

"And I was stateless. Well, that's the way the cookie crumbles. So I was stateless until I became an American citizen in 1957. I was not a war bride. War brides only had to wait three years. Immigrants wait five years. And by the time five years were up, you have to live for the past six months in one county. Well, the last six months, we lived in two counties. Every time my time was up, I made big mistake of the laws of the immigration, you know?"

When Eva married Dov, her legal identity merged with his. According to law, once she was Mrs. Dov, she acquired his national identity. Since the nineteenth century, US law, like that of many nations, based women's citizenship on marriage. If she married a foreign man, a woman lost the citizenship to which she was born. Western democracy lives on the myth of the universal citizen, but not on the actuality. Not all citizens are equal. Men did not lose their citizenship when they married foreigners. For a long time a woman could not reclaim her US citizenship birthright even if she divorced the foreign national and wanted to come back to the land of her birth.

"We stayed with your mother and father for a few days before we went to New Haven. And they took us out that first evening to the Radio City Music Hall."

"That was my mother's favorite place."

"That is a nice place. And we saw, with Ava Gardner, *Show Boat*."

The film Eva saw was the 1951 remake of an even earlier film based on the play. *Show Boat* opened on Broadway in 1927 in the era when eugenics dominated explanations of race. Eugenics, or "the study of hereditary improvement of the human race by controlled selective breeding," according to the online Free Dictionary, was used as the scientific justification to sterilize black women in the United States and by the Nazis to sterilize, euthanize, and murder various groups, such as Jews, the disabled, and the mentally challenged. *Show Boat* was written by two Jews, Jerome Kern and Oscar Hammerstein, during the golden age of Broadway musicals. While annual Nazi Party rallies, beginning in 1923 in Nuremberg, did not catch the attention of US newspapers, this show talked against racial prejudice at a time when Jews were considered a race.

So many Broadway and movie musicals by Jews had plots or subplots about racism. In *Show Boat*, a subplot has a Southern sheriff threatening to close a performance on a Mississippi River showboat because one of the stars is mulatto and married to a white man. The white man makes a small cut on his wife's arm and drinks the blood so that he can honestly tell the sheriff that he has black blood, too. In this way, he was not violating the sheriff's rules about miscegenation, and the show could go on.

Right off the boat from postwar Germany, Eva, a BDM girl with a brother and brother-in-law who fought for Hitler, and who must have been questioning her sanity after the debacle with Dov's seasickness on the ship, was exposed to a big-screen lesson in racial tolerance in *Show Boat*. Like everyone else, though, she delighted in the fluff of the music.

"We had been on the boat five days on high seas, plus two days in the harbor because they had all holiday, the Labor Day. So when I was walking down that middle aisle of that Radio City Music Hall, I walked just like a drunken sailor. My body, my nerves, was still floating on the boat.

"And we saw the Rockettes and the man on the big organ. Then a few days later, we went to New Haven, Connecticut, and HIAS arranged a nice little room with a window in a house.

"Then Dov had a job in a printer shop for a dollar an hour. And I'm gonna tell you a story of 1951 which is really worth recording. In 1951 there were tax-free for each member of your family thirteen dollars. Thirteen dollars per person tax-free. He made a dollar an hour and worked forty hours. After the thirteen dollars, we paid twenty cents' tax on each dollar. And we felt very rich. With forty dollars, we went to the store and bought five dollars' worth of groceries and could hardly carry the bag, it was so big. And it was very good.

"We went and looked for apartments in the newspaper, and we would go around. And we always wheel there the carriage, you know? No car. And most of the places were so bad, I said, 'No, no. We don't even to ask here. We don't even need to ask there.'

"So we went down one street and was cute little house. And so I went to the window, and I did look in there, you know? And I came back and I said, 'Keep on walking, can't afford it.' We had learned that you can only pay a quarter of your salary for rent. So forty dollars a month is quarter of the salary. He made forty dollars a week, so you pay forty dollars a month for rent. So I said, 'Just keep on going. We can't afford.' But cute little garden in front. Very nice.

"Lo and behold, the owners of this house saw me peeping in there. And they came running out and caught up with us and said, 'You're looking for an apartment?'

"'Yes.'

" 'Well, we saw you looking in the window.'

" 'But we can't afford it,' I said, before I even asked how much it was. I was just assuming.

"And she said, 'Well, how much can you pay?'

" 'Well, we have learned already, by word of mouth from everybody around us, you can only afford a quarter of your salary, and he makes forty dollars, and we can pay only forty dollars.'

"She said, 'Sold.'

"So we got it. And that made us really happy. That was really good. And now we could really sort of like settle down. Was really cute. Had only two rooms plus a bath and a kitchen. Was good.

"So I went down there to Yale University, and I inquired if I could type some thesis for the students. Oh, yes, they have need for that all the time. And I said, I'll get myself a typewriter. I'll be back as soon as I have a typewriter. I had to find a way to earn the money for it.

"So I saw this little ad in the paper for a job in an ice cream parlor. So I needed to go and find where that was, you know. And I wheeled my child down the Dickwell Avenue, which is a black street. I kept on walking, and I kept on walking. What can I do? I mean I was wanting to see if I could have that job, you know? And I got there to the ice cream parlor.

"And the manager said, 'Do you have experience?' and I said, 'No.'

" 'Well, start tomorrow.'

"I'm not sure if we had the Studebaker by then, but we had this little car that fell apart every time we got in it, but it did have four wheels, you know. I think that Dov brought me to work.

"So I come in there and my boss says, 'Our biggest business is when the movie is out, and we are serving ice cream after the movie.' And he said, here is strawberry. And this is sundae and this is soda and this is the banana split. God, I have never heard of any of it in all my life. I had never gone to the American base like Ursula, you know? I had no idea what I was doing. And I thought to myself, 'Good lord, how hard can it be to dish out a scoop of strawberry ice cream and put syrup on top of that? Cherry on top.' So I did that, and in comes the crowd. And I was doing pretty good.

"This was only from six to nine, was part time. And so the crowd comes in. And working hard as we can, just two of us. And the owner, of course, he was also assisting. And here was this cute man with his wife; he wanted a banana split. Oh, God! I remember, however, one scoop of each—chocolate, red, and white ice cream, you know? And then you have all the three sauces over there, and then comes all this whipped cream. And then comes the cherry on top, little nuts and everything. I got it together, and I put it in front of him. And he says, 'Where's the banana?'

" 'Oh, Lord!' So I said, 'Can I give it to you and put it on the side?'

" 'Of course you can.'

"He gave me a quarter tip! I was never so happy in all my life. I got a quarter tip for a mistake. I thought that showed a little bit of the American empathy. They really have a totally different way of looking at things than other places in the world, for that matter. And so, the next day, while we were having to prepare everything, I was talking to this young lady I worked with. I was telling her where I came from, and she said, 'What, you're only this in country three weeks?'

" 'Yeah.'

"And she said, 'Man.'

"So we talked, and I said, 'But keep a secret please. As soon as I have a hundred dollars saved, I'm out of here because I'm buying myself a typewriter and I'm going to type thesis for Yale University.'

"She said, 'You're going to save a hundred dollars to buy a typewriter?'

"I said, 'Yeah.'

" 'Why don't you go downtown tomorrow and get you a typewriter and put it on a credit?'

"You get things here on credit. I could hardly wait till Saturday. I went downtown, went to the store, got the Underwood typewriter. Still have it upstairs, still is typing. Still have that paper where I paid ten dollars a month. And every time I walked down to pay it, he made notation, 'paid.' I quit the night when I got that typewriter. I had that job for one week. That was the nicest experience. I mean, if I wouldn't have said it to her, I would have worked until I had a hundred dollars, you know.

"So I get this job typing for these boys. And then they always had a deadline. And then I had to walk to take the bus with my child on my arm. And I went on the bus and had a dollar in my hand. And I thought I was pretty good with English, you know, so I step into the bus and give him the dollar.

" 'Don't you have a token?'

"I was totally confused. I mean what is a token? What in the world have I now done? What is it that I'm doing right here? I broke down there. I cried immediately. And was a cute lady sitting there, and she said, 'Shhh. Sit right here. I put your token in.'

"She put a token in and never took my dollar, you know? Because it was only ten cents, I think, anyhow. You get maybe eleven tokens for a dollar or something like that. I never took the bus again, ever. I walked to town. It really cured me. I walked to Yale University to deliver thesis and pick up the next.

"And I got twenty cents per page. So the more pages, the more I got. But I needed to be there at ten, and Lara had her pants full. So I cleaned her up, and I raced down Davenport Avenue and cut through the middle and got there to this little office, and this young man already standing on the sidewalk, pacing. He didn't pay me. He paid that office and then they paid me. And so he grabbed that thesis and he ran to class.

"You probably never have heard this before, 'My typist didn't get here on time.' Something like that. Not the dog ate my paper. But the typist was late.

"And then I got sort of tired of that. For this twenty cents I was really spending too much time to make letter-perfect, you know, and I thought I had to do something else.

"I did all of this in the daytime while Dov was at this print shop. And then one evening I went downtown to Howard Johnson's. They had something in the paper—a waitress for three hours, from six to nine. That was sort of my speed, you know, six to nine.

"And so I went there, and he said, 'Have you ever done waitress work?'

" 'No.'

" 'Hired.'

"So I started. He gave me a little white frock of some sort, and we served hot dogs, you know, and fried clams, typical Howard Johnson food.

"Then I had to serve one time a Martini and a Manhattan, and I came to the table and said, 'Now who gets the white one? And who gets the red one?'

"So it was cute. Was nice, was fun. I got paid like probably twenty to thirty-five cents an hour for just being there, and then you're supposed to get your tips, and then that is all yours. Okay, so they paid me probably twenty-five dollars a week or something like that. And then whatever little tip I got, and plus whatever I was typing in the daytime.

"So there were two or three other girls, and they said, 'Now, how much money did you make today?'

" 'Oh,' I said, 'Two dollars, fifty cents.'

" 'And you're happy about that?'

" 'Well, when I came in here, I had none, and now I have two dollars, fifty cents.'

"The other waitresses were so complaining, 'Don't make any money here.'

"And I said, 'Well, where would you all want to work where you're gonna make more money?'

"They said, 'I want to work at Casey's. That's the fanciest place in town, and that's where you make the money.'

"I thought to myself, 'Oh, is that right? I might like to go by there and check that out.'

"So I walked in there with Lara in the morning, and I said that I was working at Howard Johnson's from six to nine, and I heard that you're the best place to work.

" 'You want to work here?'

"I said, 'Yeah, I do. Would like to work here.'

"I got the job. Walking in cold. Nothing advertised. Nothing.

"And I said, 'But I can't work on Sundays. That's when my husband is off.'

" 'Okay, you have Sunday off.'

"Those other girls never forgave me. I never worked a Sunday, and I never worked in the daytime. I worked from five to one in the morning. I made a pile of money.

"And we were across the street from Shubert Theater, and every time the theater was in town, Paul Newman and his wife Joanne—he was not yet divorced, and they were not yet married, but they were sitting right there. Also Elaine Stritch and Milton Berle. You name them, they were all there."

She's right. They were all there. The Shubert in New Haven, Connecticut, was known as the "Birthplace of the Nation's Greatest Hits." It was the first stop on the Broadway hit parade. The world premieres of *Oklahoma, Carousel, South Pacific, The King and I, The Sound of Music, My Fair Lady* with Rex Harrison and Julie Andrews, and *Call Me Madam* with Ethel Merman all took place at the Shubert. It also premiered Tennessee Williams's *A Streetcar Named Desire*, launching the career of Marlon Brando, and Eugene O'Neill's *Long Day's Journey into Night*, with top billing going to Fredric March and Jason Robards. The actors who were newcomers at the Shubert reads like a Who's Who of certain eras, including Humphrey Bogart, Kim Hunter, Spencer Tracy, Katharine Hepburn, Jimmy Stewart, Clark Gable, Mary Martin, Gene Kelly, Robert Redford, Warren Beatty, Shirley MacLaine, Andy Griffith, Jane Fonda, Sidney Poitier, James Garner, James Earl Jones, Liza Minnelli, and John Travolta.

"Some people were collecting signatures from these stars, but I didn't know who they were, you know. Now maybe it would be fun if I had them.

"So I worked there, and the girls asked me, 'Can you work tomorrow at lunch?'

" 'No. I work only nights.'

" 'Can you work Sunday for me?'

" 'No, I don't work Sundays.'

"I was not cooperative when it came to that. But I never missed a day, and until one girl—every time you turned around, she was out. And the boss said, Mr. Casey himself said, 'The next one who is out is going to stay out a week.'

"That's the day that I got the flu like I have never had before in my life. And I called in sick.

" 'You stay out till next Monday.' So I was on the receiving end of that wrath, you know.

"But that was fine because by then I was well again. He could always depend on me to be there."

"For how long were you in New Haven?"

"Well, until 1956."

"What happened then?"

"That's none of your business."

"Well, but you left Dov."

"Yes, I did."

"Did you get remarried? Was there a divorce?"

"Get it from Dov. It's your family."

"I have his point of view. I was hoping for yours."

"That's it. That's it, so we don't need to talk any more about that."

"I was just curious about his relationship with Lara, and why it was so many years before there was a connection again."

"Well, that is his fault."

"So he did know where you were? He could have gotten in touch?"

"He wrote my mother a letter and said, 'I have no address for Eva.' And my mother sent me that letter, and she said, 'What do I do?' And I said, 'All you need to do is tell him to mail the letter to me at New Haven, and it will get forwarded to me by the post office because we have forwarding address.' He chose to never do that."

Then Eva had had enough. She said, "Okay, good. We're at an end."

"That's all you want to talk about?"

"That is correct. Now you can ask me anything that you want to have clarification about the things that I have spoken about which were maybe not fully, you know, covered. So you can, if you have questions, you can ask them."

"I was curious about why you contacted Dov after a silence of so many years."

"When I had some very difficult medical problems—I'm a three-time cancer survivor, you know. And so when I came out of a cancer operation, I was all of a sudden very much concerned about Lara. So I thought, well, my daughter has a father in New York, and damn it, she really needs to know him.

"So I got up on a Sunday morning, went into my bedroom where my telephone was. Had my little booklet with Josef and Lina's number, and dialed it. Lina answered. 'Hello? Who's calling?'

"I told her what was wrong with me. I said I don't want to die and let my daughter be thinking that she has no one in America. She needs to find her father. And I'm going to help her."

When Eva got in touch with Dov, his marriage to Katja was in disarray, so her wanting to connect inspired in him fantasies of reuniting. He did see his daughter Lara, as well as his grandchildren. And when Katja returned to him, they kept in touch with Lara, but it was too late to heal Lara's wound, her resentment of being abandoned by her father.

Dov's two wives even met one another at a grandchild's high school graduation: the hidden child and the Hitler Youth—well, BDM member, since it is important to distinguish the boys' from the girls' movement in Nazi Germany. In concert with Nazi ideology, the organizations exaggerated gender differences for Aryan children, with males destined to become soldiers and females destined to produce more of them. Eva's daughter, Lara, commented on how alike Eva and Katya were—both animated and chatty. Eva said in the interview, "She is handful as much as I am handful."

When I turned off the tape recorder, Eva began to tell me a different story about her marriage, so I quickly turned it on again. Now that she's told her side of the story of Eva and Dov, she relaxes and remembers a good time.

"We would go to Savin Rock in New Haven and swim there. That Savin Rock was on the ocean. And there was nice little beach there with really nice beach sand and big stones, and I think we had to pay admission. And we would lie there in the sun in the sand, sunning ourselves and singing together. And when my mother visited in 1953, she went with us, and we had to always find shady spot for my mother. And she would sit over there in the shade in a chair. And we would spread out there in the sunshine baking. And singing."

I took a drive to Savin Rock Beach in West Haven, Connecticut, and it is a beautiful beach. There are benches on which to meditate and look out at Long Island Sound, and small cottages dot the shore. It's quite a big park, with a museum, a family outing kind of place.

Now parking is ten dollars, which is more than Dov would have earned for a whole day's work back then—though inflation accounts for about nine dollars of this fee, so if there had been a similar toll for parking, it would have been about a dollar.

"He could sing," I say.

"Yeah. He could sing. They used to call him Julius LaRosa."

Does anyone know who Julius LaRosa is anymore? He was a Brooklyn-born Italian crooner of the 1950s, a heartthrob. Lola was half in love with him and would mock swoon when he appeared on television.

"Dov and his sister performed in a nightclub in Russia."

"No. Never heard that."

"He has charisma, doesn't he? When you first met him, he must have been charming. People seem to like him."

After I compliment him, she remembers to keep on message.

"Yeah. I remember the dollar an hour after a year became old. And it was time to get a raise. And I mean, you work a year, and we had probably some kind of a discussion when a year was up.

"He was still doing the printing job. And he was doing something for the owner that was a new little line. And I said, 'You need to be proud of that. And you need to push that and say, you know, fifteen cents an hour more is probably fair—whatever.'

"But he came home and he said, 'Well, I got the raise. Guess what it is? A nickel.' So he now made a $1.05. And that was just about the end.

"So I said, 'Why don't you look for another job? If he wants to give you a nickel that seems to me as a sign you should look for another job.'

"And so he was right with it and got a job very quickly at Winchester. And he made gun parts. And had a big raise overnight because they paid a totally different scale. Maybe $2.25. But it was enormous.

"And then he said, 'I need to lose some weight. I think I'm going to buy myself a bicycle, and I'm going to ride to work on a bicycle.'"

Dov finally got the bicycle that his brother Josef had kept for himself.

"And that was perfect. I made his lunch and he took his little lunchbox, and he rode the bicycle.

"I had the car and I did take the car then to work at night. But I did not go very far in the daytime—shopping, grocery store. I didn't buy much stuff."

No, she did not buy much, true to her frugality, but with that car she cheated on Dov and drove herself and their child out of his life.

What is the story here? Eva didn't want to whore herself to American soldiers for a piece of bread. The route to self-respect was with a Jew, who could still provide that bread. And Dov, stars in his eyes, thought he had the golden girl. He was Gatsby to her Daisy.

After a while, Eva's view of Dov cleared. Dov attracted bad luck; he would always be a Jew. He became Quasimodo to her Esmeralda. My mother could not forgive this marriage with the enemy, and in her own way, she put her finger on the flaw in it. Eva, trained to love all things German and reinforced in that belief by her family, who had sacrificed a lot in the war as Germans, could not surrender her sense of superiority, which was fed by the patrons at Casey's who told her she was too beautiful to be a waitress.

Ill-conceived love drives a lot of literature. In George Eliot's *Middlemarch*, Dorothea Brooke foolishly marries the cold fish Casaubon because she imagines he is a great thinker, when he is just stupidly self-important. Henry James's *Portrait of a Lady* has lovely, gullible Isabel Archer marry the vile Gilbert Osmond for his European sophistication. Then there's Tolstoy's tragic Anna Karenina, who commits suicide because she can't choose between her son and her lover.

But those are old stories that rely on rigid rules about women, marriage, and mixing social classes. Now we live in moral Velcro, easy on and easy off. Our decisions are reversible and negotiable. We can always leave if we discover that our passions are misguided and our actions misbegotten. We can come to our senses and take another path. Bob Dylan croaks it out in that song of deluded love, "It Ain't Me Babe": "But it ain't me, babe / No, no, no, it ain't me, babe. / It ain't me you're lookin' for, babe." If it had existed then, Eva and Dov could have sung it to one another.

Eva's friend Margot, who carried the Olympic flag in front of Hitler at the age of eleven at the 1936 Olympics in Berlin, survived the war and fell in love with a man, Simon. Their marriage lasted until death did them part. Eva fell in love, as she says, to right a wrong, with an idea. As did Dov—the toss of blonde hair, the sparkling white teeth, the bikini and all it promised. What balm to his losses.

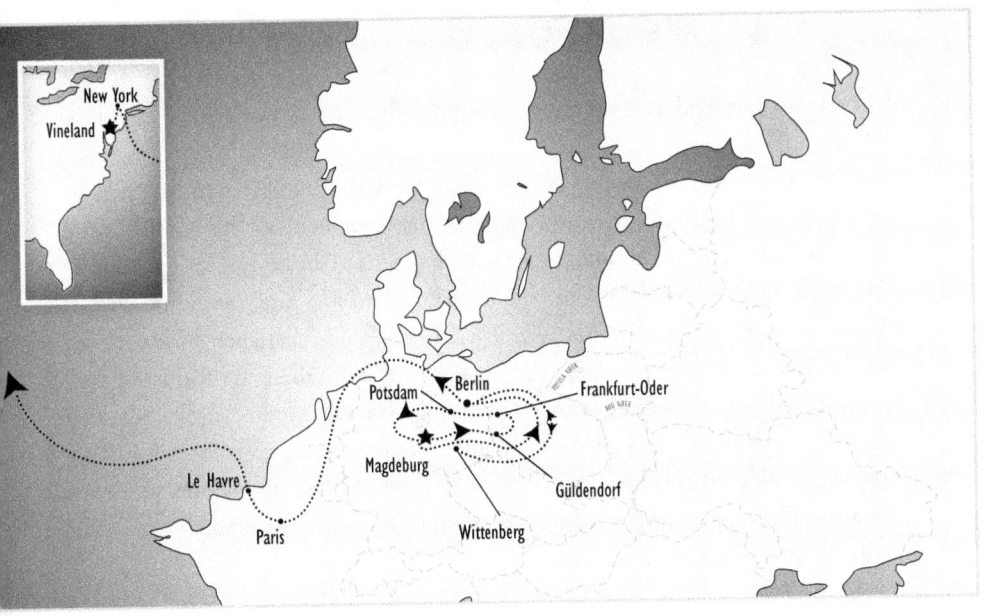

6

Katja

It is my birthday and we are at the cemetery again, as we have been on or near my birthday for the last nineteen years. Another year in my life is another year in the ground for Lola, Dov, and for the last two years, Itzak. It's the New Montefiore Cemetery in Babylon, on Long Island. It describes itself as the largest Jewish cemetery in New York. In this crowded park of the dead, my family's gravestones are located in the northeast corner. I always come on a Sunday, a popular day for funerals, and have to navigate the processions waiting to go to the newly dug gravesites. In the parking lot, where I stop so that I can go to the bathroom after the long ride to the cemetery, people who look like my uncles and parents are hugging and talking in hushed voices. Some of the older ones speak in the Eastern European–accented English of my *mishpokhe*. On this hot, steamy July Sunday, I am joined by Dov's second wife, Katja, and her two daughters and three grandchildren. Her daughters' husbands have stayed home. The only man there is my husband. It is also Katja's birthday. This is how Katja and I celebrate. We visit the dead.

Waiting for the others, my husband and I talk about whether to have a grave or be cremated. A good friend of ours was just cremated. My husband wants a gravesite. And I think, "Should I care what happens to my body after I am dead?" What do the connections of the blood require? At any rate, the future cannot know us from our gravestones—"beloved father" and "cherished husband." So few words fit on a gravestone, and the words that are there are formulas. Our immortality often comes down to the photographs of us fading in boxes stored in attics of the future. The bill for the plantings around our gravesites is an annual obligation that the future may or may not fulfill. In this digital age, won't the images of us on phones and computers disappear even more quickly than in the past, as the devices are discarded?

This year Katja is in a wheelchair. She has stopped trying to be the good Parkinson's patient; she has stopped walking with her walker. Too many falls, too much effort. Her dementia, too, has increased. Getting her now-heavy body out of the car and into the wheelchair takes three people. She allows herself to be lifted and placed in the chair. Her ankles and legs are white, thick columns, in which calves and ankles are the same diameter. Once she is settled in the wheelchair, she looks up and surveys us and comments. Her eyes fix on clothes, purses, sunglasses, shoes. She likes the cutout back of my black T-shirt. She likes her granddaughter's Gucci sunglasses and her younger daughter's Louis Vuitton purse. Her older daughter quips, "I'm glad you still remember your designers."

Her quip is full of meaning. It means that her mother squandered a lot of cash on designer goods and jewelry and had no money to send her daughters to college. It means that, despite her dementia, she still focuses on designer goods, the names of which she remembers even though she cannot remember to walk or take her pills or the dates of her grandchildren's birthdays or, increasingly, their names.

Katja complains about her orthopedic shoes. They were bought by her daughters to fit her now that her feet are too swollen for regular shoes, but they do not live up to the standard of elegance she still maintains in her clothes, which are smart, crisp, and coordinated. Her hair is a fashionable white and stylishly cut. Her fingernails are polished. When I inquire, she tells me that she applies the nail polish herself. I am amazed since her hands shake, and she can hardly bring a spoon to her mouth without spilling the contents. I can imagine the effort it takes her to maintain this dignity of her person.

I have been drawn to Katja since I first met her in 1956. It was when I was approaching adolescence, and Elvis was king of rock and roll. Oh, those swiveling hips sent a tidal wave of desire right through me. I emulated Katja. Her carriage was regal. She had been a model for a short while in Berlin. At five foot, six she was the tallest woman in our family, and she was fashion-magazine thin. My mother had a ton of clothes, shoes, and matching bags, gloves, coats, and hats, but her style was, let's face it, bargain basement, which is where she shopped—both for herself and, to my repeated disappointment at this time, for me. Katja wore couture and looked it. Because I studied her for the lessons I could take away, she trained my eye and my taste. I can see her now as if for the first time. Her shoulder-length hair arranged in a stylish twist at the nape of her neck, she wore a twirly shirtwaist dress. It was navy with a print of tiny white sailboats with red masts. The thin leather belt around her waist and her high heels were red, matching the masts. She had several plastic bracelets in navy, red, and white, along with some gold hoop earrings. Even her decision not to dye her graying hair seemed elegant to me, so unlike my mother whose hair was home-dyed and looked it. You know, that telltale reddish-brown color.

As she occupies her wheelchair, largely immobilized, somewhat blank, visibly wary, her agency reduced to complaining about her shoes, I think of the secret she had kept from everyone but Dov until I was already out of college. She was only eight years old when she was taken from the familiarity of her home and given to a family friend called Marta who kept her for a fee. This was Magdeburg, Germany, in 1940. She spent the war years with Marta in a small, remote German village for safekeeping. Her mother told her they wanted someone in the family to survive the war, and she was the oldest child—eight, while her sisters were still babies. Katja was already known as Jewish because she had attended school.

When Marta, a midwife, went to work on her motorbike and her two sons went to school, Katja hid in the basement of their cottage and was instructed not to leave under any circumstances. For five years, until close to the end of the war, Katja spent weekdays in the basement—eight to ten hours every day. She could not read very well and had no books anyway. As the Seven left Brest for the Soviet gulag and Eva taunted the nuns in her KLV camp, Katja sat silently and watched the day go by through a small basement window. Pale sunlight in winter and brighter when spring came, gray morning light to the sometimes subdued but brilliant orange and reds of dusk. She does not remember having crayons or dolls or make-believe worlds. She remembers she did nothing but fold a piece of paper over and over and look out the window, sometimes counting and marking the progression of the day. The image she paints is dismal.

Katja's sister Anna denies that she lived in a basement during the war, but Anna was an infant at the time. The sister's conviction made me look harder at the details of Katja's story. It made me think about the difference between being there to witness something and later testifying about it, recounting it. The forces of time and memory, images accumulated from films and books and other people's accounts, hold the paintbrush with you as you give your testimony. They may help you to fill the blank canvas with pictures you think you drew all by yourself, straight from lived experience.

I interviewed Katja over the course of a couple of years while she was in good health and Dov was still alive.

Me: We are looking at an affidavit for the German government dated 1967 that has a few short paragraphs about what happened to Katja during the war. It's part of her application for reparation payments. And she's letting me have a copy. "Thank you, Katja."

Katja: Absolutely. You're more than welcome.

Here is the story, translated from the German, that Katja told the officials deciding whether she deserved reparation payments from Germany for her suffering at the hands of the Nazis during the Holocaust:

> Before me, the undersigned Notary Public, came today Mrs. Katja G., living at 120-07 85th Ave. Kew Gardens, L.I., N.Y. and gave the following statement required by the German Government for restitution. She gave the statement after being made aware of the consequences and the legal ramifications for a false sworn statement.
>
> I declare, under oath, that I already, as a small child, was terribly harassed by the Nazis of Germany.
>
> I lived at the time with my mother in Magdeburg, Germany, and suffered much already as a student in an elementary school under the propaganda directed towards Jews by the Nazis.
>
> I was, as a Jewish child, not permitted to participate in playing with other children, and I was left to myself.
>
> I suffered under the mockery and cruel taunts from the other children and cried often all night long. I wished so very much for one girl friend, but I was always left alone, only to be laughed at or insulted.

Our life at home got worse and worse. The Gestapo searched our apartment over and over again. They ripped our beds apart, and the Nazis who searched our living quarters were so insolent that they cost me as a child unbelievable psychological pain. They looked at my head and said they had to make sure that I did not have lice and measured my head to establish my non-Aryan heritage.

At one of their home searches in August 1938, the Gestapo took my mother away, and I was for many, many hours left all alone. I waited for my mother's return in unimaginable fear and anguish because I thought I would never see my mother again. I was only 7 years old and all by myself.

All of those circumstances made me so nervous, and I got so very, very thin that my mother decided to take me to a friend in a small town, Guldendorf, near Frankfurt on the Oder River. I lived there without being registered with the police. I suffered terribly under the separation from my mother. I lived in constant fear that I would not see my mother again. I cried a lot and was afraid to go to sleep. I became very melancholic and could not understand why I was not permitted to live free and happy as other people did. The degrading feelings, nervous conditions, and fears I still have today, even though I am now free.

For my nervous condition, I am under constant treatment by a specialist, and without the treatment, I would not be able to live a normal and relatively healthy life.

Sworn before me . . . 1967.

She was granted a monthly stipend.

I believe Katja's story. It was the story she told her husband and eventually her daughters. Her sister Anna was too young to remember, and their mother was not one to dwell on the past, especially if there was some perception of guilt on her part.

The fury of the Holocaust threw ordinary people into extraordinary lives. It entangled them with strangers far out of their normal orbit, from what would have been exotic geographies and terrifying worlds before. Imagine a blonde, blue-eyed Hitler *Mädchen* and my big-nosed, short, Polish-Jewish uncle Dov marrying; or my staid father becoming a courier for the Soviet secret police, the NKVD; and the solidly bourgeois family of Katja giving a child away for years.

The Seven attached themselves to unlikely others in alien circumstances, thus complicating who they were and enlarging what was included in their aggregate. Even Sonia. She brought the pits of Bronnaya Gora into their range, a range that already included Komi and which would absorb Central Asia, as well as postwar Poland, Germany, and the United States—not to speak of France, where Josef's friend Chapka went, and Australia, where my father's Alexanderplatz partner immigrated.

With the addition of Katja, its reach just about embraced the entire Jewish diaspora. A sister of Katja's mother spent the war in Shanghai; another one went to Palestine in 1933 when it was still a British mandate; and her mother's brother went to Central America. Add to that the notion of hiding in Germany throughout the war even as the Germans hunted every Jew. From the impossible and unimaginable, the Holocaust forced things into the possible and imaginable. Katja's pleasure-seeking mother was bullied into becoming a double agent, serving the Stasi and the CIA at the same time. That's why I believe Katja. Any story coming out of this maelstrom is true. It happened, whether to her or someone else. I do believe that it did really happen to her.

The reparations that Germany has been paying to Holocaust survivors for more than sixty years were called *Wiedergutmachung*, translated as "making things good again." These reparations are renegotiated from time to time and over the years have been extended to more people. A few years ago the requirement of time served in a ghetto was reduced from eighteen to twelve months. How long would you have to have been in hiding in the forest to receive some cash? How much time in a concentration camp? How much money for a dead parent or sister?

Each time they renegotiate the terms of reparation payments, the Germans and Jews are icy to one another. The Germans feel they have paid and paid for a previous generation's sins, and the Jews, well, for the Jews, what can reparations be except a reminder? *Wiedergutmachung*, what a wildly optimistic name for this transaction.

I ask Katja, who was born July 22, 1931, in Magdeburg, what she remembers from her childhood.

"I still remember when Hitler came into power. I mean when I was a little girl, and I remember when things changed, when in the morning my father went to our shop, that the windows were all written 'Jews' and had the Jewish star. And in the beginning he would fix the windows, but at the end it became too costly because the next day was done the same thing. So they moved out of the neighborhood and moved someplace completely different.

"My parents owned a lovely shop, okay? In the store they had mostly children stuff—clothes and baby things. Lots of things were handmade. I know that from my mother telling me what they all had, okay? So the store was very, very beautiful.

"And I remember walking with my mom for ration cards for food, somewhere connected to my school. Right. And you know you couldn't go shopping so easily when you were Jewish. You had a plaque on the door in lots of these stores, and there I saw this terrible sign: *Juden sind hier verboten*. Jews are forbidden here.

"I was the only child at the time. And then we moved to the Werder in Magdeburg. And you had to go over two bridges to go to this place from the store. It was like a little suburban area. And on the sixth of January of 1938—Anna is seven years younger—my sister Anna was born. And then everything started going very bad.

"I went to school, and was Jewish schools all closed by then, so I went to the public school. I had to walk and was a decent, nice long walk to go over a bridge to go there. And my teacher's name was Miss Nuss. I was sitting all the way in the back, and she was always picking on me. She would come with a ruler and hit me on my paws. And when it was lunchtime and the weather was good, you all could play outside. But I had to stay in between two teachers because as far as I know, I was the only Jewish girl in the school. I was not allowed to mix with other children.

"And on the way home, it was just awful. They hit me with stones, and they called me names because I was Jewish. I remember coming home and asking my mom, 'Why are all the children so mean to me? Do I look different? Do I have a hunchback or something?'"

Katja is channeling Shakespeare's Shylock monologue from The Merchant of Venice:

Hath

not a Jew eyes? hath not a Jew hands, organs,

dimensions, senses, affections, passions? fed with

the same food, hurt with the same weapons, subject

to the same diseases, healed by the same means,

warmed and cooled by the same winter and summer, as

a Christian is? If you prick us, do we not bleed?

if you tickle us, do we not laugh? if you poison

us, do we not die?

That's the piece of the speech that gets quoted the most, but this avowal of Jewish equal humanity prepares the way for Shylock's real purpose, his declaration of his right to retribution: "and if you wrong us, shall we not / revenge?" Shakespeare's Jew is a victimizer as well as a victim—well, perhaps a victimizer because he is victimized—but not Katja. She was helpless.

"And my mother would say, 'No, you look just like the other kids; it's just their religion and our religion doesn't go hand in hand.'

"So that was the story. And we had a lovely apartment. Was furnished beautiful. But then all the trouble started. The Gestapo came to our apartment. Yeah. We had an entrance door what was glass blocks with a little wrought iron around them. And if you didn't open up the door for them, they would just smash it and then take the handle from the inside and come in, okay? And they went through all the apartment, ripped everything apart. And then also they took away the radio, the telephone, everything was taken. My father's car was taken away; everything was taken away.

"Yeah, in 1938, right. Well, then after this, when it became so bad, my parents said, 'It's no good that Katja goes to school anymore. She better stays home because it is dangerous.' And I was afraid, too.

"So, then, my other sister came around. Malina was born in 1940, and my mother was really very helpless because she didn't want a child anymore. And I remember that she went to the nuns, and she gave birth there. And they took care of her.

"And being that I was the oldest and was known because I had gone to school, my parents said, 'No good. We have to get her out of here.' So my mother made arrangements with a friend who had lived in the building. She had already moved out. And she was a midwife.

"And my mother got in contact with her. Her name is Marta. And they made a plan.

"When she was living in the building before she moved, I played with her two boys because she couldn't have cared less what religion I was. She just liked us. And I would go in her house, and I would go and eat *tunken* bread. She used to put milk and coffee in a mug, and she would give us a slice of bread and we would dunk it. I never had that in my mother's house. But there I had it. And oh, did I love it. And sugar in it, mmm, mmm, mmm. Was delicious.

"She had two sons, Helmut and Hugo. And we were very good friends. And they didn't care that I was Jewish. Because they just liked me as a partner to play ball or for ice-skating or whatever. They just were good friends with me. They were really my *only* friends. And Helmut was a little bit reserved because he was older. So anyway, they moved away to Guldendorf in Germany, about an hour and a half away from Frankfurt-Oder.

"Marta received from my parents some money, and they made some plans that I would stay with her. And to hide this plan from the Gestapo, my mother made out an invitation like I would be going to a wedding. Pretending, you know, if they should ask me why I was traveling. So they gave me a new dress and shoes, so like I would go to a wedding and carrying a gift.

"It was more or less my mom who made all the arrangements and sent me off on my own. And I went by myself in the train. And I had one little suitcase. I was still eight years old.

"And I went on the train. And Marta, she was at the train station in Frankfurt-Oder. And she picked me up. And we took a *Strassenbahn*, a streetcar, all the way to the last stop. And from the end, that's about a ride of almost half an hour, we walked twenty-five to thirty minutes to her little village where she lived.

"And she took me home. There were only three houses in the village, each very far apart—about a quarter of a mile. That's all there was around there. And she was in the last one. They were all white, and you could see the first house from Marta's because was a little bit up the hill.

"And she was hiding me. She would go in the morning to work on her motorbike. She would put me in her basement, and there I would sit all day.

"Her husband was a soldier, but the marriage was not good, so she had no contact with him. He was in the army. And she would get very early up in the morning. By six or so, at dawn.

"And she would go and wake me up. She let me sleep in the bed with her. That was wonderful.

"And she would wake me up and say, 'Katja come, come, come, come. Have a little breakfast, and then you go in the basement and you sit till I come home.'

"The basement was dark, and I didn't know really how to read or write. So I was sitting there and waiting until she is coming home.

"And her two sons knew that they had not to tell a soul that I was there. And she really must have trained them because they never said anything. Never anybody came to her house, nobody ever came and knocked and said, 'Is somebody living with you?'

"I do not know what this is called, but on top of the hill, straight up from her house, was like a concentration camp, but I don't know the name. I just don't know. Probably was not very well known like Dachau or Auschwitz or anything like this. Was just small. In front of the concentration camp were all fields with corn and sunflowers and things like that.

"So Marta, she had such a good heart. And if she could find in the hospital some bread, she would bring it home. And would give it to the sons, and they would crawl up the hill and bring the bread to the people behind the fence.

"And the fence, you couldn't touch it. And behind it were people in the uniforms, black-and-white stripes. And the people there did speak in a different language. She would take me up the hill, too, to help the people over there with a little food. I was scared, but I went with her.

"They were talking to us. We were crawling up on the belly. She always brought a whole loaf of bread, and we would crawl up there with her sons and give the people some bread. But God forbid if somebody would have noticed that.

"And Helmut and Hugo and I, we sometimes came crying down the hill when we saw how grateful the people were for the food. We took carrots up the hill, too. Carrots from the garden. And we gave it to them. And I was just shaking my head, and I said, 'What is this all here?' And the smell. And the people in the uniform with the black-and-white stripes and the hats on. And they looked all so skinny, and they looked so sad. And that's why Marta many times said to me, 'No, you not going up. You're not going to see this anymore because your heart is broken.' But I begged her, 'Take me. I want to go up there. I want to go.' We had to be very careful because the spotlight from the guards would go around the place. And if the light could catch us, God forbid, we would have been in trouble.

"So that's this experience."

Recent research records 42,500 Nazi ghettos and concentration camps throughout Europe, including Germany. Thirty thousand were slave labor camps, 1,150 Jewish ghettos, 980 concentration camps, 1,000 POW camps, 500 brothels with sex slaves, and thousands of others for euthanizing the elderly and infirm, performing forced abortions, et cetera, et cetera, et cetera. According to Eric Lichtblau, "You literally could not go anywhere in Germany without running into them. They were everywhere."

"There was no toilet inside of the house. The toilet was outside. And boy, oh boy, was I afraid to wake up during the night and go in the dark into the wooden outhouse and make pee-pee there. I was shaking.

"When the moon was out, then it was okay because then something guided me. But if the moon wasn't out, oh, my God, I was shivering from head to toe.

"She had a little goat, she had a few little bunnies. And she would bring food for them home in a big basket with straps around her shoulders. And she would say, 'Feed the animals from it.' Always at night. Never in the daytime. And that was lots of fun for me. And then she would milk the little goat. And it had horns.

"Until this day, I love goat milk, goat cheese, buttermilk from goat. And it brings a lot of memories back. She would make at night, she would let me help churn it. She would make butter from that. And we made bread sometimes. Oh, my God, was this a treat. To have bread and butter. It was like chocolate ice cream. She always fed me.

"You know, she had to struggle. But she would always find where she could bring a piece of meat home. Or she would have a chicken with the feathers still on, and oh, the smell. She would go put on the oven, and burn their feathers off. Ugh. Made me sick.

"She also was very strict of keeping yourself clean. She did not have a bathroom, so there was a bench in front of the window. And there was a round big dish with a pitcher. What you filled up from a big bucket. The water was taken out from a pump. The boys had to bring this in. That was their chore. And there was a ladle. And you put with the ladle the water in that pitcher. Cold. Ice cold water. I remember it well. And then you had to take the soap and a washcloth and a towel, and you had to strip yourself from head to toe naked and wash yourself. That's how she was. You had to smell good. You were sitting in that basement all day and had to be cleaned. So I was sitting there all day till she would come home from work. And then she would take me up and feed me, and I had to wash myself.

"And she was the same way with the boys. But of course we didn't strip together.

"And then at night, many nights, during the week, she would cover her dining room table with blankets. And she would take her radio underneath, and we would listen to the English station. She was very interested of how the war was going on and what's all happening. So, you know, what I didn't understand, she would explain it to me.

"And I saw all the planes going at night. Making the form—how do you call it? The formation? And you know, those flights would go over us *every* single night. Make terrible noise and you knew that something was on the way. But this place Guldendorf was really, for some reason, it wasn't bombed. Magdeburg was terrible bombed.

"Yes. And she was *very* good to me. She really was good to me. The only thing was, you know, when she had to go in the morning to work, that I had to come in the basement. She would say, 'Katja, Katja come. Let's go. You have to go back there.'

"Okay. So then many years passed."

"What did you do down there in the basement?"

"Nothing. Nothing. Just sitting and staring at the walls and there was small window. And I was just looking out there and doing nothing. And maybe I was counting, you know. I knew how to count. Also when I had paper, I would fold it in different ways to make shapes. And maybe I dozed off to sleep. But reading, I couldn't. I didn't learn that much yet in school. It was too short that I went to school. So that was a terrible problem.

"I was at Marta's until almost the war was over, until 1945 when it happened that the Russians came."

"For five years you did this? And the routine never changed?"

"How? No. No. No."

"You were a teenager when you came out."

"When I came out, I was a teenager, yeah. Was thirteen years old. Almost fourteen."

"You told me once that you had gray hair when the war ended."

"Yes. Lots and lots of gray hair. And when my mother saw me, she said I looked like a prune. So old my face, like I was old and wrinkled."

"Did you have any contact with your family?"

"No, I had no contact with *anybody*. Because it was too risky to make telephone calls. You don't know if somebody listens in or something like this. No. No contact with anybody. I asked Marta all the time about my family. And that was very hard and difficult, too. My parents were with my two sisters together.

"I said to my mother—later on I questioned my mother—and I said to her, 'Why did you do something like that? How could you have separated me from you guys?'

"And she said, 'Well we thought it was the right thing to do. We wanted, you know, that somebody stays alive.'

"And it's true, before I left Magdeburg, the circumstances were terrible. My mother had to go with my father to the Gestapo. They were called up. They had to go. And I was with Anna there, alone in the house. And one time they came in the house, and she's in the highchair. And they touching her head and say, 'Oh, yeah, we can tell that she is Jewish. Touch her head.'"

Anna also recalls such an incident when the Gestapo came to the house and measured her head to assess her Jewishness. Head shape was a feature of Nazi race ideology that purported the superiority of Aryan head shapes.

Katja resisted talking about her father, so I asked her sister about him. Anna told me that her father was in the German army during the war and served first in France and then in Russia. He was Lutheran and married her mother in 1931. I think she enjoyed telling me that since it means that her older sister, Katja, who she thought was preferred by their mother, was probably conceived out of wedlock.

The rabbi who married her parents talked her father out of converting. Smart rabbi. It may have saved the family once the Nazis came to power. Eventually, the father was thrown out of the army for being married to a Jew. When the Russians came into Magdeburg, he caught some stray shrapnel in his leg that left him with a life-long limp.

Katja did not talk about her father, I think, because she avoided any conversation that impugned her credentials as a Jew, which my parents, especially my father, found suspect.

"Did you practice Judaism?"

"No. No. I knew about it, but we did not practice."

"Do you know what happened to your mother's relatives?"

"My mother's relatives all left; they all left Europe. Nobody was there anymore. My mother's oldest sister went to Palestine. My grandmother with the youngest sister went to Shanghai. And one brother was in Monteverde, Costa Rica."

Anna told me that that brother committed suicide in Costa Rica. Encountering anti-Semitism even there, he shot himself. That was during the war.

"Well, then in 1945 things got bad. The Americans came from one side. We listened on the radio. We could hear the planes. And from other side came the Russians. So Marta said to me, 'If this continues, you cannot stay here.' She came originally from Russia, so she was afraid of what they would do to her since she was married to an enemy soldier. So she said you cannot stay as a young girl. You have to find your way home. The war was still going on. Must have been maybe March or early April of 1945.

"One day Marta said, 'Katja, the Russians are coming. They're coming closer and closer. And you cannot remain here anymore with me because I am original Russian. And I don't know what they gonna do to us. So I can't protect you from that. So you have to leave.' So she gave instructions to her older son, Helmut. And she told him, 'You take Katja with the *Strassenbahn*. You take her, and you put her in a train what goes to Berlin. And then she has to see how she gets farther.' Everything was in a mess by that time. It was 1945, very early spring.

"First we had to walk to the streetcar. All the way up hills and over dirt roads. And then you got to the streetcar. She gave us money that we could pay for it. And she gave me a basket with bread and something to drink, and a couple of apples, so that I would have something to eat."

I studied a map of Germany to see if the paths of Eva and Katja, two girls alone and on their own at the end of World War II, in the chaos and ugliness and uncertainty of that time, could possibly have crossed as they made their slow and anxious way back to their families. But Eva was much farther south than Katja.

"And I had a dress on. This was the same dress I had when I came to Marta. It was hand-knitted. I will never forget it. Dark red, with gray. It had in the middle something, a string, to pull in the waist. And it had pom-poms hanging. My mother knit that for me. And I had wooden clogs. Like Dr. Scholl's shoes. That's what I had on. No stockings. No nothing. That's how I walked. And so Helmut brought me to the train station at Frankfurt-Oder."

"How could it have been the same dress you came in? You were eight years old when you went there and now you are thirteen."

"Yeah, well, it stretched. Because it was knitted. So it grew with me. You know, it was very short. But we had nothing else. And it had long sleeves in the beginning, and the sleeves when I left were higher than my elbows. So, I mean, what was the wardrobe at that time, you know? It was totally unimportant. As long as you had a pair of underpanties and a little undershirt on. It was always the same dress. So I think my mother was in shock when I came home, and I still had the same dress on. She couldn't believe it. Maybe when she made it, like in Europe they did this, it was with a little extra material. You made something so that you could release it and it got longer. I wouldn't be surprised if that's what it was.

"So he bought me a ticket. He gave this to me. I had my little food basket. And he said, 'Katja, take good care of yourself. And good luck and go. And watch out. Be very careful.'

"Okay, the first train I took was a regular train. There were lots of people who were traveling. I heard a lot of German. But there were other languages talking, too. The first train I went in, you could sit down.

"So I went back to Magdeburg. I knew that address. Mittelstrasse *fünfundfünfzig*. I knew 55 Mittelstrasse. I knew that. And I figured we all meet, if my parents are still alive, somehow. We never discussed this with each other, that somehow we will all go back to the same place where I lived with them. And they should come back there, too.

"So now I'm taking the train, and I'm going. And then the train stops, and someone is shouting, 'Out out out!' You see all the soldiers with rifles. 'Everybody out of the train! Everybody out of the train!'

"Okay, out of the train. So what's next? Then they announcing, 'We don't know when the next train is coming.'

"Well, we stood there, and I was sitting on the floor. And people were talking and nobody knew what was going on. And then came a next train, and it was a train for animals. How do you call this now again? Cattle car. Okay. With straw inside.

"Okay, so we went into this. And then came Potsdam, what is close to Berlin, and we had to get out again. 'Everybody out! Everybody out!'"

"You had no papers?"

"Papers? I had nothing. I had like Dr. Scholl's little wooden shoes. And a little dress on. And it was cold. And there was no heat. The train was like for animals where you go in. And it would go and it would stop, and it would go and it would stop. And I had no idea how to get home. I said I have to go to Magdeburg to see my parents there. That's all I knew.

"So we all had to get out of the train. It was such a mess already by this time; it was unbelievable. And when you looked at the street, you saw people walking with wagons, horses, or a cow. And on top with furniture and bed things and blankets. And they were hitting the animal and making noises to make the animal go.

"And then always in between would come the soldiers. And they yelling: 'Move on already.' Or 'Don't be so slow.' And they would scream at the people. They taking the gun and shoot up in the air. It was unbelievable scary.

"But many people had each other, was traveling together, and I had nobody. But I wouldn't connect with anybody anyway. I was way too smart to do that. Because who knows what would happen to me then? So I wait for the next train, and I would at least be going somewhere again.

"When you got off at a station, then people would say, 'You can go over there and you get some water.' Okay. I go over there and get some water. And somebody would say, 'There's a bakery over there, and they're baking some bread. You can get a piece of bread.'

"So I would go there, stay on line, and I would get a piece of bread. And I had a cup, a metal cup for water. And that I kept with me. And that was about it.

"And I was more times hungry than I was not hungry.

"Oh, it was like in the Wild West movie. How the people were shouting and screaming and crying. And the horses neighing. They didn't want to go anymore, and they had the white stuff on their mouth, the foam. And was disgusting.

"But now came night. And then what are you going to do then? And I would go and sit under a tree. And freezing cold. Freezing cold. I have no blanket. I have nothing. Just my little dress. Luckily, it was wool. Sometimes when I was warm during the day, I hated it. But at night, it was good that I had it.

"Okay, so it had stopped somehow with the trains at Potsdam. We had to get off, and the trains didn't go anymore. And then you heard people saying you had to walk. And I walked with other people, but you couldn't go and understand their language. They all didn't have a place to live. They didn't have a home. They had nothing. They were all wandering around like wandering Jews. You know, maybe they came from Poland; maybe they came from Czechoslovakia. Who knows where they all came from. It was awful! And the smell and the crime. I mean, it was just awful. Well, and then I saw how everything was bombed out. All to the ground level.

"'Oh, my God,' I thought. I had not seen that in Frankfurt-Oder. There was hardly anything smashed up there. So I walked and walked and walked. And you know, there were all these signs still—how to go, with the names from the cities on the signs. And I said to myself, 'Well, maybe eventually it will come a sign, and it says Magdeburg.'

"And because I couldn't read, I had to ask people, 'What is the sign saying?' And people would say, 'Oh, you're going there? The sign says this way.' So then all of a sudden, the sign said, it's going to Magdeburg. So I kept walking, and finally I got there."

From Frankfurt-Oder to Magdeburg is more than 126 miles; from Potsdam to Magdeburg, about 72 miles.

"I couldn't believe how the city looked. It was totally bombed out. I knew how to go on foot, and I knew where I was living because I walked so many times as a little girl in the city. And we were living on the outskirts. I had to cross bridges twice to go to the place where our house was.

"And I walked over the water. The bridge was damaged. The next bridge was damaged, too. But you could still walk over it. And my heart started to go like this—pounding, pounding.

"'Oh, oh, oh. I'm almost home.'

"And I came to our house. Our apartment building. And it was also very much ruined. And wood was protecting the windows. And I did run up the steps like wild. And I got to my apartment in Magdeburg. And I couldn't believe it that I was home.

"'Mom, Dad. Mom, Dad. Anna, Malina.'

"And they opened the door. They were in the apartment. Was not to believe. It was not to believe that they were there. And then I became very sick. I had pneumonia, okay? But my mother, God bless her at that time. That time she was terrific. She found a doctor. She found some food. And she cooked me some nice chicken soup. And she had the doctor give some medicine. And she nursed me back to health.

"I became fourteen years old that summer; in July, I turned fourteen."

"Where did your parents spend the war—in Magdeburg?"

"My parents were not in Magdeburg. They went all the way to the Bavarian mountains near Munich with my two younger sisters. In a little town by a lake. I don't recall the name of it. But that's where they stood. In Bavaria, nobody knew my parents or maybe somebody hid them. The story from that I really don't recall because I wasn't there. They had some money, and some relatives made a connection for them."

Katja's sister Anna adds to this story. Sometime after her father was dismissed from the army in 1942—he was on the Russian front—her mother, Gerda, with her two younger daughters in tow, came back to Magdeburg from Bavaria. Her father, Fred, bought a car and managed some gasoline, and every morning before dawn, they would drive to the mountains for the day to avoid encounters with the Gestapo, who were more likely to be prowling around the city during daylight. Every night they would drive back home and spend the night in a Magdeburg public bunker. They depended on a nightly air-raid siren to deflect Gestapo searches. They used their apartment as little as possible, but they were there when Katja came home.

They were very lucky. When the father received the letter of dismissal from the army because he had a Jewish wife whom he did not divorce, he was on the

Russian front. He went to his superior officer, with the resealed letter in his hand, and told him that he was ordered home. Had the officer opened the letter, he would have seen the reason for Fred's new orders and might have shot him on the spot.

The first anti-Jewish laws in Nazi Germany excluded people over the age of sixty-five, Jewish war veterans, and also Jews married to Aryans, as well as the children of those marriages. These exemptions prevented people in these categories from being deported, but only at first. Eventually, most of these privileged Jews were taken to Theresienstadt and then to the eastern death camps. By 1943 the Nazis declared Germany *judenrein*, free of Jews, but there were still an estimated twenty thousand Jews living in Germany, either in hiding or passing as Christian or classified as *Mischlinge*. Katja and her family were among them.

Mischlinge was a strange Nazi category that illustrates the sinister and elaborate Third Reich's obsession with blood. In 1935 the Nuremberg Laws defined a Jew by blood, as someone with at least three Jewish grandparents, no matter whether they practiced Judaism or Hinduism or Christianity. However, if you had two Jewish grandparents, practiced Judaism, and married someone Jewish, you were a *Mischling* of the first degree. With one Jewish grandparent, you entered the *Mischling* second-degree category. An Aryan convert to Judaism was considered Aryan but also a race traitor.

What to do about *Mischlinge* occupied the Nazi hierarchy at the Wannsee Conference in 1942 and at some subsequent conferences. The decision was that first-degree *Mischlinge* would be sterilized; second-degree *Mischlinge* would be considered German. However, if a *Mischling* looked Jewish, deportation was an option. Hitler himself adjudicated the fate of about a thousand *Mischlinge* in difficult cases. However, this relative leniency applied to German *Mischlinge* only. Those in the east were considered Jews—unless of course you found a Nazi you could bribe.

Katja's family was a complicated case. By Nazi standards, her mother was clearly Jewish, though she didn't look it. Her husband, Fred, was an Aryan and a soldier. None of the three daughters looked Jewish, despite the Gestapo harassing them by measuring their heads. Katja and her sisters had two non-Jewish grandparents, and they did not practice Judaism. Nevertheless, their identification papers read *Mischling ersten grades*, Mischling first degree.

"You know my family; they just had money, and when you had money, you could do something. My mother's youngest sister, Alyce, was in the concentration camp. And in the beginning, when you had money, you could go and get them out. And my grandmother got her youngest out, and they left for Shanghai.

But she was in the camp almost a year, 1937 to 1938. They stood in Shanghai many years. They came back after the war. Maybe a year after the war."

Katya's sister Anna also told me that Alyce was imprisoned with her first husband—she had five husbands altogether. When she was released, she somehow got hold of two boarding passes for passage to Shanghai. But she took her mother and not her husband. Shanghai was then an open city and did not require visas or passports. You just got on a cruise ship in Genoa and entered the city. It was one of the only places on earth where Jews could go legally and without papers.

After *Kristallnacht*, the Jewish population of Shanghai went from about fifteen hundred to more than twenty thousand. Before the Germans found more efficient means to deal with Jews, Adolf Eichmann and other Nazis thought it was a good place to send Jews to get rid of them. This escape route, which was legal, ended on October 23, 1941, with the law prohibiting Jewish emigration.

In Shanghai, Jews were ghettoized by the Japanese, who controlled parts of the city, in a section known as Hongkew, a slum. They declared it a district for stateless refugees. When the Germans wanted the Jews to be handed over, the Japanese administrator asked the delegation representing Jews, "Why do the Germans hate you so much?" Rabbi Kalish, who headed the delegation, shrewdly answered that it was because the Jews are short and dark-haired. They were not handed over. When I followed the source of this Wikipedia story to the book *The Rabbi of 84th Street*, Kalish is quoted in Yiddish as responding, "*Zugim weil mir senen orientalim.*" Tell him the Germans hate us because we are Oriental. Regardless, they were not handed over.

Alyce, at the age of twenty-two, was an accomplished fabric-cutter and seamstress. She acquired a second husband there, but by the time she left, she had finished with him. All five of Alyce's husbands were Jewish. Anna was emphatic about that.

"And then Magdeburg became a terrible disaster, too. The Americans came in first. And my mother went on the street, and she would say to the Americans, when they passed by with a jeep, 'I'm Jewish. Is there anything you have for me, some food? I have three children.'

"And they said, 'Yes.' And she got Nescafe, and for the first time in my life I ate white bread. And she would bring us the things up into the apartment. And they asked where we lived, and they would come the next day and bring us more food. They were very kind to us.

"And then they all of a sudden, they said to us, 'We're leaving. The Russians are coming and we have to leave.'

"Okay, so then before the Russians came, they blasted the bridges. There were no more bridges."

"Who blasted them? The Americans?"

"No, the Germans blasted the bridges because they didn't want that the Russians come over. So now that the Russians were there, my mother went up on top of the roof, with the white rag on a stick and said, how do you call it? Oh, yes, to surrender. Right, I surrender. Okay? That nothing should happen to the building anymore."

Anna remembers the Russian soldiers throwing furniture, food, pots, blankets, whatever struck their fancy, out of apartment windows and into the courtyard. Then they would sit there on the broken furniture and eat and drink until they were drunk. One day the youngest of the three sisters, who was only five, stuck her head out of the window and said, "Heil Hitler" to the Russians. Her father, laid up with his injured leg, catapulted himself out of bed and grabbed her. But the Russians only laughed. They were forgiving of children.

"Being that I was the oldest," Katja continues, "my mother dragged me all over the place. She went to Russian commandant, the officers. She told them that we are Jewish, and so they gave us something to pin up on our door that showed that we were Jewish, so that people would leave us alone. She also would go with me every night to the bridge to get some information. What is going on? And my mother it was who always talked to the Russians. Some of the Russians, they could speak a little bit of German.

"And one of the nights, a Russian says to us, '*Geh weg, geh weg, geh weg.*'

"And my mother said, 'Why? Why should we go away?'

"'Go! Go! Go! Away away away.'

"And there suddenly comes a truck with Russian soldiers. And they're picking my mother and myself up. And they all have guns and they take people on the truck.

"Okay. And my mother is on the truck with me, and she's saying to those soldiers: 'Let us off! Stop this truck. We don't belong on this truck. We are Jews.'

"'Doesn't matter, doesn't matter. You gonna go with us.'

"They picking other people up. And all of a sudden, the whole truck is full of people. I think I was the youngest on the truck. And we're going to a *lager*, a refugee camp, you know, a DP camp.

"It turns out they want us to clean up clothes. It was all international Jews who were coming there, got deloused, got new clothes. And so on and so forth. And my mother disappears.

"I'm standing here working alone and wondering what is she doing.

"My mother is looking for the highest officer. I'm telling you, Ellen, in that respect, my mother had some chutzpah. God bless her. What my father was not capable to do, but she was capable of doing. And she told this high officer, commandant, or whatever he was, with stars and everything, you know, and he took his hat off and talked to my mom. And he talked some German. And then, she motioned to me that I should come, too. Stop working with putting the clothes on the wagon and come where she was.

"And he told my mother, no, we don't have to do this work. And he was saying to another Russian soldier, 'Go and get something for them to eat.' And we got cans of ham and fish and coffee and sugar.

"Unbelievable. Unbelievable. And then he had somebody to drive us home in a private car, like in a jeep. They took us home. But this was unbelievable. When we came home, my mother and I, we went into the bathtub with hot water to scrub ourselves off. And throw the clothes in a trash bin because who knows what we had on ourselves. Right? So, but that was some experience.

"And the people who were there in the DP camp were Jews, refugees from different countries. Like Dov and your parents. Right.

"We left Magdeburg because you couldn't live there. Everything was bombed out and destroyed. And I had a grandmother in Wittenberg, Elizabeth. That is the mother from my father. She had a house, and she ran two stores in the house. And she said for my parents to open up a store there. So we made a decision to go to Wittenberg."

Anna told me that their dad's brother was one of the biggest Nazis in Wittenberg and threatened to put his mother in a concentration camp if she would open her mouth again to defend her Jewish in-laws. Then he spit in her face.

"My grandmother Elizabeth had there a smoking store—pipes and things like that. My father made out of this a department store with lots of beautiful things. And it was very hard after the war to find things to sell. And we had a lot of Russians coming to us and buying this and that. They brought us butter and they brought us meat because for it we had some fabrics to sell to them, and they would take it to the tailor to have some clothes made. You know, there are a lot of women, Russian women, in uniform, and, oh, they went crazy. They were crazy to go get pretty things.

"What did I do? I cleaned the house. I made breakfast in the morning for everybody. My two sisters went to school. And I cooked lunch and I made dinner. Oh, boy, and if things sometimes didn't work out the way my mother wanted it, I would get it. And when I cleaned the house, she would put on a pair of white gloves, and she would go around and see if I dusted everything. And God help me if I didn't do it like she wanted."

"Did you attend school?"

"No, no. We tried that I would go to school. *Ach*, my God! I was put in sixth grade, and I was so tall. How could I go to school? I was a laughingstock.

"And I said, 'No. I'm not going to that school. How could you put me in school like this? They know more than I do and I'm older. You can't do it.'

"So arrangements were made and a tutor came in, and I learned how to read, to write, and to do arithmetic. And that's it. Just reading and writing and some arithmetic. It was very important because then, you know, I educated myself. Then I knew how wonderful a book could be. You know, I learned fast, and I was very eager to learn because I wanted to go and read books. Okay? So what was my first book? I read there a book, I think it was *Rebecca*, the movie version what my mother somehow got a hold of. And I read that book, and I couldn't put it down. So that was fun when you knew how to read, and I love books and magazines still to this day."

Rebecca is a Gothic romantic novel by the British writer Daphne du Maurier. Its opening lines may be familiar:

> Last night I dreamed I went to Manderley again.... I came upon it suddenly; the approach masked by the unnatural growth of a vast shrub that spread in all directions.... There was Manderley, our Manderley, secretive and silent as it had always been, the gray stone shining in the moonlight of my dream, the mullioned windows reflecting the green lawns and the terrace. Time could not wreck the perfect symmetry of those walls, nor the site itself, a jewel in the hollow of a hand.

Any Alfred Hitchcock fan would recognize them since he directed an American film version of the book in 1940, starring Laurence Olivier and Joan Fontaine.

An edition of the script, perhaps even the one that Katja seems to have read in a German translation, was used by the Germans in World War II as a key to the encrypted messages to be hidden from the Allies. According to one source, the page number of the text, followed by the line number, followed by the position in the line were used to compose coded sentences. Field Marshall Erwin Rommel kept a copy of it at his headquarters. Ken Follett wrote the spy novel *The Key to Rebecca* about a German secret agent who uses the book to pass information to the Nazi Rommel.

Why did Katja's mother have a copy of the film script rather than the book? Was it also used by the Stasi, for whom she worked?

"Then came back my Aunt Alyce and my Uncle Hans from Shanghai with my grandmother. And she had no children, and she was much younger than my mother. She was very funny and lively and she was just terrific. And she said to my mother, 'I'll take her back with me to Berlin. You have three children, you need only two. Let her come with me.'"

"You liked the idea."

"And how! Because she was so warm and cuddly and she cared so much for you.

"First of all, also, she was a tremendous dressmaker, and that's how she survived in China. In Shanghai. She was a cutter for material—silk. She would cut so-and-so many blouses from silk. And she would be so clever to cut it, so there was always a piece from it left over. And at night she would go and take it home. It was the extra material from the garment. She would pack it into her things at work, and when she was finished for the day, she would go and get food for supper and for next morning by selling the fabric. So that's how she survived in Shanghai with her husband and my grandmother. So it was not an easy life in Shanghai for the Jews there either.

"When I lived with her, her husband worked for the Americans, driving the car. And he would bring home delicious food and also the cigarettes, and we went always somewhere out. I must have been seventeen, eighteen years old. Her husband was a pianist on the boat from Shanghai, and that's how they meet."

This was husband number three.

"And my grandmother of course, from my mother's side, was also on the boat. Like my mother, she was all cold and saying, 'Don't touch me.' I remember this as a child. She wanted me to stay away. She was always worse than a winter chill, and she was always, 'Don't touch me, don't make me dirty.' See? I guess my mother got that from her.

"With Alyce, it was the most wonderful time I remember—in Berlin, with my aunt. She would say to me, 'We have money, we can go and pay for our hot chocolate. We can buy our own ice cream. We don't have to look for any handouts from anybody.' And that was the truth. They were doing well. He played the piano at different nightclubs and was driving a big-shot American around during the day. I had the most beautiful clothes from her.

"And they were just wonderful, but they didn't like it in Germany. She complained about everything. And she would say, 'For goodness sake, the stupid Germans. I can't take this. I'm getting sick and tired of them.' She didn't like to go in the subway. She didn't like to go on the street. Every day she found something that the Germans did wrong."

When I was a guest professor in Frankfurt, I was anxious much of the time. German families on trains, especially the comic-strip ones that were ruddy and a bit beefy. Beerhalls with lots of young, loud German men. I saw them with uniforms on. Really any concentration of Germans, including the students in my own classes or the audience that had kindly come to a lecture I was giving. Encounters with German bureaucracy when some document was required. They all evoked Nazi Germany for me.

One night while I was walking home from dinner, I found myself shaking with terror when two policemen holding two muzzled German shepherds by their leashes walked toward me. Automatic, visceral, completely unreasonable—that was my response. It had little to do with the objects of my anxiety. They were going about their normal affairs. The dogs were probably drug-sniffers.

Germans in uniforms with guns and German shepherds, a Hollywood cliché. My connection to its symbolic meaning was tenuous—inherited, vicarious, second-hand only. Nevertheless, eliciting very real and helpless panic. I understand Alyce. After the war there was no resumption of normal life for her in Germany. She had been imprisoned in a concentration camp for a year just for being Jewish. And then she fled to Shanghai to save her life. Unrelieved unease and anger must have accompanied day-to-day life in Berlin. Those memories, first- or second-hand, insidiously invade the present, like a cataract that blurs your vision. Can exiles ever truly return? I feel I am an exile as well—though in some lesser sense.

Perhaps we should study the model of justice in the *gacaca* court system after the 1994 Rwanda genocide that claimed the lives of an estimated one million Tutsi people. Over an eleven-year period, beginning in 2001, about 400,000 suspected perpetrators, mainly Hutus, were prosecuted without lawyers and judges in *gacaca* courts; they used plea-bargaining in a local community setting. Almost every Rwandan has participated as witness, defendant, or observer at these hearings. The idea is that the survivor describes the crime, the perpetrator confesses, and the community adjudicates the case. The goal is for the survivors and the community to forgive the perpetrators and to reintegrate them into the community. Most of the convicted perpetrators were given commuted sentences and work doing community service in—so the hope was—peaceful coexistence with those they had victimized or whose families they had victimized. *Gacaca* justice—the idea of it—inspires my awe. Even if the results of such courts, as reported, fall short.

"And before I knew it, the packing boxes came to Alyce's apartment. The wooden crates came, and everything was packed in. And she left Germany, and she went to Israel with my grandmother; they went to Israel. I went back to my mother and father in Wittenberg.

"If she would have asked me, I think I would have gone with her to Israel. No doubt. She had a sister in Israel, in Haifa—Ilse. Ilse adopted a black Moroccan Jewish baby. Aunt Ilse was a clothes designer, like Calvin Klein. The most gorgeous clothes you could design.

"So that's that part.

"It wasn't that easy at home with my mother. She would push me aside, as if Katja isn't here. It was for many, many, many, many, *many* years like this. She handled me like I was her stepchild. When I ask her why she left only me with strangers, she says, 'Oh, that's what we had to do, we had no other choice. And you have to make the best out of things, you know.' And she could be very mean. She lost her temper, and she would hit me. She was very cold, very cruel. Very cruel. She would give me the food three times the same if I didn't eat it. Morning, lunch, and dinnertime. Already as a little girl, she was hitting me. Pang! Like this. And she had beautiful jewelry on, which cut me, and the blood would come running out of my nose like crazy. And my nose was already so sensitive. She just had to touch it and the nose would bleed. Forget anything normal from her. She wouldn't even say goodnight to me.

"You know what my youngest sister said? 'Oh, Mother should have never been having children.' She was not a woman to have children. She shouldn't have had anybody.

"You know, it's so sad. Now I have from my grandmother this story about me. My mother told her that 'In the first bath I should have let her go.'"

Mean mother stories link Katja to her sisters; all of them spill out bitter tales of their mother's cruelties. Anna confirms that Katja walked around with a perpetual bloody nose. Her mother hit her with a wooden ladle when Katja flagged in her duties as family cook and caretaker of her sisters.

When Anna had the measles, her mother told her she was sorry she had ever given birth to her. Shipped off to her German Protestant grandmother in Wittenberg when she was a baby. Anna, her mother told her, was too ugly to keep at home.

Born in 1906, Katja's mother, Gerda, lived until 2004, when she was ninety-eight—fueled by selfishness, her children say. Like Katja, she had Parkinson's disease.

I usually like mean mother stories because they counter the self-sacrificing mother stereotype that has held so many women hostage. But I have to admit, I only like these stories when they are fictional and symbolic rather than real.

Yet the woman had grit. During the postwar starvation in Germany, it was Gerda who had the courage to illegally forage for food in the middle of the night on nearby farms.

And she had intuition. The father was in the hospital with shrapnel in his leg when Gerda swept into the hospital and collected him and brought him home. The next day the Russians emptied the hospital of German men. They sent them east, to the frozen *gulags*.

Gerda also had chutzpah. After the family moved to Wittenburg, like Magdeburg controlled by the Russians, the German secret police, the Stasi, knocked on Grandmother Elizabeth's door, looking for Gerda. It was 1951. When they found her working in the family store, they took her to their headquarters. They told her that they wanted her to spy for them. When she refused, they countered that if it weren't for them, she wouldn't be alive.

"How do you know that?" she asked.

They showed her a Nazi detainment and transport document, in which she and her family were all due to be picked up and, as they told her, gassed. They showed her the papers issued in Magdeburg for their deportation. Seeing them, Anna said, she nearly had a nervous breakdown. Yet she still refused to spy for the Stasi. They threw her into an isolation cell where she lasted twenty-four hours before she relented and agreed to their terms.

After they let her go, Gerda plotted to elude their surveillance long enough to sneak into the American embassy in Berlin to see what she could negotiate. The embassy people told her that she and her family would be granted asylum in West Berlin if they could manage to get themselves there.

She was followed constantly, so the family had to be clever and very, very careful with their escape plans. She knew a man whom the Stasi killed and a woman who hung herself after the Stasi raped and tortured her. In the meantime, Gerda was a double agent, reporting to the Americans about what the Stasi ordered her to do and, at the same time, with the consent of the Americans, spying for the Stasi. To test her, the Stasi asked her to go to West Germany and retrieve a Czech couple who interested them and bring them east into their jurisdiction. When she told the Americans about it, they said it was a ruse, because that couple, Judith and Stephen, was already in the east and already arrested.

A historian of the Stasi, John Koehler, compares the Stasi to an octopus; their tentacles were everywhere. Every apartment house had an agent of the secret police spying on the inhabitants. Stasi spies included priests, professors, even students under the age of sixteen. If you count the entire Stasi machine, including regular informers, there was one spy for every six citizens. In any gathering of a dozen or more people, you had to assume that the Stasi were there watching you.

Hunted by the Germans and exploited by the communists, Gerda managed to steer her family to a safe harbor in the West. One summer day, the family took a Sunday walk in the woods with their dog. Grandmother Elizabeth met them and took the dog with her. Gerda and her family made their way through the woods to a country road. There they had arranged to meet a German friend of her husband's who had a car and knew a circuitous route to West Germany. When they got there, they hopped on a train to Berlin.

"No suitcases, nothing. Just the stuff which we had on our backs. And we went into the train, and then when we arrived close to Berlin, we jumped off the train. We were rolling down the grass hill. All of us. In the dark. And then we found the subway, the S-Bahn. So we got into this train. Oh, my God.

"What year was this?"

"1951."

"So it's the same year that they recruited your mother."

The same year Katja's family escapes to West Berlin, Eva and Dov leave it to emigrate.

"Yes. Right. And there we went the following day to the Americans, and they said, 'Yeah, we know about you all.' They said not only did you have trouble before, with Hitler, now you are having the Stasi on your back. So we all got passports from them, and we had something to walk around with.

"So that was that. And then my mother went to work, and my father went to work.

"My mother, she worked in a nylon stockings factory. Looking if they had runs in them or holes. Yeah. Had to go make money. She had three children. Right? And my father, he went into the business of wool. Yarns. Knitting needles and whatever you need for knitting. That he did to the end of his life. So he made a decent living with that.

"We lived in the Kreuznacherstrasse, in a suburb of Berlin. And that was a beautiful place. We were on the top floor. What was it, a walk up. One, two, three, four—the fifth floor, with a balcony. Yeah, with red carpets on the stairs. Was beautiful. French doors. Oh, do you know how hard it was to get an apartment in Berlin? *Ach*, unbelievable. Unbelievable. The Americans helped us get it."

"At this time you are twenty years old. Your schooling is finished."

"Right, and then I went to work and modeled."

"How did you get into it?"

"I ask. I just go and ask. Like I did it when I went to this Bloomingdale's when I came to this America and said, 'Can you use somebody to help as a salesperson?'

"So I did this too in Berlin. No, I just have chutzpah to do that. Put on some nice clothes, and I go to the store and ask. Horn was the name of the store. And I got the job. I walked in and, you know, customers were sitting on the couch, and they said, 'Oh, this dress and this dress and this suit and this jacket and all that—I would like to have that. And would somebody put it on and I see how looks on a person?' And that's what I did. Was not a big thing.

"Then one day I was going to lunch.

"And the boss she said to me, 'You cannot go to lunch now.'

"And I said, 'Yes, I do. I go every day to lunch at this hour.' Was about 2:00.

"And she said to me, 'No, you can't go.'

"And I remember putting the collar up on my coat, looking in the mirror, and walking out. And she came running after me, 'You Jewish pig, you. You have the nerve to do that?'

"Well, I didn't take that from anybody anymore. Okay? So I went to Mr. Galinski from the Jewish organization. Heinz Galinski. He was the big shot in Berlin who took care of the Jews.

"I told him, 'Oh, my goodness! Listen what happened to me.'

"And he said, 'Now this is here outrageous! We're going to do something. We're taking this to court.'

"And we took it to court. She was fined. She had to pay me money. I don't know, maybe eight hundred or a thousand marks.

"And in court, when she gets the judgment, and the judge hit that gavel and told her she had to pay, she was saying again, 'Oh, look what that Jewish pig does to me. I have to pay her now money.'

"And the judge says, 'Now you have to do it double because you are saying it again.'

"So, that was that.

"I worked there a few years, maybe was 1955 already. Yeah, I worked there a long time. I was very well known in Berlin. You know, it's not such a big city. You get to know people and they get to know you."

Katja's savior, Heinz Galinski, was a survivor of Auschwitz, Buchenwald, and Bergen-Belsen. In contrast to most German-Jewish survivors of the camps, Galinski returned to Germany after the war. He was the first postwar chairman of the Berlin synagogue and worked to advance the cause of Jews in Germany for the rest of his life. A Berlin Jewish elementary school still bears his name. In the late 1990s two bombs destroyed his gravestone.

Katja's second great abandonment was by her fiancé.

"Yeah, I was engaged, yes, to a Jewish boy. It's also very sad story, and okay, it became very hard for me to be in Berlin because he married my best girlfriend. And everything was ready. We wanted to go to Paris."

Anna told me that his name was Gerhard Besch, and he was half-Jewish. Anna herself had a crush on him. He drove a Hudson, an American car. He had lived in Australia during the war, where he got malaria. With his brother, Richard, he owned a pharmaceutical company. I found their common headstone in the Judischer Friedhof Ohlsdorfer, a Jewish cemetery in Hamburg, Germany—no other markers for wives or children. Anna remembered that Gerhard's baby died around the time that Katja left for the United States.

Not a best friend, but a younger woman, according to Anna, seduced him away from Katja. He wrote her a letter to break off the engagement.

Anna said that after the war there were no men in Germany anymore. They had all died or left. In 1946 Germany had seven million more women than men. There was no one to date. Katja was popular, but there were very few men with whom to be popular. And if you were interested in a Jewish man, well, forget about it. She had had her chance with Gerhard and lost it.

When Dov first wrote to Katja, she was looking at her twenty-fifth birthday—old in those days to be single. Also she must have found the lure of America hard to resist. How glamorous to be invited to go by ship to the United

States on a romantic escapade, not to speak of the excitement of New York City. It must have smelled like rescue from a site of abandonment and from the indignity and shame of running into her ex, being reminded that she had been discarded—again.

"I would go to the movies, I would be in the theater, and I would bump into him with his wife. It was unbelievable to cope with.

"So then I got this wonderful letter from Dov. The sixth of January 1956, the letter came. It was my sister's birthday. On that night when I came home from work, there was the letter, and oh, I couldn't believe it. The paper was powder blue and red and white stripes. And I became very excited. And then I opened it up and it said his name, and he hopes that now is the time that we really would sit and write to each other. And he tells me how old he is and that he lives in New York. And please answer this letter as soon as possible.

"And I took some paper from the kitchen, and I answered the same night the letter because if I don't do that right away, it could have been forgotten, and Dov would have never heard from me. So it came that on a weekly basis that we wrote to each other. Even sometimes I had two letters. And even in the beginning, Dov writes to me that he wants me to come and meet him.

"And he writes to me, 'Katja, I want you to come to this country and to me for good. And hopefully we like each other, and we find things in common and you will stay here for good. And we get married.'

"And I was laughing. I thought his proposal was so funny and so very romantic."

"After how many letters did he make this offer?"

"After a few weeks of writing back and forth. Dov's best friend, Simon, and his wife, Margot, got us together. Dov said as a joke, when she went on the boat to come to Europe for visiting her parents, he said, 'Find me a nice girl.' And the day before Margot left Berlin, my sisters were in the house, but not me. And she came to our apartment, my sisters were cooking, and she said, 'Well I'm leaving tomorrow to go back to the States, but your sister isn't here, so do you have a picture of her?'

"And they said, 'Yeah, we can get you a picture.' So they cut out a picture from me in a photograph, and they give her just a little picture from me. And that's what Margot gave to Dov."

After Margot visited Katja's family on Dov's behalf, he tried to reunite with Eva. But it did not work out. The first letter from Dov was brief and alludes obliquely to the death dance of the relationship with Eva:

New York, January 6, 1956

Dear unknown Katja,

For a long time I've wanted to write this letter, but different circumstances prevented me from doing it, and it was always pushed off.

My friend Margot, who was recently in Germany to visit her parents, told me that you are open to start a correspondence to get acquainted. I have your photo already for quite a long time. Even though it's a small one, it's enough to see that I like you. You are very pretty.

The first letter is always so difficult because we don't know each other personally. That's why I hope you will answer very soon and write a nice, long letter.

The ladies are usually better correspondents than men. They know how to write.

So I will come to the end of my letter today and look forward to a response very soon.

My regards to your parents and sisters even though I don't know them.

Yours,

Dov G.

She did respond right away. Even in her first letter, she focuses on aspects of herself that she thinks will attract him—her appearance, her love of family. She also provides a personal reference as if she were applying for a job. Toward the end of the letter, her tone turns flirtatious, especially when she gives him a verbal image of her sunning herself, presumably in a bathing suit.

Berlin, January 12, 1956

Dear Dov,

A few days ago your letter arrived here and I was very happy. I am thanking you for this.

Also, thanks for the photo. I like the picture very much. You have a very sweet little daughter.

That you liked my picture and that you liked the way I look made me very happy.

Now I will go to the photographer so I can send you a picture that is big, and you can put it on your night table.

Today my mom visited Mrs. S. [the friend of Margot]. My mother told her how nice you wrote to me. Through my mother I heard only good things about you.

Is that not nice for you?

It is terrible that Berlin is so far away from New York. It would be much better to meet in person.

I think it is wonderful to have good friends that stand by you in good and in bad times.

If you want a more personal introduction from me, you could visit or call an old friend of mine. I believe he lives in the States since 1935 and comes on business many times to Berlin. He would be very happy if you would see him and bring him personal greetings from me. He is not young, approximately sixty-five years of age.

So if you wish to see him, I will send you his name and address. He knows me very well from the past.

I believe New York is a beautiful and exciting city, and you do not get bored there. A lot is happening here also. It is Mardi Gras here, but I will not go anywhere. I find it is too cold. At the moment we have twenty degrees here. It is terrible. I hate cold. I could sit on a stove and still be a frost bump.

But it will not take long, and then the sun will shine and we can go swimming again.

I love to go swimming and love to lie in the sun and daydream. . . .

Now the weekend is almost over and tomorrow starts the six-day run again.

So, for today, I am sending you heartfelt greetings and best wishes.

Yours,

Katja

In his letter from New York, dated January 20, Dov is also flirtatious and aggressively pursues her. He is relieved that she likes his photo and writes,

> How I would love to take you out tomorrow evening for a nice date with dancing—but, unfortunately, is the ocean between us. Nevertheless, I have big hopes that this wish, in time, will become true. My intentions are real; that is my dream for the future; what is yours?

He can't believe that Katja is a "frost bump" since her picture "gives out so much warmth that I get heart palpitations looking at it."

On January 25 from Berlin, Katja adds to her self-description:

> Now you want to know everything about me. So, pay attention, here I go. My name you already know. I was born on July twenty-second in the year of 1931. Soon I will be twenty-five years old, and I stand with both feet on the ground. I have a profession that sustains me.
>
> I live with my parents and we get along extremely well. That is the reason I am at home a lot. The men in this country are neither trustworthy nor nice. I cannot see wasting my time.
>
> I love to dance, boogie-woogie—only I need a partner.
>
> I go a lot to movies, theater, operas, concerts, and also to good sport events.
>
> Whatever is coming up—for those things I spend a lot of money.
>
> In addition, I am 5'6" tall, I am thin—my weight is 113 lbs. My hair color is dark blonde, maybe even considered brown?? I can be very entertaining and keep a lot of people on their toes.
>
> You see, I feel like you, it is not easy to write about yourself.
>
> Above all things, I love children. . . .

Dov responds, enticing her with his ability to provide, his intelligence, his love of children and family:

New York, 1 February 1956

On the tenth of November 1921 I was born. I'm 1 meter 68 cm tall. I have dark hair and I weigh 145 American pounds. I know Berlin very, very well since I lived there from 1946 until I emigrated in 1951. I lived in Berlin all those years, and I know the neighborhood where you live very well. I'm almost five years in America and I love it. It's wonderful here. I would not change this country for any other one. Right now I'm driving a taxi in New York City, and I earn good money. I hope to become my own boss pretty soon. . . .

As you know, I'm going through a divorce right now, and my daughter Lara is with my ex-wife. Here in USA it is very difficult for a father to remain with his child. The child is usually going with the mother, even though she doesn't deserve to be the mother of the girl because of the way she acted, to have such a daughter. . . .

As I see from your letter we have common interests. I love music, sports, theater. I like to dance and like to be happy. I also love children. . . .

I look forward to an answer very soon and I hope for it. I hope this letter reaches you in good health and that you enjoy the letter.

If you have any questions, just ask. I send regards to you, Katja.

Yours, Dov

It was a six-month courtship by mail, ending with Katja on a ship to the United States, the SS *United States*. By February 24, in a special-delivery letter, he invites her for a visit and assures her that he will take care of all arrangements for her travel to the United States. He is happy, he writes, for the opportunity to "play teacher" while she learns English. He cannot wait to show her the "miracle of architecture" that is New York City. He asks her to raise a glass with him and say "*L'chaim*," drink to their new relationship, and seal their feelings with a "kiss from far away." He writes that from now on he will end "German formalities" and address her with the familiar *du* rather than the more proper *Sie*.

In her response dated a week later, Katja does virtual cartwheels:

Dear Dov,

Now how do I say it? I am so excited and mixed up and my thoughts have to calm down....

When the doorbell rang and your letter arrived by special delivery, I thought I would have a heart attack I was so happy. My delight was enormous that you thought so well and much about me.

In my mind I give you a loving kiss for this. I may do this, don't you think?

After all, we drank to our friendship and health!!!!

Now, dear Dov, to the most important item of your letter. Your invitation. I feel like a fairy princess in a story where the prince comes in her dream, but it is not a dream but reality.

My happiness I cannot describe in writing. At work I could not think of anything else, and last night I could not sleep. I was so excited and very happy, oh, dear Dov. Can you possibly know how I feel?

So if you are really sure you want me to come to get to know me, and I will get to know you, then I will come....

Your "frost bump" is now melted since your letter. Your picture stands before me and you are watching me as I write to you....

They wrote multi-paged letters, spaced a few days apart—she in a cramped, tiny script, and he in an expansive, large-looped cursive. Eighty letters survived, about evenly divided between those from Dov and those from Katja. In a matter of a few fevered weeks, they had plans for Katja to come to New York not only for a visit but permanently, setting the goal of Katja arriving around her birthday on July 22. Their letters were eager and romantic. The letter from Katja dated March 13 declares:

> I hope you do not get the wrong impression, but I believe that you understand me well. After your loving letters and your pleasing photo, I am not afraid nor do I have any thoughts other than of you, and you will not believe it, and it is totally surprising, but I fell in love with you.

Without meeting, they fell in love. Just like Eva, Katja in prewar times would have been out of Dov's league in terms of class and status. German Jews with a purchase in the middle class looked down on the Jews from the East, whom they thought of as uncultured and dirty. The Holocaust equalized them.

In the early letters to Dov, Katja is charming in her blatant transparency. After an elaborate description of a meal—soup to nuts, so to speak—that she cooked for her family, she asks in the same letter, "When may I cook for you? You know the saying, 'The way to a man's heart is through his stomach.'"

After she became Dov's wife, she did not actually cook much. My mother was the family cook. All family holidays were celebrated at our house. Lola truly showed her love through the food she cooked, dish after dish after dish of it, miraculously coming out of the tiny kitchens in our rented apartments—erasing with each meal the deprivations of the past. One of her staples was roast turkey—a beautiful, luscious browned and stuffed affair. Fighting over the drumsticks was one of our rituals. Who would get them? When my cousins and I started to have our own kids, it was the kids who competed for them. Hoping to please us one night, she served a platter of turkey drumsticks, without the rest of the turkey. As the dish settled on the table, we all waited, thinking the rest of the bird would follow. We were silent and then finally accepted that it wasn't coming. Such disappointment. No one really wanted the disembodied drumsticks. It just wasn't the same.

In the very next letter, Dov tells Katja he is flying to Las Vegas, where he can get a divorce in less than two months:

> You can see, it is my biggest wish as fast as possible to get a divorce and to meet you as a free man. Otherwise, dear Katja, I do not think it would be fair to you.

In her response of March 18, she promises Dov to "do everything to be a good wife." She adds, "That will not be difficult if you love somebody very much."

He sends her two dozen long-stemmed red roses, a lucky charm from Las Vegas for her charm bracelet, and stockings. In Berlin she sees Oscar Peterson and "Big Ella," meaning Ella Fitzgerald. In Las Vegas he sees the comedy team of Dean Martin and Jerry Lewis and the singer Eartha Kitt, and helps a new friend with his goldmine. They both love the movies. She sees *Daddy Long Legs* with Fred Astaire, the French thriller *Rififi*, Clark Gable and Susan Hayward in the Cold War film *Soldier of Fortune*, and with her whole family, *Gone with the Wind* for the second time.

Their letters are confined to their small, personal spheres in those six months of 1956. They are wrapped in a lovers' insularity. They do not write about the world outside themselves. As their letters crossed the Atlantic, Arthur Miller, around the time of his marriage to Marilyn Monroe, was subpoenaed to testify before the House Un-American Activities Committee (HUAC), which he did on June 21, 1956. Nineteen fifty-six was a year before the Soviet Union sent up the space satellite Sputnik, launching what would become known as the space age; and a year earlier, Rosa Parks, a forty-three-year-old seamstress and activist, refused to surrender her seat at the front of a bus to a white man, and was arrested in Montgomery, Alabama.

In 1956, as Elvis released *Heartbreak Hotel* and Little Richard brayed *Tutti Frutti* from car radios, Khrushchev denounced Stalin, the Suez Canal crisis brought Israeli troops to Egypt, and dynamite was thrown onto Martin Luther King, Jr.'s porch. On Broadway the Tony Award for best musical went to *Damn Yankees*. My mother would sing "Whatever Lola Wants, Lola Gets" from that play around the house in defiance of something my father had denied her.

The adaptation of Anne Frank's diary into a play also won a Tony that year. The play reminds me how Anne was betrayed by the stage version of her diary. It was adapted to communicate an optimism palatable to American audiences that was not in her writing.

It also made me think about Anne Frank's life in the attic as compared with Katja's in the basement. In hiding, Katja was not surrounded by her loving and protective family. She had no schoolbooks or writing materials or new clothes as she outgrew her old clothes. Anne could worry about her relationships with her sister and parents, fall in love with Peter, the teenaged boy in the attic. She could listen to the radio and dream about becoming a writer and learn new languages. Kitty, the name she gave her diary, was an eager ear for the contents of her inner life. Except for a few precious hours at night, Katja spent her days waiting for time to pass. She waited for years as her childhood tediously faded.

Anne's life was sacrificed to a murderous delusion, while Katja survived and enjoyed a normal lifespan—yet the unanswered needs of her young years must have shaped her as an adult. In her letters to Dov, she writes in detail about the decoration of her room, of a crocodile handbag that she has nobly denied herself, of the good quality of the stockings he sent to her. When I think of her, she is always dressed to the nines in designer goods. The various apartments and houses she had with Dov looked as if they were ready to be photographed for *House Beautiful*. She had tons of gold jewelry, gifts from Dov, which she draped around her neck and hung from her ears, and with which she weighted her wrists, halfway up to her elbows; she wore rings on several fingers of each hand. She was the material girl before Madonna.

"And then I had to go for my papers to come to the United States. And all of a sudden, I am called, and I have to come to the American consul, personally, in his office. So he says to me, 'You cannot leave Germany till you have proven to me that you left Wittenberg and came to Berlin for political asylum. You have to have papers from this. And until you bring this to me, I will not release that you can go to the United States.' The consul himself.

"So I made a frantic call to home, and I told my father, who was luckily home in that moment, and he said to me, 'Katja, take it easy, take it easy. I have the papers. You can prove it. You can go tomorrow back and you can show it to him.'

"So that's what I did. I went the following day. And I saw the consul again. And he saw the papers. He said, 'Okay. Everything looks in order. You're getting your visa. You can go. You can leave.'"

Her sisters teased her, calling her a mail-order bride.

"And I was *extremely* excited.

"And Dov was in Las Vegas for his divorce from Eva, and he sent me a little gold horseshoe with a penny in it to put on my chain. For good luck. And I sent him little packages with chocolate. And the letters got nicer and nicer and nicer. So it was really an exciting six months to come to this country.

"And on my way to America, I saw my relatives in Paris, and stood with them for a few days. And then they put me on the train to go to Le Havre where the boat, the *United States*, was anchored. And from far away you could already smell on the train the ocean. Ah, was delicious. It was sunset, and you could see the boat. I thought that boat never ends. Blue, white, and red. Such a magnificent ship, the *United States*.

"Could it be more perfect? To be on the *United States* and also going there? And I was so excited.

"When I came out of the train, there were all over people who would help you with everything, with what cabin you would go in and things like that. And I was in my cabin, and then came a knock on the door.

"'Katja?'

"And I was very surprised that everybody called you right away by your first name, like you never had another name.

"And I opened the door. And again I got *twenty-four* dark red, long-stemmed roses from Dov.

" 'Bon Voyage. I love you. See you in a few days in New York.'

"I could not believe it. I just could not believe it. And he never changed.

"I could not speak English, so every day, when I ordered my breakfast, lunch, or dinner, I was pointing to something on the menu, and I got always such a surprise what was coming on the plate.

"And I arrived on a Monday morning, and the view from New York! It was a *very* beautiful morning. And the ship comes in. And you see *all* the homes on the mountains. And I stood there with my mouth open. I couldn't close my mouth. And then you go a little farther and farther and farther. And then you see the beautiful lady with the torch in her hand, the Statue of Liberty.

"So everybody got off the ship. And Katja was the last one coming off the boat."

"Why was that?"

"Why was this? Because they started taking pictures from me. And it was for the newspaper. And I was in the newspaper. They misunderstood me. They thought I came to the United States to marry a GI. But that wasn't so.

"But you know, communication in different languages makes some misunderstandings. But nevertheless the next day I was in the paper."

The next day the front page of the now-defunct New York *Daily Mirror* carried a photo of Katja sitting on the steps of the ship, looking beautiful. The caption under the picture reads, "THE PRETTIEST ARRIVAL ON THE SHIP HERE TO MARRY AN EX-GI FROM THE BRONX."

The *Mirror* jumped on the GI angle. In the middle of the Cold War, GIs mattered.

"So my friend Dov stood on the pier, and couldn't understand what happened to me. Why I don't come. Everybody else came down.

"And then finally I waltzed down, and I said, 'Here I am!'

"And Dov said to me, 'Katja! What took you so long?'

"And I said, 'Well, they took pictures from me.' They didn't leave me alone. They were running after me, saying we have to take pictures from you.

"Okay. So that was it.

"And I mean, Dov and I liked each other. We talked. His experience from the war. My experience from the war. And I was very sad to hear Dov's horrible story about his family. And my heart was broken what he went through. And I really felt very, very bad about him. And I said to myself, Well, how could you not love a man like this? Who went through such sad stories and lost his family—little children, brother, sisters, nephew, nieces, and everything.

"And he listened to my story, and he said, and he was holding my hand, and kissing my hand, and he said, 'We both have so many things in common. And we will go and have a good life together.'

"And I said to him, 'Definitely.'

"We both like classical music. We both liked to read books. We both liked walking on the beach, going to the theater, going to see movies. Laugh together, cry together."

The stories I remember that Dov and Katja told of one another about those early days are these: Katja remembers that Dov bought her a shower cap because he knew there were no showers in Germany. It spoke to his thoughtfulness, his awareness of her needs.

Dov remembers that shortly after they met, she asked him whether he would wear elevated shoes. He was shorter than she was, and when she wore heels, which she liked to do, he was much shorter than she was.

"Okay. So I was here maybe two weeks, and we took the car and went to New Jersey to visit his brothers. I knew he had two brothers in this country.

"And I took a piece of paper with me to show his brother Itzak—because Dov was before married, and she was not Jewish. And she did not convert. And Itzak wanted to make a thousand percent sure that the second wife was definitely Jewish. So I brought a piece of paper from the rabbi from my mother to prove to him that I was Jewish. After I met him and we talked, maybe after an hour, he said, 'Where's the piece of the paper?'

"And I went into my pocketbook, and I said, 'Here it is in black and white; you can see it.'

"And he said, 'Okay. Very good.'

"And then, Josef came over to his brother Itzak's place where we were with his children and with his wife, Lina. And I met all them. And Lina, of course, she's from Germany, and she spoke to me in German. And it was all very nice. And when I knew that I will meet Dov's family, I remember that Margot said, 'Katja, it's not that hard. They all will like you.'

"And that is true, you know. So that was my first visit with Dov's family. And it was nice."

In fact, except for me—I don't know how my cousins felt—no one liked Katja. My father found her Jewish credentials suspect, and he liked criticizing his brothers no matter what.

My mother—well, no one ran after her to put her picture in the paper when she landed at Ellis Island. She was a sewing machine operator, paid according to the number of items she finished. Katja became a stay-at-home mom. Only when her kids went to school did she get a job. She went to work in the designer dress department of Bloomingdale's, a place in which my mother never set foot. It was for the rich. Warsaw Ghetto girls just didn't cross that line.

"We married September the ninth, after the Jewish holidays. We went to the rabbi. We talked everything over with him.

"Max and June, the family friends I lived with in Long Beach when I was first in US, were very much against that I should marry Dov. They thought maybe I could do better. I should go and learn English, go into a profession. They thought what's the hurry to get married?

"And I told them, 'No. I'm going to marry Dov.'"

"Why didn't you follow their advice?"

"Dov wrote me already in the letters that 'Katja, when you come here, I am ten years older than you. And when we get married, I want you to become pregnant, and we have a baby because you're twenty-five, I'm thirty-five. How long should we wait to have a baby?'

"And that's exactly what happened. A year later I had my baby in my arms. She was born in Long Beach. And that's how it happened.

"And you know, there was nobody really who could talk me out of it, that I should go and get married to Dov. Maybe it wasn't the greatest love in the beginning, but enough that I knew that I could go and get married to him.

"And he was absolutely crazy about me. That's what he told me. *Ach, ach, ach.* He never stopped. Always looked at me, 'My Katja, my Katja, my Katja.'"

Katja's mother and two sisters immigrated to the United States a year after her marriage to Dov. Katja's sister Anna was nineteen in 1957, when they arrived. She had attended the university in Berlin for two and a half years, focusing on math.

With just a little English, Anna landed her first job at Macy's, in the accounting department. Personnel gave her a book to read, and she read it phonetically, only pretending to understand it although she hardly understood a word. She aced the math test, though, and got the job.

I love these immigrant stories that delight in besting the native authorities. I know a Russian *refusenik* who got a job as a librarian in an Ivy League school the same way. She had memorized certain "job interview" phrases and, triggered by a word or phrase from the interviewer's question, used them. Nothing beats chutzpah, made up of confidence, a dash of desperation, and luck.

Anna met her husband, another Holocaust survivor, in 1958 on the F train while commuting to work. She took the subway ten stops from Kew Gardens to 34th Street, Herald Square, the location of Macy's. Her first winter in the United States, she noticed a guy who entered her subway car every day. It turned out that he was a diamond setter on 47th Street, one stop before hers, in the New York City diamond district. He and his father left Frankfurt am Main in Germany in 1938, when he was seven.

One morning he walked up to her and sat down and said that since they ride together, "Let's talk." They rode the train together for about half an hour every day. Then he stopped coming. She learned later that he hated her German accent and half expected her father to be wearing black SS boots. He needed to extricate himself before it was too late. He told her that he was going to a South African diamond mine for a while on business and wouldn't be in the city.

In the fall of 1959, he was with a friend and, forgetting himself, entered the car where she sat. There she was on a warm September day without a coat, revealing her Jewish star on a gold chain around her neck. They were engaged by November and married in May.

How do two Holocaust survivors from Germany find one another on the New York City F train and get married? What did they recognize in one another that drew them to one another?

Five years after they married, Dov, Katja, their four-year-old daughter, and their new baby moved to a chicken farm that he bought down the road from his brother Josef. Stars must have been in their eyes. I imagine Dov thinking that he could live off the land. Collect eggs and sell them and thrive—not worry every time someone opened the taxi door that in moments a gun might be pointed at his head. By then he had already been robbed several times. He had a young family and a beautiful wife. He had already lost one beautiful wife. On the farm he could be with them 24/7. Katja must have rubbed her hands together at the thought of decorating a whole house. Yes, she was a conspicuous consumer but also a natural artist, in love with material beauty. Once furnished, the house was the talk of all the refugees in Vineland.

"So much money on furniture!"

"He's crazy. He doesn't know what he's doing."
"How will they pay back all the money?"
"Who does she think she is? The Queen of England?"
"Why do they need such fancy things?"
"A waste of money."
"It will all go to the next owner at ten cents on the dollar."
"They will go bankrupt before the year is out."

Loudest among the critics were Dov's brothers. Itzak, to his face, predicted he would lose his pants. On the farm, his daughters developed asthma, as did Dov, from the chicken feathers and dust the chickens kicked up. He hated the work—chickens were stupid and cannibalistic, pecking one another to death if you let them—but Katja loved the house; so many rooms to which to apply her artistry. He bought a rifle after an incident with an intruder. One of his workers made a pass at Katja. As the loans got larger, he began to drive a truck into the city to deliver eggs and chickens, leaving the farm to take care of itself. Which it didn't. They lasted a year and a half before they declared bankruptcy. Dov couldn't find a buyer. The farm went to the bank in foreclosure.

I loved having them so close to me. Katja was more girlfriend than aunt. I talked to her, really talked to her. My parents would drop me off at their farm while they went to their stalls in the farmer's market. I sat in a soft armchair with my books and my French tapes in the utter luxury of peace, quiet, and a gloriously adorned space.

My parents and I lived in a cramped, rented one-bedroom apartment on a major thoroughfare, and I had no privacy. Katja and Dov were permissive and not critical. I could smoke in their presence and bury myself in books, away from my mother's worried hovering and without the disturbance of the neighbors' fights or the clunking high heels overhead from the upstairs apartment.

By the time Katja and Dov left the farm, I had made my escape to college and stopped paying attention. The next I knew, they were back in the city, with Dov driving a cab again—but he drove for tips now. He still made a decent living, but this failure must have taken its toll. He had sold his taxi medallion to buy the farm and added a ton of loans to that investment. He gave the farm up when the Stern brothers, who supplied all the baby chicks in the area, stopped delivering to him because he owed them so much money.

I was best friends with the daughter of one of the Stern brothers and still see her. She gave Meg O'Day to the National Museum of American Jewish History in Philadelphia. Meg is the white leghorn chicken that gave my friend's father,

Gus, his fifteen seconds of fame. Ordinarily chickens live for about two years, but Meg lasted six months longer than that, 25 percent over the usual chicken lifespan; and then Gus stuffed her and put her on the dining room table. He bestowed this honor on her because she held two world records, both for the most eggs laid in 1956 and for the most consecutive days of laying eggs in one year. Meg O'Day laid an egg for 284 days in a row and then, after taking a short break, continued to lay eggs for 362 out of 365 days, breaking the old record of 354 held by a white leghorn on an Oregon farm in 1949. The average white leghorn lays 240 eggs annually. In Gus's words, "She worked her tail off." He meant that literally, since Meg lost her tail feathers in old age. For a while, weekly articles about Meg's laying prowess appeared in the newspapers. It was a time when Vineland was America's "egg basket." Gus told reporters that it took him thirty-two years of selective breeding to produce Meg O'Day.

Sometime in the late-1980s, Katja and Dov separated for a year and a half. Eva had come back into the picture. And Dov was interested. He did not accept at first that Eva thought she was dying and wanted not him but to reconnect him with their daughter. The marriage of Katja and Dov by then had settled into a routine, with periods of bickering and money problems. Unlike other immigrants they knew, he was still struggling, and he felt that his best self was in the past. So when Eva contacted him and gave him the chance to see her and their daughter, he wanted to grab it. His eagerness terrified Katja. She wanted nothing to do with Eva or Lara.

When he insisted, she left him before he had the chance, as she feared, to repeat the past and abandon her.

Her years in therapy and on Prozac were supposed to help her cope with this fear of being abandoned, as she had been by her family during the war and by her fiancé after. But how can therapy and drugs manage the coming-to-life of the feared reality?

I am looking at a black-and-white photograph of my husband and his younger sister as small children, probably aged four and seven. She still has her milk teeth, though an incisor is missing. The photographer has posed them so that their bodies are touching. Wearing a light-colored dress with puff sleeves and a white Mary Jane collar, she is sitting on his left knee, a position that makes them both smile bashfully. Her body faces the camera, and her face is turned toward his. Her round, pudgy, dimpled right hand cups his chin. Her curly dark hair is bobbed and has very short bangs. Both of their noses are sweet little knobs, as yet undefined. He is wearing a short-sleeved polo shirt with multicolored stripes tucked into wool herring-bone pleated pants, hiked up by suspenders to his chest. His body is turned toward her. He looks down, too shy in his young maleness to face her as directly as she faces him. His lovely, rounded right arm with a dimpled elbow is bent so that his fingers graze hers, which lie on her lap, as the photographer probably placed them. He tried for a portrait of sibling affection and succeeded; the photograph is very convincing, so convincing that it brings me to tears, and it depresses my husband, so we keep it out of sight, in the basement. The difference between the closeness and love the photo communicates and my husband's relationship to his sister today is too great to bear. It evokes a time that perhaps never was, except as staged for the occasion, but oh, how that Neverland is longed for. Photographs like that force us to calculate the distance from the present reality, and we are heartbroken.

If the children in the photograph are victims of ordinary life, how much more extreme are the disappointments of Dov and Katja? With the sepia-tinted image of Eva in postwar Berlin—the beautiful blonde in the white bikini—in his head and Katya, the now middle-aged woman in full color in front of him, Dov, given the chance, would have tried to transport himself to the past. But unlike the characters in *Back to the Future*, Dov would have chosen not to return to the present in which his back hurt him, his heart was failing, making the rent was a monthly effort, and his wife was seeing a shrink for her depression.

For Katja, there was not even the solace of an old posed photograph to put nostalgic pictures in her head. The past had betrayed her again and again. For Katja, I think, the solace to be had was possible only in the present moment, in the material world and the pleasures she might reap from it, from the accumulation of shiny new things—things that gave her status and that she could touch and clean and replace at will. Looking down at her orthopedic shoes, she must realize that she has lost control over the decision of what things are properly hers. With that loss, the present also slips out of her reach, the present that addresses itself to her in an ever-thickening cloud.

7

Legacy

It has been a year since I began to write Katja's story and my birthday has come around again, so we will visit the cemetery as usual. This birthday is one of those big ones, marking another decade gone. My loved ones will give me a party. Not one of the original Seven will be there. Not one of them is on top of the earth any more. Their stories remain—although they are no longer their own. They are now in my uncertain hands. I will visit the three to whose graves I can drive. I will tell my mother about the party. I will not tell my father because he would think only about the waste of money, that it should be in the CitiBank account accumulating interest.

Lola loved parties. My parents used to drive from Vineland to Brooklyn or the Bronx once or twice a month for card parties with their immigrant friends. Before I had my own life, beginning at about the age of fifteen or sixteen, I would go with them and hang out with their friends' kids. On the car ride back, they reviewed the evening. My mother astonished at the inadequacies of the food. My father railing against the duplicity that lost him twenty-five dollars in the game. These card friends were with them in Warsaw, the lice-infested cattle cars, the prison settlement in Nyuvchim, on the Soviet labor front, or in the DP camp: Mische, who supervised my father's illegal black market territory in Berlin, and Heniak, who bought stolen tobacco leaves from him in Kyrgyzstan, for instance. I have said before that our resentments help to glue us together; we feel the sting, and we remember one another; especially, we are reminded of the immense weight of our shared history. Pain can be an efficient cue to memory.

As I look out at the party crowd, I will see that six of the original seven—the six related to me—have multiplied more than sevenfold. What did they pass on or what was passed on through them? In photographs and from stories, I can detect the traits that may have been handed down: the wary look in my grandmother's eyes, the high cheekbones of my grandfather on my mother's side, the big, luscious lips of my Aunt Sonia, the open-handedness of my grandfather on my father's side and his mercurial temper, my mother's compulsion to take care of people that now drives her granddaughters, the dark hair of most of them, the raw brain power that draws so many in the family to books and degrees. Among them are PhDs, a DMD, an MD, advanced engineering degrees, law degrees, MA and BA degrees. They play piano, clarinet, violin, cello, tenor and alto saxophone, flute, and trombone. Like Sonia and Dov, some of them also sing. Only one of them has spent much of her adult life dependent on the government, and all but one, thank God, are somewhere in the middle class. They are a family who survived the Holocaust, and their history, a version of it, my version of it, has now been told. Meeting any one of us, who could guess our provenance? The seven youths who left Warsaw were, except for my mother, poor and working class, and minimally schooled, and yet they bested their circumstances. They had community among themselves, whatever its quality, and just often enough, they had the help of strangers.

They say that post-Holocaust generations feel that the past subjugates them, that the past is more compelling in their lives than the present or the future. I have felt that and am trying to make peace with it. The past counts for a lot, but it never captures us completely. The engine of time moves us forward despite ourselves. Births and birthdays, graduations, weddings, and the holidays that mark the progression of the year, such as Thanksgiving and Passover, outnumber the trips to the cemetery. Never forget, but there is room for not forgetting and also for moving on.

Like the twenty-nine pilgrim travelers in Chaucer's *Canterbury Tales*, the people in this book tell their stories, revealing themselves as they do. But Chaucer's pilgrims, unlike my family, return home. So too, in Boccaccio's *Decameron*, do the storytelling characters—ten of them—who have left their city to escape the Black Death, return home when it is safe. While they were alive, the Seven were exiles, no matter what passports they possessed. They included Dov's wives and Chapka, Josef's friend who stayed in Poland, but who as a Jew was in a kind of exile in his own country. When he fled to Paris in the 1960s to save his and his family's lives, his exile just changed its address.

They accumulated so many miles of exile, totaling more than half the circumference of the Earth: approximately 127 miles from Warsaw to Brest, 216 from Brest to Minsk, 443 from Minsk to Moscow, 169 from Moscow to Yaroslavl, 440 from Yaroslavl to Kotlas, 205 from Kotlas to Syktyvkar, 31 from Syktyvkar to Nyuvchim, 2,385 from Nyuvchim to Osh, 384 from Osh to Frunze, 200 very steep miles to the Tian Shan Mountains, 1,568 from Aravan to Chelyabinsk, 1,113 from Chelyabinsk to Moscow, 3,128 from Frunze to Stettin, 94 from Stettin to Berlin, 3,972 from Berlin to New York City, 639 from New York City to Cincinnati, and 613 from Cincinnati to Vineland. That's not counting all the circuitous reroutings to let troop trains pass or all of their separate routes, or Shanghai, Costa Rica, and Palestine, where Katya's relatives went.

I include Cincinnati since that is where UNRRA sent my family from the Great Hall at Ellis Island when we first immigrated. They gave us an attic apartment, and at six, I was placed in first grade. I did not know a word of English. A six-year-old boy was assigned to help me because he could speak German. He hated the idea, and who could blame him? At that age, in that time, boys and girls came from different and hostile species. I don't remember him ever speaking to me, in fact, in any language, just looking longingly at another corner of the schoolyard where his buddies were playing, while the teacher kept him pinned to me with her glance.

One time I sat at a desk while the class took a spelling test. The teacher had given me spelling test paper, just as she had all the first-graders. Out of boredom I copied the words the girl next to me printed on her test. I did not expect to be graded, but the teacher took my test along with the others and after lunch, returned it with three gold stars at the top. The girl whose test I had copied exactly received no gold stars and had red Xs on her paper, which I understood as signifying wrong answers. I hated being held to a different standard. Rather than encouraging me as the kind teacher must have intended, it only emphasized my difference, my not-belonging.

The burden of exile, estrangement, and strangeness, a sense of *Unheimlichkeit*, of never quite being at home, is my family burden but, I realize, it is also yours. There seems to be a cultural contagion about exile. Hitler bequeathed the condition of exile to the twentieth century, and it has made itself at home in the twenty-first.

The story of Jews during World War II has become a touchstone in our time. A friend of mine worked for some years in an NGO located in Rwanda, the country that practices *gacaca* justice to deal with the perpetrators of genocide there. She brought some Rwandans to her house in New Jersey for medical treatment. When she asked them what they would like to do while they were in the United States, one of them said he would like to meet Jews. Someone told him that they had a genocide, too.

ACKNOWLEDGMENTS

Many people helped me through this journey. I want to thank my graduate and undergraduate students for helping to transcribe my audio tapes. The biggest thanks goes to Kathy Engle Voinier, who did the bulk of them. Kathy Starz, Matthew Fuhrmeister, and Eric Elberty also contributed. I am grateful to polyglot David Stillman for help with YIVO-preferred transcriptions of Yiddish and other language questions; Inken Rothschild for German; Annette Berkovits for Polish; and my daughter Rebecca Friedman, Jon Mogul, and Aleksey Berg for Library of Congress–preferred transcriptions of Russian. I greatly valued the stories of growing up in Vineland that Lana Stern, Paula Laufer, and Ben Glezer told me, some of which found a place in this book. I appreciate Marsha Levin Schumer's generosity with her family's archives about the history of Norma. My colleague Jo Carney gave me a wonderful story that I have included in this volume. Maureen Gorman, librarian at the College of New Jersey (TCNJ), helped me to puzzle out maps and distances and also to locate people I subsequently interviewed for this book. My former student Scott Bowen, himself a writer and editor, provided incisive editing of an early draft. Rosalie Siegel, a retired literary agent, looked at an early draft and was generous with her time and advice. Annette Berkovits read an early draft and contributed her expertise as the author of a book about her father, who was also a Polish-Jewish exile in the Soviet Union. I was lucky to find Margot Krumholz, whose husband, Simon, was Dov's best friend. She told me wonderful stories of postwar Berlin, some of which found their way into this book. I thank her for her generosity with her memories.

Maxim D. Shrayer, a memoirist and scholar, encouraged my work and also led me to John and Carol Garrard, who put together the Brest-Litovsk Ghetto Passport Archive and donated it to the United States Holocaust Memorial Museum, where the historian Jude C. Richter found it for me—I thank all of them.

I am very grateful for the friendship of Timothy Snyder, which began when he gave a memorial lecture in honor of my father at the College of New Jersey in April 2012. From then on he has been a faithful supporter of this book and an astute reader and editor.

I am enormously thankful for my friend and colleague David Haven Blake, who read my manuscript with great intelligence, compassion, and a literary sensibility.

Institutional support for this project's many needs has been generous from the College of New Jersey, where I teach English and where I helped to launch a Holocaust and Genocide minor. TCNJ's English department provided funds for students to work on the transcriptions. The Support of Scholarly Activities (SOSA) and Sabbatical Committees provided time away from teaching so that I could write this book. The dean's office mini-grants and travel funds allowed me to buy recording devices and software for the recordings and transcriptions and supported my travel for interviews. A TCNJ travel grant funded my first trip to the Soviet Union to follow the footsteps of my family. And Suzanne Pasch, acting provost, gave extra funds for transcriptions that helped bring the process to completion. I was also encouraged by the Faculty Senate–sponsored colloquium where I read an early draft of a chapter.

I have read from my manuscript at the Biography Center at the University of Hawaii, Manoa, twice and served there as visiting scholar. I also have read various sections at Åbo Akademi University, Instutum Judaicum, in Turku, Finland; the Steven J. Green School of International and Public Affairs, Global Jewish Studies Program, and the Jewish Museum of Florida of Florida International University; the 34th Biennial Conference on the Holocaust & Genocide at Millersville University; and the Jewish and American Holocaust Literature Symposium in Miami Beach, Florida. These readings were invaluable for pushing me forward.

Louis de Vries, publisher of Hybrid Books, was among the first to confirm that I had a manuscript worth publishing. Kathryn Wildfong and the readers at Wayne State University Press gave detailed and expert editorial advice, which has made this book much better than when they first found it. Thank you as well to Kristin Harpster, Kristina Stonehill, Emily Nowak, and the entire staff at Wayne State University Press.

I give thanks to Brenda Morano, whose big heart helped me in many ways. I am grateful to the people at the center of my life: to my dear friend Miriam Fuchs for her love, support, and advice during the long process of this book; to my brilliant daughters, Rebecca Friedman and Sonia Friedman, who read the manuscript with love and sympathy and who gave me the motivation to see this project through; and to the love of my life, Max.

NOTES

Who and Where

1   Historians are increasingly addressing the experience of Polish Jews in the Soviet Union. They calculate that from 250,000 to 300,000 Polish Jews survived the Holocaust in the USSR. For various reasons their stories have not been widely told: Their stories were overshadowed by the stories of the gas chambers and concentration camps, which have dominated the narrative of Jews during World War II. Immigration to the United States in the Cold War climate necessitated keeping silent about their association with the USSR. Postwar displaced persons (DP) camps in Germany, which gave refuge to many Polish Jews, were first populated by concentration camp survivors who dominated camp hierarchies and thus the narrative coming from the Jewish experience. Polish Jews in the USSR represent by far the largest percentage of survivors, and thus their stories must be heard. The sources I found especially insightful on this topic include Timothy Snyder's *Black Earth: The Holocaust as History and Warning* (New York: Random House, 2015); the essays by John Goldlust, Mark Edele, Wanda Warlik, Natalie Belsky, and Atina Grossmann in *Shelter from the Holocaust*, ed. Mark Edele, Sheila Fitzpatrick, Atina Grossman (Detroit: Wayne State University Press, 2017); the article by Yosef Litvak, "Jewish Refugees from Poland in the USSR, 1939–1946," in *Bitter Legacy: Confronting the Holocaust in the USSR*, ed. Zvi Gitelman (Bloomington: University of Indiana Press, 1997); Natalie Belsky's PhD dissertation, "Encounters in the East: Evacuees in the Soviet Hinterland during the Second World War" (University of Chicago Press, 2014); Feliks Tych's "The Polish Jews in the DP Camps," in *Jewish Exodus Out of Europe, 1945–1948*, ed. Sabine Aschauer-Smolik and Mario Steidl (Innsbruck: StudienVerlag, 2010); Laura Jockusch and Tam Lewinsky's "Paradise Lost? Postwar Memory of Polish-Jewish Survival in the Soviet Union," in *Holocaust and Genocide Studies* 24 (Nov. 3, 2010): 373–99; and two articles by Markus Nesselrodt, "From Russian Winters to Munich Summers: DPs and the Story of Survival in the Soviet Union," in *Displaced Persons*, ed. Rebecca Boehling, Susanne Urban, and René Bienert (Göttingen: Jahrbuch des International Tracing Service, Band 3. 2014), 190–98; and " 'I bled like you, brother, although I was a thousand miles away': Postwar Yiddish Sources on the Experiences of Polish Jews in Soviet Exile During World War II," in *East European Jewish Affairs* 46, no. 1 (2016): 47–67. An interesting discussion of relief efforts for Poles in the Soviet Union after the 1941 Soviet amnesty

of Poles may be read in Keith Sword, "The Welfare of Polish-Jewish Refugees in the USSR, 1941–1943, in Relief Supplies and Their Distribution," in *Jews in Eastern Poland and the USSR, 1939–46*, ed. Norman Davies and Antony Polonsky (London: Macmillan, 1991), 145–60 (in association with the School of Slavonic & East European Studies, University of London). Sword is also the author of *Deportation and Exile: Poles in the Soviet Union, 1939–48* (London: Macmillan, 1994).

2   Historical scholarship is not fulsome regarding how common it was for group bonds to facilitate survival among Polish Jews in the gulags. Yosef Litvak writes that most of the Polish-Jewish exiles were single young males (135). Based on testimonial accounts, John Goldlust, who writes that some extended family groups of five or six people left Poland for the USSR, also writes that, more commonly, single young males followed this route. See "A Different Silence: The Survival of More than 200,000 Polish Jews in the Soviet Union During World War II as a Case Study in Cultural Amnesia," *Australian Jewish Historical Society Journal* 1 (2012): 18–21.

4   A body of scholarship is growing around received memories of the Holocaust. These inherited memories, representing experiences that one has not lived through, go by terms such as "absent memory," "inherited memory," "belated memory," "prosthetic memory," "vicarious witnessing," "received history." The most common name for them is "postmemory," a term popularized by Marianne Hirsch, who describes it as "the relationship of the second generation to powerful, often traumatic experiences that preceded their births but that were nevertheless transmitted to them so deeply as to seem to constitute memories in their own right." My sources for this scholarship include Richard Crownshaw, *The Afterlife of Holocaust Memory in Contemporary Literature and Culture* (Basingstoke, UK: Palgrave Macmillan, 2010); Elke Heckner, "Whose Trauma Is It? Identification and Secondary Witnessing in the Age of Postmemory," collected in *Visualizing the Holocaust: Documents, Aesthetics, Memory*, ed. David Bathrick, Brad Prager, Michael D. Richardson (Rochester, NY: Camden House, 2008), 62–85; Marianne Hirsch, *The Generation of Postmemory: Writing and Visual Culture after the Holocaust* (New York: Columbia University Press, 2012), and *Family Frames: Photography, Narrative and Postmemory* (Cambridge, MA: Harvard University Press, 1997); Brett Ashley Kaplan, *Landscapes of Holocaust Postmemory* (London: Routledge, 2010); Lori Hope Lefkovitz, "Inherited Holocaust Memory and the Ethics of Ventriloquism," *Kenyon Review* 19 (Winter 1997): 34–43; Erin Heather McGlothlin, *Second-Generation Holocaust Literature: Legacies of Survival and Perpetration* (Rochester, NY: Camden House, 2006); Gabriele Schwab, *Haunting Legacies: Violent Histories and Transgenerational Trauma* (New York: Columbia University Press, 2010); Esther Faye, "Missing the 'Real' Trace of Trauma: How the Second Generation Remember the Holocaust," in *American Imago* 2, no. 2 (2001): 525–45; Alison Landsberg, *Prosthetic Memory: The Transformation of American Remembrance in the Age of Mass Culture* (New York: Columbia University Press, 2004).

5   Speaking of her position as a child of survivors with responsibilities to their memories, Lefkowitz writes, "From puppet to puppeteer, in reciprocal ventriloquism" (41).

NOTES

Dov

13 This section is adapted from audio tapes I recorded on August 18, 1983; September 8, 1983; February 24, 1984; and March 3, 1984. The people in this book spoke many languages—Polish, Yiddish, Russian, German, English, as well as more local languages and dialects. Their speech reflected the richness of this linguistic cross pollination. The languages also had different alphabets—Cyrillic, Hebrew, and Latin. For purposes of clarity, I have used the Library of Congress recommendations for transliteration of Cyrillic and YIVO recommendations for Yiddish—except when the particular word has entered common English vocabulary. The two exceptions for the Cyrillic are referenced in the notes to the page where they first appear.

16 Mikhail Aleksandrovich Sholokhov, *And Quiet Flows the Don*, trans. Stephen Garry (London: Putnam, 1934). This reference is to an early English translation, but of course Dov would have read a translation in Polish.

16 Joseph Marcus paints this picture of the Bund in Warsaw during those years in *Social and Political History of the Jews in Poland, 1919–1939* (Berlin: Mouton Publishers, 1983), 280–84. Marcus Nesselrodt thought that the Po'ale Tsiyon might be a better fit, given Dov's leftist activism, and led me to an online article by Samuel Kassow in the *YIVO Encyclopedia of Jews in Eastern Europe* ("Po'ale Tsiyon," http://www.yivoencyclopedia.org/article.aspx/Poale_Tsiyon, October 11, 2010; accessed September 5, 2016).

21 Isaac Bashevis Singer, *In My Father's Court* (New York: Farrar, Straus, Giroux, 1966).

22 See Marcus, "1930s home-workers," in *Social and Political History of the Jews in Poland, 1919–1939*.

27 Timothy Snyder, *Bloodlands: Europe between Hitler and Stalin* (New York: Basic Books, 2010).

31 I have used the Library of Congress transliteration rules for Russian except for the place names *Nyuvchim* and *Yaroslavl*. The "y" spelling makes an internet search for those places easier.

36 *Echelon* as "special train" is probably what he meant. Credit goes to John Goldlust, who helped me figure this out via a personal email dated August 26, 2016.

38 The irony of a gulag paradise is well expressed in the title "Paradise Lost? Postwar Memory of Polish-Jewish Survival in the Soviet Union" (Jockusch and Lewinsky), an article examining the testimonies of other Polish Jews with similar feelings about their experiences.

40 A. S. Nemerov, *City of Bread* (*Tashkent—gorod khlebnyi* [1927]).

40 Aleksander Wat, *My Century: The Odyssey of a Polish Intellectual*, trans. Richard Lourie (Berkeley: University of California Press, 1988).

42 Michel Foucault, *Discipline and Punish: The Birth of the Prison*, trans. Alan Sheridan (New York: Vintage, 1975).

48 Schlachtensee DP Camp. The seminar referred to was the Leo Baeck Summer University in Jewish Studies, which took place at Humboldt University, Berlin in 2008, led by Atina Grossmann (http://dp-camp.shalom-berlin.net/home). See also Atina Grossmann, *Jews, Germans, and Allies: Close Encounters in Occupied*

Germany (Princeton, NJ: Princeton University Press, 2007), especially chapter 4, "The Saved and Saving Remnant," 131–82. In addition, see Angelica Königseder and Juliane Wetzel, *Waiting for Hope: Jewish Displaced Persons in Post–World War II Germany*, trans. John A. Broadwin (Evanston, IL: Northwestern University Press, 2001). The book lists the number of DPs in each camp in the US zone. Beginning October 1946, Düppel housed about 3,500 Jewish refugees (see p. 223). Also Feliks Tych's "The Polish Jews in the DP Camps" summarizes additional reasons that surviving Polish Jews left Poland for the DP camps. They include avoiding the communism they had observed in the Soviet Union and the appropriation of their property by Poles.

Josef

55 This section is adapted from audio tapes I recorded on May 22, 1984; May 29, 1984; June 9, 1984; June 15, 1984; June 30, 1984; and July 7, 1984.

72 See Nesselrodt, "I bled like you, brother, although I was a thousand miles away" (p. 49), on the reasons for Soviet deportation of Polish Jews.

78–80 Sources I consulted for what may have happened to Sonia and the Jews of Brest include John Garrard and Carol Garrard, "Barbarossa's First Victims: The Jews of Brest" [1998], republished in *East European Jewish Affairs* 28, no. 2 (2008): 3–48; Yitzhak Arad, *The Holocaust in the Soviet Union* (Comprehensive History of the Holocaust), trans. Ora Cummings (Lincoln: University of Nebraska Press, 2013); and Yitzhak Arad, Shmuel Krakowski, and Shmuel Spector, *The Einsatzgruppen Reports: Selections from the Dispatches of the Nazi Death Squads' Campaign Against the Jews, July 1941–January 1943* (Washington, DC: United States Holocaust Museum Press, 1990).

79 Her identity papers were found by Jude C. Richter, a historian at the Holocaust Survivors and Victims Resource Center, United States Holocaust Memorial Museum. They are on reel 23 of the collection USHMM Acc.1996.A.0169. They are part of the Brest-Litovsk Ghetto Passport Archive collected and donated to the museum by John Garrard and Carol Garrard, scholars of this history.

84 The importance of the loss of citizenship for European Jews is eloquently argued in Snyder's *Black Earth: The Holocaust as History and Warning*.

85 See Litvak, "Jewish Refugees from Poland in the USSR," p. 134, about the second passportization. John Goldlust confirmed these consequences in a personal email on August 21, 2016.

90 Jan Gross, among many others, records this anti-Semitism toward returning Jewish Poles. See *Fear: Anti-Semitism in Poland after Auschwitz* (New York: Random House, 2006), 36.

92 Brenda Gayle Plummer, "Brown Babies: Race, Gender, and Policy after World War II," in *Window on Freedom: Race, Civil Rights, and Foreign Affairs, 1945–1988*, ed. Plummer (Chapel Hill: University of North Carolina Press, 2003).

95 These DP numbers come from Jockusch and Lewinsky, "Paradise Lost?" 380.

Itzak with Lola Interrupting

101 This section is adapted from audio tapes I recorded on August 4, 1984; August 9, 1984; August 10, 1984; and August 18, 1984.

109 See https://lesterresduklezmer.com/2014/05/20/yidl-mitn-fidl/ (accessed May 6, 2017).

125 See Marcus, *Social and Political History of the Jews in Poland*, 313–14.

127 See, for instance, Jan T. Gross, *Fear: Anti-Semitism in Poland after Auschwitz; Neighbors: The Destruction of the Jewish Community in Jedwabne, Poland* (Princeton, NJ: Princeton University Press, 2001); and "Polish-Jewish Relations During the War: An Interpretation," in *European Journal of Sociology 27* (1986): 199–214.

138 Marci Shore, *Caviar and Ashes: A Warsaw Generation's Life and Death in Marxism, 1918–1968* (New Haven, CT: Yale University Press, 2006).

148 Katherine Jolluck, *Exile and Identity: Polish Women in the Soviet Union during World War II* (Pittsburgh, PA: University of Pittsburgh Press, 2002).

158 Snyder, *Bloodlands*.

164 John Maynard Keynes, *The General Theory of Employment, Interest and Money* (London: Macmillan, 1936).

Eva

165 This section is adapted from audio tapes I recorded on June 4 and 5, 2005.

170 https://www.jmberlin.de/1933/en/05_03_letter-from-the-bismarck-lyceum-to-parents-requesting-proof-of-descent.php/ (accessed May 4, 2017).

171 Goebbels's letter can be found in Kimberly Ann Redding, *Growing Up in Hitler's Shadow: Remembering Youth in Postwar Berlin* (Westport, CT: Praeger Publishers, 2004).

172 Information about the KLV curriculum came from J. Noakes and G. Pridham, eds., *Nazism: A History in Documents and Eyewitness Accounts, 1919–1945*, vol. 1 (New York: Schocken Books, 1984).

173 Jean-Francois Lyotard, *The Postmodern Condition: A Report on Knowledge* [1979], trans. Geoff Bennington and Brian Massumi (Minneapolis: University of Minnesota Press, 1984).

185 Keith Lowe, *Savage Continent: Europe in the Aftermath of World War II* (New York: St. Martin's Press, 2012).

185 Mary Louise Roberts, *What Soldiers Do: Sex and the American GI in World War II France* (Chicago: University of Chicago Press, 2013).

185 Quote from the American general appears in James Heartfield's *Unpatriotic History of the Second World War* (Winchester, UK: Zero Books, 2012), 333.

Katja

209 This section is adapted from audio tapes and digital voice files I recorded on April 18, 2004; June 6, 2004; and June 10, 2005.

218 Eric Lichtblau, "The Holocaust Just Got More Shocking," *New York Times*, Sunday Review, March 1, 2013.

NOTES

227 See Warren Kozak, *The Rabbi of 84th Street: The Extraordinary Life of Haskel Besser* (New York: Harper Collins, 2004), 177.

235 John O. Koehler, *Stasi: The Untold Story of the East German Secret Police* (New York: Basic Books, 2008).

239 These letters were translated by Inken Rothschild.

www.ingramcontent.com/pod-product-compliance
Lightning Source LLC
Chambersburg PA
CBHW070756230426
43665CB00017B/2384